Territorial Force Regulations 1908

Printed and bound by Antony Rowe Ltd, Eastbourne

CONTENTS.

Part I.—TERRITORIAL FORCE.

Part II.—COUNTY ASSOCIATIONS.

APPENDICES.

PREFACE.

THE Regulations for the Territorial Force which form Part I of this volume replace the Regulations for the Imperial Yeomanry and the Regulations for the Volunteer Force, which are now formally cancelled.

The Regulations for the County Associations are included in this volume as Part II. Under the Territorial and Reserve Forces Act, associations may have assigned to them the duty of establishing or assisting cadet battalions and corps and rifle clubs (Section II, Subsection 2); the registration of horses for the regular army; and the care of reservists and discharged soldiers. Pending the further development of the organization of the Territorial Force proper, the Army Council have not thought it expedient to call upon associations to take up these duties, but instructions with regard to them will be issued at a later date. The instructions on various matters which have been issued to associations by circular memoranda will remain in force and will, where necessary and where they have not been incorporated in these regulations, be read in connection with the regulations contained in Part II. But future editions of the Regulations will be made to contain as complete a statement as possible of the duties of the associations.

It is not claimed for these Regulations that they are definitive in character. This first edition is issued provisionally and to a certain extent tentatively. Although certain portions have already been issued in other forms (*e.g.*, the finance and training regulations), the book has of necessity been prepared without the advantage of any considerable experience of the working of the new system, and it is recognised that, until the regulations have stood the test of being acted upon, they must be regarded as liable to modification and amendment, and also as susceptible of improvement in consistency, arrangement and clearness.

There are also subjects which it has not been possible to deal with in this edition, or with which it has not been possible to deal fully. Amongst these are:—medals and decorations, the unattached list, mobilization and embodiment.

The formation of a Chaplain's department and of a Veterinary Corps for the Territorial Force are under consideration. No references to the appointment of chaplains and veterinary officers (other than civilian veterinary officers) are therefore contained in this edition. Regulations dealing with these matters and amendments of the regulations on the subjects dealt with where they are found to be necessary, will be promulgated from time to time in Army Orders. It is consequently contemplated that a second edition of the regulations will be required at an early date, but it is not intended to issue a further edition until 1909, before the training season of which year it is expected that it may be possible to deal in a more complete manner with the various matters on which these regulations should ultimately contain directions. At the same time it may be possible to dispense with regulations on some matters which it may be found are better left to the discretion of general officers commanding, or of the county associations.

The regulations published in the Special Army Order dated 18th March, 1908, so far as they deal with the transition, are not republished. Part II, however, of that Army Order is reprinted, with certain slight modifications, as Section 7 of Part I of this book, and Part II of the Special Army Order is accordingly cancelled.

For convenience of reference, the Territorial and Reserve Forces Act is reprinted as Appendix 1, and the model scheme for the Territorial Force Associations as Appendix 2. A manual is, however, in course of preparation, summarizing and explaining the law relating to the Territorial Force as contained in statutes, &c., and dealing in some detail with the composition, powers and duties of the associations.

Separate regulations are published dealing with the Officers' Training Corps.

By Command of the Army Council,

1*st July*, 1908.

9
General No.
39

ORDER BY HIS MAJESTY.

WHEREAS it is provided by Section 7 of the Territorial and Reserve Forces Act, 1907, that, subject to the provisions of Part II of that Act, it shall be lawful for His Majesty, by Order signified under the hand of a Secretary of State, to make orders with respect to the government, discipline, and pay and allowances of the Territorial Force, and with respect to all other matters and things relating to the Territorial Force; and that subject to the provisions of any such Order the Army Council may make general or special regulations with respect to any matter with respect to which His Majesty may make orders under that section:

And whereas His Majesty has been pleased to approve of certain consolidated regulations relating to the Territorial Force which have been submitted to him by the Army Council.

Now therefore His Majesty, in exercise of the powers conferred upon him by the said Act, and of all other powers him thereunto enabling, is pleased to order, and it is hereby ordered, that the regulations above referred to (which are printed as Part I of the appended "Regulations relating to the Territorial Force and to County Associations") shall be orders made by His Majesty under the said Section of the said Act, and shall be the sole and standing authority on the matters whereof they treat:

Provided always (i) that the Army Council shall be the sole administrators and interpreters of the said regulations, and shall, in any matters not affecting the rates or quantities therein laid down, have power to alter them from time to time as may appear to them to be expedient, until His Majesty's further Will and Pleasure be made known;

(ii) That the Territorial Force, when embodied, shall be governed by the provisions contained in the several Royal Warrants, Regulations, and Orders for the time being governing the Regular Forces, so far as such Warrants, Regulations, and Orders may be applicable to the Territorial Force.

His Majesty is further pleased to order, and it is hereby ordered, that all pay, allowances, and other pecuniary advantages granted by the appended regulations relating to the Territorial Force, which shall not have been claimed within a period of twelve months from the date on which they might have been claimed, shall be deemed to be forfeited, except under such exceptional circumstances as shall be approved by the Army Council, or by an officer duly authorised by them; and that the pay and all other emoluments granted by the said regulations to an officer, non-commissioned officer, or man of the Territorial Force shall be held liable to be stopped, on the order of the Army Council, to meet any public claim (as defined in the Royal Warrant for the Pay, Appointment, Promotion, and Non-effective Pay of the Army, but including any similar claim of a Territorial Force County Association) that may be outstanding against him, any regimental debt that may be due from him, or any regimental claim that the Army Council may direct him to pay.

By His Majesty's Command,

R. B. HALDANE.

PART I.

TERRITORIAL FORCE.

SECTION 1.—ORGANIZATION AND ESTABLISHMENTS.

ORGANIZATION.

1. The Territorial Force is composed of :—

(*a*) Divisions.
(*b*) Mounted brigades.
(*c*) Army troops.
(*d*) Special troops for defended ports, consisting of artillery and engineers.

2. Each district in Great Britain furnishes one division, except the London district, and districts Nos. 3, 5, which furnish two divisions each.

ESTABLISHMENTS.

3. The tables in Appendix 3 contain the authorised establishments of the different arms of the Territorial Force, and show in detail the numbers of personnel, horses and equipment which may be taken out for annual training.*

4. As a general principle, the establishment of personnel therein laid down follows, except where otherwise shown, the Regular War Establishments.

5. The following numbers of unpaid lance ranks are allowed :—

Units.	Numbers of acting bombardiers or lance-corporals (unpaid).
Yeomanry...	2 per squadron.
Artillery—	
Horse, Field, Mountain, Howitzer, and Heavy batteries	4 per battery.
Ammunition Columns—	
Horse Artillery, with mounted brigade	3 for the column.
Field Artillery brigade	6 ,, ,,
Howitzer brigade	3 ,, ,,
Mountain Artillery brigade ...	6 ,,
S.A. Ammunition section	1 ,, section.
Heavy battery	1 ,, column.
Garrison company	2 ,, company.

* These establishments will in future be published annually in "Regimental Establishments," which are issued with Army Orders.

Units.	Numbers of acting bombardiers or lance-corporals (unpaid).
Engineers—	
Field company...	4 per company.
Wireless Telegraph company ...	1 „ „
Divisional Telegraph company ...	1 „ „
Cable Telegraph company	3 „ „
Air-Line Telegraph company ...	6 „ „
Balloon company	1 „ „
Railway battalion	12 „ battalion.
Coast Defence units—	
Works company	2 „ company.
Electric-Light company	1 „ „
Infantry	2 per company.
Cyclist Battalion	2 per company.
Army Service Corps—	
Divisional Transport and Supply Column—	
No. 1 Company	2 per company.
Nos. 2, 3 and 4 Companies... ...	1 „ „
Mounted Brigade Transport and Supply Column	1 „ „
Medical Corps—	
A Mounted Brigade Field Ambulance	2 per unit (1 per section).
A Field Ambulance	3 „ (1 „).

During training, these acting non-commissioned officers will be granted separation allowance (*see* paragraph 399). On mobilization, the same number of paid lance ranks as in the regular army will be allowed.

PERMANENT STAFF.

6. Instructors, paid by the public, are allowed in the proportion shown in the Tables of Establishments in Appendix 3, the actual distribution among companies being left to the discretion of the officer commanding the unit.*

7. When a company is stationed at such a distance from head-quarters or from another company that, in the opinion of the commanding officer, an additional instructor is necessary, application for the same may be made, on Army Form E 671, through the usual military channel; the general officer commanding-in-chief, in forwarding such applications, will invariably give his opinion as to the existing means of access to the outlying detachments and the need for the proposed increase.

8. Should an outlying company or companies, for which an additional instructor has been authorised, be moved to another station, the general officer commanding-in-chief will report the fact, together with his recommendation as to the retention or otherwise of the additional instructor.

* The establishment of the permanent staff will also be shewn in "Regimental Establishments."

SPECIAL SERVICE SECTION.

Composition.

9. The Special Service Section of the Territorial Force will for the present be composed of members of Territorial units, who offer to serve, in case of national emergency, for the purposes of defence, at such places in the United Kingdom as may be specified in their agreement, and whose services are accepted by His Majesty the King.

Conditions of service.

10. The conditions for service in the Special Service Section will be as follows :—

(*a*) They will engage to serve in case of national emergency, when called upon to do so under the authority of the Secretary of State, for a period not exceeding one month, in the coast defences or other specified place mentioned in their agreement, even though no order calling out the Territorial Force for actual military service is in force at the time.

(*b*.) When called out on special service they will retain the rank which they held in the Territorial Force.

(*c*.) They will be medically examined, before joining the Special Service Section, by the medical officer of their unit, and will not be accepted unless they are certified as fit for the duties they will have to perform. They will be afterwards medically examined at least every third year, and if found unfit they will be discharged from the Special Service Section.

(*d*) They may at any time terminate their agreement by giving their commanding officer three calendar months' notice in writing ; provided that, if before such notice has expired they are called out for special service, they will be required to complete their period of special service as defined in (*a*).

(*e*) They may at any time be discharged from the Special Service Section by the authority of the general officer commanding-in-chief, and will thereupon revert to the ordinary conditions of service in the Territorial Force.

(*f*) Enrolments in the Special Service Section will be carried out by the officer commanding any unit concerned. Lists of such units, and the quota which they are invited to furnish, will be communicated to general officers commanding-in-chief, who will issue the necessary instructions.

(*g*) On joining the Special Service Section each officer and soldier will be required to sign a declaration on A.F. E 622 in the presence of the officer commanding the unit to which he belongs. This form, in the case of a soldier, will be preserved with the enlistment form.

SECTION 2.—APPOINTMENT, PROMOTION, AND RETIREMENT OF OFFICERS.

General Rules.

First appointments in lowest rank.

20. Applications for appointments to commissions in the lowest rank in the Territorial Force should be addressed to "The Secretary, Territorial Force Association," for the county in which candidates desire to serve, and should be accompanied by a copy of the

candidate's birth certificate. Recommendations for such first appointments, together with Army Form E 536 and a copy of the candidate's birth-certificate, will be forwarded by Presidents of County Associations to general officers commanding-in-chief for submission to the Secretary of State for War.

Procedure. **21.** The procedure in connection with first appointments to the unattached list of the Territorial Force for service in the Officers' Training Corps, and in connection with appointments to the command of Officers' Training Corps units and with the granting of local rank to officers appointed to the command of Officers' Training Corps units, is laid down in the "Regulations for the Officers' Training Corps."

Appointments not in lowest rank. **22.** Applications for appointments to commissions other than in the lowest rank should be addressed to general officers commanding-in-chief, and should be accompanied by a copy of the candidate's birth certificate.

Dual commissions. **23.** Officers are not permitted to hold more than one commission in the Territorial Force.

Regular officers. **24.** Officers of the regular forces, on the active list, will not be allowed to hold any commission in the Territorial Force.

Service in other branches. **25.** In the case of a candidate who has previously held a commission in the territorial or other force, the general officer commanding-in-chief will, before recommending his appointment to a unit of the Territorial Force, obtain a certificate from the candidate's late commanding officer that his services were satisfactory, and that his retirement or resignation did not arise from any matter affecting his character or efficiency.

War service. When a candidate has served in any campaign, a statement which has been certified by a senior officer who is personally cognizant of such service will accompany the recommendation.

Rank service. In the case of a candidate who has previously served in the ranks (whether in a regular or other unit), the discharge certificate or certified copy of it will accompany the application for a commission.

If an applicant for a commission has already served in the Army in any capacity, the particulars of his service must be stated in his application.

Selection for promotion. **26.** Promotion will, except where otherwise stated, be governed by establishment, and will as a rule be given according to regimental seniority, but in the interests of particular units it may be necessary to appoint or promote officers who are not next in seniority or who have not served in the lower ranks.

Recommendations. **27.** Recommendations for promotion will be forwarded by commanding officers to general officers commanding-in-chief for submission to the Secretary of State for War.

Brevet promotion. **28.** A captain after at least six years' service, a major, or a lieutenant-colonel, may be promoted to the next higher rank by brevet in the Territorial Force for distinguished service in the field, or for meritorious or distinguished service of an exceptional nature other than in the field. If the officer dies before the date on which the notification of his promotion for distinguished service in the field appears in the London Gazette, the promotion shall bear the date which it would have borne had the officer not died.

29. When a vacancy in a unit occurs, the commanding officer will submit, through the usual military channel, to the general officer commanding-in-chief the name of the officer he recommends to fill it. Vacancy.

When recommending an appointment or a promotion by which any officer will be superseded, the commanding officer will state in writing the circumstances which have led to such recommendation. Supersession.

30. His Majesty's approval of appointments, promotions, transfers, secondings, restorations to establishment, removals, and retirements, and His acceptance of the resignations of officers in the Territorial Force, will be notified by publication in the London Gazette. Notifications in London Gazette.

The general officer commanding-in-chief in submitting any recommendation for approval, will name the date from which it is to take effect, for insertion in the Gazette.

31. An officer granted leave for the purpose of going abroad for a period of more than two years may, at the termination of his second year's absence from the regiment, be seconded for a period not exceeding three years from that date, on the recommendation of his commanding officer. Leave abroad.

Commands and Staff.

32. Officers will be selected as follows, viz. :— Division.

(1) Headquarters of Division, from regular officers on the active list :—

1 General officer commanding.
1 General Staff Officer, 2nd or 3rd grade.
1 Deputy-assistant-adjutant and quartermaster-general.

(2) Headquarters of (*a*) Mounted brigade, and (*b*) Infantry brigade, from regular officers on the reserve or retired lists, or territorial officers having special qualifications :— Brigades.

1 Colonel commanding.
1 Brigade-major.

(3) Divisional Artillery, from regular officers on the active, reserve, or retired lists, or from territorial officers having special qualifications :— Divisional artillery.

1 Colonel commanding
1 Staff officer.

(4) Headquarters of divisional Engineers, telegraph groups, and fortress groups, from territorial officers :— Divisional engineers, &c.

1 Field officer (paid during training only).

From regular officers :—

1 Adjutant.

(5) Headquarters of divisional transport and supply column, from territorial officers :— Divisional transport and supply

1 Colonel or Lieutenant-Colonel.

From regular officers on the active list (not seconded) :—

1 Adjutant.

(6) Headquarters of divisional Army Medical Service, from territorial officers :— Divisional A.M.S.

1 Colonel (A.M.O.)
1 Sanitary officer.

From regular officers on the active or retired list :—

1 Staff officer to A.M.O.

Seconding. **33.** Officers on the active list of the regular forces, or territorial officers selected for staff appointments, will be seconded in their units during their tenure of appointment.

Rank. Officers appointed to command brigades or divisional artillery will, if they do not hold the rank of colonel in the regular army, be granted such rank temporarily.

Tenure, regular officers. **34.** The tenure of commands and staff appointments by officers of the regular army on the active list will be governed by the conditions applicable to similar appointments in the regular army.

Tenure, retired officers. **35.** The tenure of commands and staff appointments by officers on the retired list, or by officers of the territorial force, will be, as a rule, for four years, though extensions beyond that term may be given if considered desirable in the interests of the service. Colonels commanding, appointed under paragraph 32, will, however, vacate their appointments at the age of 65, and staff officers at 55. (Age limit.)

Commanding Officer.

Tenure of appointment. **36.** Appointments to the command of units will be made for a term of four years. Extensions will be for terms not exceeding four years, not more than two extensions being allowed.

Qualification for Staff, &c.

Certificate (Q) or (q). **37.** In selecting officers of the Territorial Force for—

(*a*) extra-regimental appointments, or

(*b*) commands of units,

special consideration will be given to those who hold certificates (Q) or (q).

Subalterns.

Age **38.** Candidates for first appointment must be not under 17 years of age.

Vacancies. **39.** When a vacancy for a second-lieutenant occurs, the officer commanding will inform the President of the Association for the county, and will render any assistance required in selecting a suitable person as successor.

Extra second-lieutenants. **40.** Where vacancies exist in the rank of lieutenant, owing to no second-lieutenant having qualified for promotion, extra second-lieutenants may be appointed, provided that the total establishment of subalterns be not exceeded.

Quartermasters.

Qualifications. **41.** First appointment to a commission as quartermaster will be made on the recommendation of the President of the County Association. Candidates, other than quartermasters who have retired from the regular army, must not be over 40 years of age.

Continuance in service. **42.** Commanding officers will report through general officers commanding-in-chief to the War Office whether they recommend the continuance in the service of the quartermasters serving under their command on completion of 10 and 15 years' commissioned service respectively. These reports should reach the War Office one month before the completion of the periods referred to.

43. Subject to Appendix 4, a quartermaster may be granted honorary rank as follows, viz. :— **Honorary rank**

On appointment	Lieutenant.
After completing 10 years' commissioned service	Captain.
After completing 15 years' commissioned service	Major.

Royal Army Medical Corps.

44. The following are the ranks of officers :— **Ranks.**

Lt.-Colonel	Promoted into fixed establishment.
Major	Promoted after $8\frac{1}{2}$ years' service as Captain.
Captain	Promoted after $3\frac{1}{2}$ years' service as a Lieutenant.
Lieutenant	On first appointment.

45. The promotion of sanitary officers and of officers appointed *à la suite* of general hospitals will be governed by establishment. **Establishment promotion.**

46. The usual number of medical officers of the Royal Army Medical Corps attached to a battalion is two. A proportion of officers for each regimental district in excess of this number is placed at the disposal of the principal medical officer, who will post them for duty where their services are considered most necessary in his district. **Distribution.**

47. The conditions of training and qualifications necessary for appointment and promotion are laid down in the Appendices. **Training, &c.**

48. Officers, warrant and non-commissioned officers who have served as such in the regular army may be appointed without further examination to the rank for which they have already qualified whilst serving with the colours. **Exemption from examination.**

49. A commission as quartermaster may be conferred upon officers, non-commissioned officers or other suitable persons of the Royal Army Medical Corps under the conditions of paragraph 41. **Quartermasters.**

50. A transport officer without medical qualifications may be appointed to each Field Ambulance, in which case he will replace one of the officers on the establishment. The rules governing his appointment, rank and resignation will, if he is not a medical officer, be the same as for quartermasters. **Transport officer.**

51. An appointment as acting transport officer may be held by an officer of the Royal Army Medical Corps not above the rank of major. **Acting transport officers.**

Honorary Colonels of Regiments.

52. Recommendations for appointments of honorary colonels of regiments or corps will be made by commanding officers through the usual military channel to the general officer commanding-in-chief for submission to the Secretary of State for War. **Method of appointment.**

King's Aides-de-Camp.

King's A.D.C. **53.** Officers appointed aides-de-camp to His Majesty the King will be granted the rank of colonel in the Territorial Force. The tenure of their appointments will be for life.

King's Honorary Physicians and King's Honorary Surgeons.

King's physicians. **54.** Officers appointed honorary physicians or honorary surgeons to His Majesty the King will be granted the rank of colonel. These appointments will be tenable by officers as long as they remain in the Territorial Force.

Transfers and Exchanges.

Transfers. **55.** Applications for transfers will be submitted to the general officer commanding-in-chief by the officer commanding the unit to which the officer wishes to be transferred, accompanied by the recommendation of the officer commanding the unit from which the officer wishes to be transferred.

Exchanges. **56.** Applications for exchange will be severally submitted by the commanding officers of the two units concerned.

Seconded Officers.

Period allowed. **57.** An officer may be seconded in his unit for a period not exceeding four years if employed in any special appointment approved by the general officer commanding-in-chief, subject to the approval of the Secretary of State. (*See* also paragraph 31.)

M.Ps. **58.** Officers who are Members of Parliament will not, on that account, be seconded, except on mobilization

Age for Retirement.

Age limit. **59.** Officers, except those referred to in paragraph 35, will be required to relinquish their commissions in the Territorial Force on attaining the age of 60, unless granted an extension of service. Such extension will not be granted for more than two years at a time, nor beyond the age of 65.

Duty of inspecting officer. **60.** The inspecting officer, when submitting his annual inspection report, will examine the ages of all officers given in Army Form E 657, and satisfy himself that no officer who has exceeded the age limit is serving.

Rank on Retirement.

Qualifications and certificate required. **61.** Officers who have completed 15 years' commissioned service may be recommended by their commanding officers for the privilege of retaining their rank on retirement, and of wearing the uniform of the unit in which they last served, with the addition of "R" on the shoulder-strap. The services of officers so recommended must be certified as good and satisfactory, and the officer must be in possession of a qualifying certificate for his substantive rank.

Death and Resignation.

62. Commanding officers will report without delay through the usual military channel to the general officer commanding-in-chief the deaths and voluntary resignations of officers of their units. Duplicates of death reports will be sent direct to the War Office. *Report of death or resignation.*

SECTION 3.—RECRUITING, DISCHARGE, &c.

8 / Terr. Force / 5

RECRUITING.

73. Recruiting will be carried out under the authority of the County Associations, with the assistance of the adjutants and permanent staff of the units concerned. *Recruiting.*

74. The County Associations will define the recruiting areas for the units for which they are responsible, and will endeavour to maintain such units at the establishments fixed for them. In the case of a unit recruited in more than one county, the several Associations concerned will arrange between themselves to maintain its establishment. *Areas.*

75. Officers in charge of recruiting for the regular forces will give every assistance in carrying out recruiting for the Territorial Force within their areas, and in the medical examination and attestation of recruits. *Assistance.*

76. The age for enlistment or re-enlistment for all arms will be from 17 to 35 years. The term of service 4 years. The standard of height will be as laid down in Appendix 5, Table A. The tests for recruits, showing the weight and chest measurement according to the height and age of recruits, will be as laid down in Appendix 5, Table A. Trades for Royal Engineers and the procedure in regard to rating of men for engineer pay will be as laid down in Appendix 12. *Age.*

77. Each recruit will be enlisted for a "county,"* and will be appointed to serve in such corps for that "county," or for an area comprising the whole or part of that "county," as he may select, and if that corps comprises more than one unit within the "county" he will be posted to such one of those units as he may select, provided the establishment of the corps or unit is not exceeded. *Enlistment for a "county."*

78. Every man offering for enlistment will be served by the recruiter with a notice paper. *Notice paper.*

79. A recruit may be required to give the name of some person of respectability from whom a personal reference can be obtained; where necessary, Army Form B 64 will be used for this purpose. Should a recruit appear to be under the age standard, enquiries should be made before final approval. *Personal reference.*

---

* *i.e.*, an area for which a County Association has been formed.

Medical examination.

80. Every recruit on enlistment will be required to pass a medical examination, which will be conducted :—

(*a*) by officers of the Royal Army Medical Corps when available ; or

(*b*) by the medical officer of a unit of the Territorial Force ; or

(*c*) by civilian medical practitioners specially appointed for the purpose.

Military examination.

81. The primary military examination, attestation, and final approval will be proceeded with as in the case of recruits for the regular army. One attestation form only will be prepared.

Boys.

82. Boys between 14 and 17 years of age may, with the consent of parents or guardians, be attested for appointment as trumpeters, buglers, or bandsmen, or for the purpose of being trained as such. The number of boys in excess of establishment of trumpeters or buglers will not exceed one for each squadron, battery, or company. Such excess must count in the total establishment of the unit.

Classes ineligible.

83. The following classes will not be allowed to enlist (or re-enlist) into the Territorial Force :—

(*a*) Men belonging to any corps of the Royal Navy, Regular Army, Royal Marines, Army or Special Reserve, Territorial Force, Militia, Irish Yeomanry, or any Royal Naval Reserve force.

(*b*) Men who have been discharged from those forces or from the Royal Irish Constabulary (1) as unfit for further service (except as provided in paragraph 84); (2) for misconduct ; (3) or with a bad or an indifferent character.

(*c*) Men who have been convicted of a serious offence by the civil power.

(*d*) Foreigners.

Discharged men.

84. Men who have been discharged from the Army, Army or Special Reserve, Militia, Imperial Yeomanry, or the Territorial Force, as medically unfit, but are pronounced by the medical authority (having complete knowledge of the cause of discharge) to be fully fit for service in the Territorial Force, may be enlisted, provided that their character on discharge was at least "fair." If men in receipt of temporary pensions are found fit for service, and accepted, a notification will be sent to the Chelsea Commissioners.

Attesting officers.

85. In addition to the officers and justices of the peace authorised to attest recruits for the Regular Army and the Special Reserve, a recruit for the Territorial Force may be attested by any lieutenant or deputy lieutenant of any county in the United Kingdom, by a regular officer, or by an officer of the Territorial Force.

Re-engagement.

86. A soldier of the Territorial Force desiring to re-engage must do so during the 12 months prior to the expiration of his current term of service. He will make the prescribed declaration on Army Form E 611 before a justice of the peace or an officer.

Approving officers.

87. The final approval of recruits of the Territorial Force will, as a rule, be carried out by officers not below the rank of field officer of the units concerned, or by regular adjutants of units ; where this is impossible, the following may approve :—

Officers in charge of recruiting areas.
„ commanding regular units of cavalry, artillery, engineers, infantry, or army service corps.
„ „ at military stations.

88. Re-engagement in the Territorial Force will be for 1, 2, 3, or 4 years. The term will be fixed at the discretion of the County Association. Term of service.

89. When a man who has previously served in the Royal Navy, Regular Army, Royal Marines, Army or Special Reserve, Militia, Yeomanry, or Royal Irish Constabulary, enlists or re-enlists in the Territorial Force, he will be required to state the particulars of his former service and cause of discharge, and to produce, if possible, his certificate of discharge, which will be returned to him conspicuously endorsed in red ink as follows :— Former service to be declared.

..........................enlisted as a soldier of the Territorial Force, on the..

90. The enlistment of men who have previously served in the army will be notified to the officer in charge of their records, in order that the notification may be placed with their documents. Men with army service

91. Soldiers of the Territorial Force may enlist into the regular army, and shall thereupon be deemed to be discharged from the Territorial Force, but shall nevertheless be liable to deliver up in good order, fair wear and tear only excepted, all arms, clothing, and equipment, being public property, issued to them. Enlistment into regular army.

92. Soldiers of the Territorial Force may enlist into the Special Reserve. If they enlist into the Irish Yeomanry or the Special Reserve of the— Enlistment into special reserve.

(*a*) Royal Field Artillery, Royal Garrison Artillery, Royal Engineers (Siege and Railway Companies), or Infantry of the Line, they will be deemed to be discharged from the Territorial Force.

(*b*) Army Service Corps, Royal Army Medical Corps, Army Railway Corps, or Army Post Office Corps, they will while so serving be supernumerary to the Territorial Force, until their service in the Territorial Force has expired.

TRANSFER, DISCHARGE, &c.

9 / Gen. No. / 121

Transfer to other Units.

93. Soldiers of the Territorial Force who change their residence to another county, may, if they desire it and both commanding officers consent, be transferred to a unit of the county in which they have taken up their residence. On transfer they will be allowed to count drills performed with their old unit towards the number required annually in the new unit, provided the transfer When allowed.

is to the same branch of the service. They may also, with the consent of both commanding officers, be transferred to another unit of the same county.

Discharge.

Definition of term "O.C." **94.** The expression "O.C." in paragraph 95 will mean :—

Yeomanry ...	O.C. the regiment.
Artillery ...	O.C. unit.
Engineers ...	O.C. company.
Infantry ...	O.C. battalion.
A.S.C. R.A.M.C.	O.C. unit.

Discharges. **95.** The following are the instructions as to the procedure in the various classes of discharge :—

Cause of discharge.	Competent officer to		Special instructions.
	Authorise discharge.	Carry out discharge.	
1.—Termination of engagement.	O.C.	O.C.	Discharge should be confirmed for the day on which the man completes his engagement.
2.—Having reached the age for discharge.	O.C.	O.C.	Applies to men who have reached the age fixed for discharge (*see* para. 99); on reaching such age they should be discharged whether their period of engagement has expired or not.
3.—At his own request.	O.C.	O.C.	On giving three months' notice, or such less notice as may be prescribed (*see* also para. 101 for discharge by purchase).
4.—Conduct unsatisfactory.	Brigade Commander.	O.C.	Applies to men who conduct themselves in such a way as to render their retention in the Territorial Force undesirable.

Cause of discharge.	Competent officer to		Special instructions.
	Authorise discharge.	Carry out discharge.	
5.—Having made a false answer on attestation.	O.C.	O.C.	Discharges under this heading are provided for in Section 99* of the Army Act, and when a man has been convicted of false answer, the O.C. will decide whether he is to be retained or not.
6.—Having been irregularly enlisted.	O.C.	O.C.	Discharges under this heading are provided for in Section 100* of the Army Act.
7.—Having been claimed as an apprentice.	O.C.	O.C.	Discharges under this heading are provided for in Section 96* of the Army Act, and when the requirements of the Act are fully complied with the man should be discharged forthwith.
8.—Having made a mis-statement as to age on enlistment.	O.C.	O.C.	Applies to men of the Territorial Force who on enlistment stated their age as not less than 17 years, and for whose free discharge application is made by their parents on the grounds that they are less than 17 years of age at the date of application.

* Made applicable to the Territorial Force by Section X. (1) of the Territorial and Reserve Forces Act, 1907.

Cause of discharge.	Competent officer to — Authorise discharge.	Competent officer to — Carry out discharge.	Special instructions.
9.—Medically unfit.	Brigade Commander.	O.C.	When a man is discharged under this heading he will be examined by a medical board, if his disability appears to have been in any way caused by his service in camp or during embodiment (*see* para. 100)
10.—Not being likely to become an efficient soldier.	Brigade Commander.	O.C.	Men who are not likely to become efficient soldiers of the Territorial Force and cannot be discharged under any other heading.

Discharges. **96.** Discharges in cases other than those specified in the preceding table, will be submitted to the general officer commanding the division.

Discharge Certificates.

Discharge certificate. **97.** Each man on discharge will receive a certificate of discharge on A.F. E 511. To ensure uniformity in recording a man's character, the following terms will be strictly adhered to :—

I. Very good.
II. Good.
III. Fair.
IV. Indifferent.
V. Bad.

Certificate of good service. **98.** A certificate of good service, A.F. E 510, will be given to each soldier of the Territorial Force on discharge, provided that he has served not less than 6 years, and that his character on discharge is at least "Good."

Age-limit for discharge.

Age limit. **99.** The age for discharge of soldiers of the Territorial Force will be as follows :—

Serjeants, other than those on the permanent staff, will be discharged on reaching the age of 50 years, except in very special cases, when the brigade commander may sanction their retention up to 55 years of age. This limit will in no case be exceeded.

In the case of rank and file, trumpeters, &c., the age for discharge will be 40 years. The brigade commander may sanction retention up to 45 years of age.

Miscellaneous.

100. The documents of men who have been discharged as medically unfit for further service, and who have claims to pension, will be submitted to the Secretary, Royal Hospital, Chelsea, accompanied by A.F. B 179. **Documents to Chelsea.**

101. Men of the Territorial Force will be permitted to purchase their discharge under the conditions laid down in Section 9 (3) of the Territorial and Reserve Forces Act, 1907. **Discharge by purchase.**

102. The undermentioned details connected with the service of a man of the Territorial Force will be entered in the statement of service on the third page of his attestation :— **Documents.**

(1) Re-engagements.
(2) Promotions.
(3) Reductions.
(4) Transfers to other units.
(5) Details of service showing whether present at, or absent from, each annual training

103. When a man of the Territorial Force becomes non-effective his attestation and other documents will be dealt with as follows :— **Documents of non-effective.**

Causes of becoming non-effective.	How disposed of.
Death....	Destroyed.
Discharge	Retained by unit for 35 years and then destroyed.
Enlistment into regular forces	Retained by unit for 35 years and then destroyed.
Desertion or absence	Retained by unit for 35 years and then destroyed.
Recruits rejected by approving officer	Retained by approving officer for one year and then destroyed.

104. When a man who has previously served in the Auxiliary Forces enlists or re-enlists in the Territorial Force the documents relating to him in his former unit will (if in existence) be obtained and preserved with his documents in his new unit. **Documents on enlisting in Territorial Force.**

105. When a man who has previously served in the Territorial Force enlists into the Special Reserve the documents relating to him in his former unit will (if in existence) be obtained and preserved with his documents in his new unit. **In Special Reserve.**

108 Gen. No. 1547

SECTION 4.—DISCIPLINE, PRECEDENCE, &c.

I.—DISCIPLINE.

1. General Regulations.

When subject to military law, officers.

116. Officers are at all times subject to military law.

Residence.

117. The permanent residence of all officers of the Territorial Force must be in the United Kingdom.

N.C.Os. and men.

118. Non-commissioned officers and men are subject to military law—

(*a*) When they are being trained or exercised, either alone or with any portion of the regular forces or otherwise;

(*b*) When attached to or otherwise acting as part of or with any regular forces;

(*c*) When embodied;

(*d*) When called out for actual military service for purposes of defence in pursuance of any agreement.

"Trained or exercised," meaning of.

119. A soldier when on parade, or performing any military duty required of him by these regulations or ordered by his commanding officer, is "being trained or exercised" within the meaning of Sub-section 6A (*a*) of Section 176 of the Army Act. He is, consequently, subject to military law, and may, under the Army Act, Section 45, be placed in military custody as there defined. The commanding officer may proceed in the manner detailed in Section 46 of the Army Act. Where a commanding officer deals with any case, he has, in addition to his powers of punishment under Section 46 of the Army Act, the power of awarding dismissal as a punishment.

Treatment of soldiers.

120. An officer of any rank will adopt towards his subordinates such methods of command and treatment as will not only ensure respect for authority, but also foster the feelings of self-respect and personal honour essential to military efficiency. Non-commissioned officers will be guided by the foregoing principles in dealing with each other and with private soldiers. They will avoid the use of intemperate language or the adoption of an offensive manner.

Reproof of N.C.O.

121. An officer will not reprove a non-commissioned officer in the presence or hearing of privates, unless it is necessary for the benefit of example that the reproof be public.

Sections of Army Act which apply to Territorial Force.

122. The following sections of the Army Act apply to the Territorial Force:—

Section 80, relating to the mode of enlistment and attestation.

„ 96, relating to claims of masters to apprentices.

„ 98, imposing a fine for unlawful recruiting.

„ 99, making recruits punishable for false answers.

Section 100, so much as relates to the validity of attestation and enlistment or re-engagement.

" 101, relating to the competent military authority.

" 143, for the purposes of which and of all other enactments relating to such duties, tolls, and ferries as are in that section mentioned, officers and men belonging to the Territorial Force, when going to or returning from any place at which they are required to attend, and for non-attendance at which they are liable to be punished, shall be deemed to be officers and soldiers of the regular forces on duty.

" 153 } relating to deserters and desertion, on embodi-
" 154 } ment.

" 163, relating to evidence.

" 164, relating to evidence of acquittal or conviction by a civil court.

" 166 } as regards prosecutions before a court of sum-
" 167 } mary jurisdiction and recovery of fines.
" 168 }

123. The sections of the Army Act enumerated in paragraph 461, King's Regulations, together with the notice regarding the liability of persons who endeavour to seduce soldiers from their allegiance, &c., will be read over to a unit of the Territorial Force when first assembled for training, and at such other times as the commanding officer may deem expedient. Army Act, portions to be read out.

124. During the period between the issue of the writ for an election in any electoral district and the termination of the election, a commanding officer will not assemble his unit in that district. A general officer commanding-in-chief may, however, make exceptions in such cases as :— No assembly during Parliamentary elections or for party purposes.

(1) Camps.
(2) Drills of less than 100 men.
(3) Class-firing and musketry practice.
(4) Regimental prize distributions or similar occasions, for which the unit concerned may be assembled in their drill hall, but without arms.

An assembly of soldiers will not be sanctioned for any day when, by reason of local circumstances, such assembly might be made to subserve party purposes.

125. Officers and soldiers training in camp, &c., who are qualified to vote and are desirous of doing so, will be granted the necessary leave for the purpose, and the period of such leave may be reckoned as attendance at training. To be allowed to vote.

Officers, non-commissioned officers and men will not take part in or attend any political meetings or demonstrations in uniform, nor will military bands be permitted to play at such meetings. Political meetings.

126. An officer, non-commissioned officer or man cannot be compelled to serve as a peace officer or parish officer, and will be exempt from serving on any jury. A field officer cannot be compelled to serve in the office of high sheriff. Exempt from juries.

Officer responsible for discipline. **127.** When detachments of units of the Territorial Force are brought together for any military purpose, the senior officer present will be held responsible for the due maintenance of order and discipline.

Unit not to leave command without sanction. **128.** A unit of the Territorial Force will not quit, as a military body, the command to which it belongs, without the sanction of the general officer commanding-in-chief. When a movement into another command is desired, the general officer commanding-in-chief will obtain the concurrence of the general officer commanding-in-chief concerned.

Praise or censure of superiors forbidden. **129.** Deliberations or discussions by officers, non-commissioned officers and men with the object of conveying praise, censure, or any mark of approbation towards their superiors or any others in His Majesty's service are prohibited.

The publication of laudatory orders on officers quitting a station or relinquishing an appointment is forbidden.

Presents. No presentations of plate, swords, &c., will take place, without the previous sanction of the general officer commanding the division.

Testimonials not to be forwarded to W.O. **130.** An officer is forbidden to forward testimonials relating to his services or character, with any application he may make to the War Office. In the event of an officer wishing that the opinions of officers under whom he has served should be brought to notice, he will submit their names, so that if necessary they may be referred to. Officers, non-commissioned officers and men are forbidden to write private letters on military matters to officials at the War Office.

Bankruptcy, &c. **131.** An officer who becomes a bankrupt, makes a composition with his creditors, or is otherwise unable to meet his engagements, will at once notify the fact to his commanding officer. The latter will report the circumstances for the information of the Army Council, who will decide whether the officer can be permitted to continue to hold His Majesty's commission.

Uniform, wearing of. **132.** Officers while in foreign countries will not wear uniform except at court, or on the occasion of State ceremonies to which they have been invited, or when employed on duty. An officer will not attend in uniform the manœuvres of foreign armies without the permission of the Army Council.

Headdress in civil courts. **133.** In a civil court an officer or soldier will remove his headdress while the judge or magistrate is present, except when the officer or soldier is on duty under arms with a party or escort inside the court.

Not to act as press correspondents. **134.** Unless by special permission of the Army Council, officers, non-commissioned officers and men are forbidden to act as press correspondents with any army in the field, or at foreign manœuvres, or, in this connection, to publish or communicate either directly or indirectly to the press any military information. If permitted to act as press correspondents, they will not use their military rank, or describe themselves as military correspondents in their published communications.

Permanent Staff N.C.O. **135.** A non-commissioned officer serving on the permanent staff will not accept employment outside his military duties without the sanction of the brigade commander concerned, which will not be given if such employment interferes with the performance of any military duty, but instructors may be employed as drill instructors of cadet corps or battalions affiliated to the corps to which the instructor is attached.

136. If a serjeants' mess is established in a unit under the authority of the commanding officer, that officer will be responsible that it is organized on the lines laid down in the King's Regulations, that discipline is maintained, and that the accounts are properly kept and audited. Serjeants messes.

2. Courts-Martial, Courts of Summary Jurisdiction, Courts of Inquiry, Committees, and Boards.

137. Courts-martial, courts of inquiry, committees, and boards will be conducted in accordance with the Rules of Procedure and the King's Regulations. One officer at least of the Territorial Force will be detailed to serve on courts of inquiry, committees, and boards, as well as on courts-martial. Mode of conducting.

138. Regimental courts-martial and courts of inquiry involving expense will not be held without the authority of the general officer commanding the division. Involving expense.

139. Offences committed by members of the permanent staff will be dealt with under the Army Act and the King's Regulations, but the powers of a commanding officer, as regards any award involving an entry in the conduct sheet will be exercised only by and under the authority of the officer commanding the district who has the custody of the regimental conduct sheets. The adjutant is personally responsible for the custody of squadron, battery or company conduct sheets. Permanent staff, offences of.

140. Whenever it is necessary to try an instructor by court-martial, the commanding officer will make application to the officer commanding the district as to the assembly of the court. Courts-martial on.

141. Non-commissioned officers and men are liable, while subject to military law, to be tried by court-martial for any offence committed by them against the Army Act while so subject, and they are also liable to be so tried for such an offence even though they have ceased to be subject to military law, provided the trial commences within three months after they have ceased to be so subject. Offences whilst subject to military law.

142. (*a*) The following offences are cognisable either by a court-martial or by a court of summary jurisdiction :— Offences cognisable either by court-martial or civil court.

(i) Offences under Section XI (1) of the Territorial and Reserve Forces Act, 1907 ;

(ii) Failure to appear at the time and place appointed for assembling on embodiment* ;

(iii) Offences under the Army Act committed by a man when not embodied.

---

* Failure to attend on embodiment or to attend at annual training or drills is only an offence when not due to such sickness or other reasonable excuse as may be allowed in the prescribed manner, or when leave has not been lawfully granted (see Territorial and Reserve Forces Act, Section XX. (1) and (2)).

Offences cognisable by civil court only.

(*b*) The following offences are cognisable by a court of summary jurisdiction alone :—

(i) * Failure to appear at the time and place appointed for annual training, or failure to attend the number of drills and fulfil the conditions relating to preliminary or annual training laid down for the arm or branch of the service to which the man belongs ;

(ii) Offences against Section XXII of the Territorial and Reserve Forces Act, 1907.

Offences cognisable by court-martial only.

(*c*) The following offences are cognisable by a court-martial alone :—

Offences under the Army Act triable by court-martial if committed by a man of the Territorial Force when embodied.

But any offence under the Army Act which is cognisable by a court-martial may be dealt with by the commanding officer under, and in accordance with, Section 46 of the Army Act. Where a commanding officer deals with any case, he has, in addition to his powers of punishment under Section 46 of the Army Act, the power of awarding dismissal as a punishment.

Time within which offences are to be dealt with.

143. Proceedings against an offender before either a court-martial or his commanding officer or a court of summary jurisdiction in respect of an offence punishable under the Territorial and Reserve Forces Act, 1907, and alleged to have been committed by him when a man of the Territorial Force, may be instituted before a court-martial, or the commanding officer, or a civil court (whether the offender's term of service has, or has not expired), at any time within two calendar months after the time at which the offence became known to the commanding officer if the alleged offender is then apprehended, or, if he is not then apprehended, then within two calendar months after the time of apprehension.

General rules as regards disposal of certain offences.

144. Of the offences cognisable both by a court-martial and a court of summary jurisdiction :—

(i) Failure to attend on embodiment* will, as a rule, be tried by court-martial ;

(ii) Offences under Section XI (1) of the Territorial and Reserve Forces Act, 1907, will, as a rule, be tried by court-martial ;

(iii) Serious military offences committed by soldiers when attending individual drill will ordinarily be disposed of by the commanding officer under Section IX (4) of the Territorial and Reserve Forces Act, 1907 ;

(iv) Military offences committed by men of the Territorial Force while at continuous training will ordinarily be disposed of by the commanding officer or by court-martial.

Court of summary jurisdiction resort to.

145. In respect of any offence mentioned in paragraph 144 which has not been dealt with in the manner prescribed in that paragraph, and in respect of any other offence which is cognisable both by court-martial and a court of summary jurisdiction, a court of summary jurisdiction may be resorted to, but proceedings before such

* Failure to attend on embodiment or to attend at annual training or drills is only an offence when not due to such sickness or other reasonable excuse as may be allowed in the prescribed manner, or when leave has not been lawfully granted (*see* Territorial and Reserve Forces Act, Section XX (1) and (2)).

court shall not be taken until the sanction of the commanding officer of the unit concerned, or of a military authority superior to such commanding officer, has been signified in writing to the court before which the proceedings are to take place, and such proceedings shall not be taken if—

(i) the case has been dealt with by the commanding officer or a court-martial;

(ii) proceedings are not commenced within the time-limit mentioned in paragraph 143.

146. A man charged with an offence cognisable both by a court-martial and a court of summary jurisdiction may be taken into military custody, notwithstanding that proceedings are intended to be taken before the civil court. **When a man may be taken into military custody.**

147. Proceedings before a court of summary jurisdiction under the Territorial and Reserve Forces Act, 1907, should be either by summons or (where it is advisable that the accused should be promptly made amenable to justice) by warrant, except where the accused shall have been apprehended and brought before the court in military custody. A summons may issue upon a statement to a justice of the facts constituting the offence, but a warrant is obtainable only upon a sworn information. In cases of doubt or difficulty, application should be made to the police for advice. **Mode of taking proceedings in civil court.**

148. Any person who designedly makes away with, sells or pawns, or wrongfully destroys or damages, or negligently loses anything issued to him as an officer or man of the Territorial Force, or wrongfully refuses or neglects to deliver up on demand anything issued to him as an officer or man of the Territorial Force, will, on complaint to a court of summary jurisdiction by the County Association, be liable to repay the value of such article, or articles, and will also, on information being laid by the County Association, by any officer or by any other person, be liable on conviction under the Summary Jurisdiction Acts to a fine not exceeding five pounds (£5) if the article, or articles, have been designedly made away with, sold, pawned, or wrongfully destroyed. **Punishment for making away with, &c., articles.**

149. If a non-commissioned officer or man illegally absents himself from his duty while subject to military law, either on embodiment or while at continuous training, a court of inquiry, under Section 72 of the Army Act, will be assembled at the expiration of 21 clear days from the date of such absence, whether the period during which he was subject to military law is less than 21 days, or has expired before the 21 days have elapsed. **Court of inquiry on absence.**

150. A non-commissioned officer or man who enlists into the Special Reserve without being discharged from the Territorial Force will be held to serve on his reserve attestation. On joining the Special Reserve, a soldier of the Territorial Force is to declare his service in the Territorial Force. **Enlisting in Special Reserve.**

3. Improper Enlistment.

151. A soldier who has made a false answer on his attestation will be proceeded against under Section 99 of the Army Act, by virtue of Section X of the Territorial and Reserve Forces Act, 1907. **False answer on attestation.**

Apprentices. **152.** A soldier who, being an apprentice, has denied on his attestation that he is an apprentice will be liable to be proceeded against under Section 96 of the Army Act, by virtue of Section X of the Territorial and Reserve Forces Act, 1907. If, however, the requirements of Section 96 of the Army Act are fully complied with, the soldier will usually be discharged forthwith.

Fraudulent enlistment. **153.** A soldier who, while belonging to the Territorial Force, when embodied, without having obtained a regular discharge therefrom, or otherwise fulfilled the conditions enabling him to enlist, enlists, or enrols himself in His Majesty's regular forces, or in any force raised in India or a colony, will be amenable under Section 13 (1) (a) of the Army Act for fraudulent enlistment.

Improper enlistment into regular forces. **154.** When information is obtained of the improper enlistment of a soldier of the Territorial Force into the regular forces, a report of the fact on A.F. E 530 will be sent by the officer commanding the Territorial unit to the officer commanding the unit in which the man is supposed to be serving, with a duplicate of his Territorial attestation, and a certificate, as laid down in the King's Regulations, paragraph 530.

Man of naval forces enlisting. **155.** When a man belonging to any section of His Majesty's naval forces has enlisted in the Territorial Force, the case will be referred to the Admiralty, before any steps are taken for prosecuting the man before the civil power.

Soldier of Territorial Force entering naval forces. **156.** In the cases of soldiers of the Territorial Force who have improperly entered any section of His Majesty's Naval Forces or the Royal Marines, similar reports will be made to the Secretary to the Admiralty, who will be requested to make the stoppages required by the Pay Warrant, and a duplicate return on A.F. E 530 will at the same time be forwarded to the War Office.

4. Complaints and Appeals.

During training. **157.** During continuous training all applications and complaints by soldiers will be made through officers commanding companies, who will ascertain whether any men wish to see the inspecting officer upon any point. They will investigate and endeavour to settle complaints as far as possible. If they cannot satisfactorily settle such complaints, a return in duplicate of the names of the men and the subjects of complaint will be laid by the commanding officer before the inspecting officer, leaving a column for his remarks and decision, and a column for the decision of the general officer commanding the division when necessary.

At other times, except during embodiment. At all other times, except during embodiment, applications and complaints will be made through the squadron, battery or company commander, or adjutant, to the officer commanding the unit. On no account will such applications or complaints be made direct to the War Office.

During embodiment. During embodiment, complaints will be made in accordance with Section 43 of the Army Act.

Appeal against discharge. **158.** Should a non-commissioned officer or man who has been discharged by his commanding officer under the provisions of Section IX (4) of the Territorial and Reserve Forces Act, 1907, desire to appeal against the commanding officer's decision, he is to forward his appeal to the Army Council, whose decision will be final.

5. Orders.

159. An officer may be authorised to issue orders on behalf of a military authority under Part II. of the Territorial and Reserve Forces Act, and any order, instruction, or letter purporting to be so signed on behalf of such military authority shall be evidence of the officer who signed it being so authorised. Authorised officer.

160. An officer in temporary command of a unit will not issue any standing orders, or alter those which are at the time in force, or authorise the application of regimental funds to any purpose other than the ordinary current expenditure, without reference to the permanent commanding officer, or to the brigade commander. An officer while absent from, and not in the exercise of, his command cannot issue regimental or other orders relating to such command. Officer in temporary command.

161. All officers will acquaint themselves with regulations and orders. Ignorance of published orders will not be admitted as an excuse for their non-observance. During annual training all orders specially relating to the non-commissioned officers and men will be read and explained to them immediately after such orders are received. Officers to make themselves acquainted with orders, &c.

162. An officer who has been on leave of absence will, on rejoining, make himself acquainted with all orders issued in his absence. On rejoining from leave.

163. The commanding officer will cause every order issued for general information and guidance either to be re-published in regimental orders, or otherwise circulated to all in the unit whom it may concern. Re-publishing of orders.

The commanding officer will also afford all officers under his command facilities for becoming acquainted with changes in the regulations and orders of the Territorial Force. Changes in regulations.

6. Absence Without Leave.

164. A soldier who without leave lawfully granted or other reasonable excuse fails to appear at the time and place appointed for assembling on embodiment will be guilty of desertion or absence without leave according to the circumstances, and the provisions of Section 154 of the Army Act and the King's Regulations with respect to deserters will apply to such offenders, who may, whether otherwise subject to military law or not, be taken into military custody and tried either by court-martial or by a court of summary jurisdiction in accordance with paragraph 144 (i). On embodiment.

165. At the end of one week from the date fixed for embodiment, a list on A.F. B. 124 of all soldiers whose absence has not been satisfactorily accounted for will be forwarded by the commanding officer to the Editor of the Police Gazette. A copy of this form will also be sent in each case to the police of the locality in which the absentee last resided. The instructions contained in the King's Regulations with regard to deserters will apply to soldiers of the Territorial Force who absent themselves after they have joined on embodiment. Report to police.

166. When a soldier who has been reported to the police authorities as liable to arrest under paragraph 165 ceases to be liable to arrest, an immediate intimation of the fact will be made to the police authorities by the commanding officer. Report when ceasing to be liable to.

Absence from annual training. **167.** A soldier who fails to attend for annual training, and whose absence has not been satisfactorily accounted for, will not be taken into military custody, but he will be liable to be proceeded against by the Association through the officer prescribed by them before a court of summary jurisdiction, as laid down in Section XXI of the Territorial and Reserve Forces Act, 1907.

Absence after joining for training. **168.** A soldier who, having joined for annual training and having, therefore, become subject to military law, absents himself, will be dealt with under Section 15 of the Army Act.

When struck off strength. **169.** At the end of 21 days from the expiration of the annual training, a soldier whose absence is not satisfactorily accounted for, and who has not been dealt with under paragraphs 167 or 168, will be struck off the strength.

Liable to additional service. **170.** When a soldier is liable to additional service, under the provisions of Section XX (3) of the Territorial and Reserve Forces Act, 1907, an entry will be made in the last column of his record of service, on the 3rd page of his attestation, as follows :—

"Deserted on embodiment; liable to serve for an additional period of......................................"

This does not refer to soldiers guilty only of absence without leave on embodiment, or of absence from annual training.

Rules of evidence. **171.** In courts-martial proceedings the facts constituting compliance with Section XIX of the Territorial and Reserve Forces Act, 1907, must be proved according to the usual rules of evidence.

II. PRECEDENCE.

Territorial Force. **172.** The Territorial Force of Great Britain takes precedence immediately after the Special Reserve.

Precedence of arms. **173.** The relative precedence of the different arms is as follows :—

Honourable Artillery Company—Yeomanry—Royal Artillery—Royal Engineers—Infantry—Army Service Corps—Royal Army Medical Corps.

Precedence of units. **174.** The precedence of units within the different arms is governed by the precedence of counties, which is shown, for the different arms, in the Army List.

Officers. **175.** Officers of the Territorial Force when serving with officers of the regular forces or special reserve will take rank as the junior of their degree.

Officers among themselves. **176.** The precedence of officers in the Territorial Force is determined by their rank and the dates of appointment to that rank in the force; of officers of different units in the same rank and appointed to that rank on the same date, by the date of their next lower rank; of officers in the same unit in the same rank and appointed to that rank on the same date, by the order in which their names appear in the Army List.

Adjutants. **177.** An officer of the regular forces, appointed adjutant of a Territorial Force unit, who is a substantive field officer, will not for regimental purposes take precedence over the majors of the regiment or battalion to which he is appointed; he will rank as junior major. If holding the army rank of captain he will rank as senior captain. When holding the army rank of lieutenant he will be appointed to serve with the rank of captain in the territorial unit, and in such case will rank among the captains according to the date of his appointment.

III. APPOINTMENT AND DUTIES OF PERMANENT STAFF.

1. Adjutant and Acting Adjutant.

178. The appointment of adjutants will be governed by the regulations laid down in the Pay Warrant and King's Regulations. Appointment.

179. The selection of adjutants will be made by the Army Council. Candidates will not be nominated by officers commanding Territorial Force units. Selection.

180. When a vacancy occurs in the appointment of adjutant, or when the adjutant is on certified sick leave, an officer may be appointed as acting adjutant by the general officer commanding-in-chief. If no officer of the unit is available, an officer of the regular forces will be selected. In all other cases an application for an acting adjutant must be made to the War Office. Acting adjutant.

181. The adjutant is subject to the orders of his commanding officer, and is required to assist him in carrying on the military duty of the unit. He will not take any part in the non-military affairs of the unit, or follow any other profession, or fill any other appointment whilst holding an adjutancy. He will not reside away from headquarters unless specially authorised to do so by the general officer commanding-in-chief. General duties.

182. The adjutant will frequently visit each part of his unit, and also the practice ranges. The number of visits will be determined by the commanding officer. Adjutants' visits to outlying units.

183. The commanding officer will take care that any duty he may have to assign to the adjutant in connection with a squadron, battery, or company distant from headquarters shall, whenever practicable, be performed during the usual visit for military instruction. Duties at usual visits.

184. The commanding officer will, with a view to suit local convenience, arrange in advance, with the officers commanding outlying squadrons, batteries, companies, or detachments, the days on which the adjutant will visit each of them. Adjutant's visits.

185. The adjutant will inspect the arms and equipment of outlying squadrons, batteries, companies, or detachments at his visits. Inspection of arms.

186. The adjutant is responsible to the commanding officer that all official books, documents, and returns connected with the military administration and training of the unit are correctly kept and rendered. Responsibility of adjutant.

2. Serjeant-Instructors.

187. Vacancies for non-commissioned officers serving on army engagements on the permanent staff will be notified by the commanding officer to the officer i/c records concerned, and will be filled as directed for permanent staff of Volunteer corps in the King's Regulations as far as they are applicable. Re-transfers from the Mode of appointment.

permanent staff will also be dealt with as directed in those Regulations.

Pensioners, discharged soldiers.

188. Pensioners, discharged soldiers, or qualified soldiers of the Territorial Force, may also, with the approval of the general officer commanding-in-chief, be employed as temporary instructors.

Instructors on parade.

189. Non-commissioned officers of the permanent staff will, on parade, rank as senior to all Territorial Force non-commissioned officers.

Acting serjeant-major.

190. Acting serjeant-majors of the permanent staff may be appointed as follows :—

1 to each infantry battalion of 8 companies (except cyclist battalions) ;

1 to each group of Royal Garrison Artillery units shown in Appendix 3, to which is allotted 3 or more serjeant-instructors. (Two acting serjeant-majors will be allowed to the Glamorgan and Pembroke Royal Garrison Artillery.)

1 to a school of instruction, Royal Army Medical Corps.

When a unit is entitled to an acting serjeant-major on the permanent staff the commanding officer may appoint one of the instructors to be acting serjeant-major, and will notify the appointment through the usual channel to the general officer commanding-in-chief. A commanding officer may deprive the instructor of his appointment as acting serjeant-major, for any sufficient cause, but when he finds it necessary to do so, he will notify the fact through the usual channel to the general officer commanding-in-chief.

Supervision of adjutant, and report of irregularity, &c.

Serious offence.

191. All instructors are under the supervision of the adjutant, who will report to the officer commanding any irregularity of conduct, incompetence, or want of attention. The commanding officer, when the offence is of sufficiently grave nature, will report it to the brigade commander, who will either dispose of the case, or report it to the general officer commanding the division. The instructor will be kept in arrest until orders are received as to his disposal.

Genera duties of instructors.

192. An instructor may, in addition to his ordinary duties, be entrusted with the custody of the arms, or be employed as caretaker of a rifle range of the unit, or charged with such other military duties as devolve on a non-commissioned officer, such as orderly-room work, superintending the cleaning of guns, harness. and arms, and looking after clothing and accoutrements in the regimental store. He will not be required to clean arms. He will not in any circumstances be employed in connection with a canteen or any regimental institution, or on any other duty which is not directly connected with the instruction or training of the unit.

Visits to outlying squadrons, &c.

193. An instructor will not visit outlying squadrons, batteries, or companies more than once a week without special authority of the brigade commander.

Inspection of arms of outlying companies.

194. The commanding officer may order a qualified instructor to proceed at the public expense to an outlying squadron, battery, or company not having a certified armourer, for the purpose of making a quarterly inspection of arms.

Drill of outlying companies during illness.

195. During the illness of an instructor posted to an outlying squadron, battery, or company, an instructor of the unit may be sent once a week to assist in the training of such squadron, battery, or company.

196. Non-commissioned officers of the permanent staff below the rank of colour-serjeant will always appear in uniform unless the general officer commanding the division gives special permission in individual cases for plain clothes to be worn. **Uniform to be worn.**

197. Instructors will not be employed in receiving or disbursing money. **Instructors not to disburse money.**

198. Each instructor will keep a diary on A.F. E 574. **Diary.**

IV. LEAVE OF ABSENCE.

199. Leave of absence may be granted to an adjutant by his commanding officer for any period not exceeding a fortnight, but such leave, when more than one day, will be reported to the brigade commander. Ordinary or sick leave for continuous or intermittent periods of absence not exceeding in the aggregate 61 days, reckoning from the 1st April in each year (including leave granted by the commanding officer), may be granted by the brigade commander. Applications for leave of absence will be made on A.F. E 539. **Period of adjutant's leave of absence. Application for leave.**

200. A general officer commanding-in-chief may, on the recommendation of a medical board, grant an extension of leave to an adjutant for a period not exceeding six months. If unable to resume his duties at the expiration of this further period, he will cease to hold his appointment. **Sick leave.**

201. An adjutant employed as a recruiting officer, or as a sub-accountant, will, before applying for leave, arrange with the brigade commander, or the accountant, for the performance of his recruiting or financial duties. **When employed as recruiting officer, &c.**

202. All officers are required to be present at the training of their units. Leave will only be granted in very exceptional circumstances. **Officers.**

203. In transmitting applications from officers for leave the commanding officer of a unit, after having obtained full information as to the circumstances of the case, will express his own opinion as to granting it. An officer, in asking for leave, will not content himself with stating urgent private affairs as the ground of his application, but will give good reason why such leave is absolutely necessary. Applications for leave (except in case of sickness) must be made not less than a fortnight before the date fixed for the assembly of the unit for training. General officers commanding divisions will decide upon each case. **Application for leave. Decisions of general officer commanding.**

204. An officer who applies for leave on account of sickness will forward a medical certificate on A.F. B 175. **Sick leave.**

205. Under instructions received from the divisional, mounted brigade, or coast defence commander, the officer commanding a unit may excuse an officer or soldier from any portion of the annual training (as defined in para. 284) on account of sickness duly certified, or for any other urgent reason which they may consider sufficient. **Power to excuse individuals from training.**

206. A commanding officer may grant leave with pay to an officer or soldier of the Territorial Force during annual training in camp for a period not exceeding one night in the case of an officer or soldier attending for a shorter period than 15 days, and for not more than 48 hours if attending for the full period of training. **Officers and soldiers of Territorial Force.**

Leave without pay. **207.** In very special cases leave for a longer period without pay may be granted subject to the approval of the general officer commanding the division, which should be obtained at the termination of the annual training.

Leave, drills to be performed. **208.** In cases where leave for one night is granted, not more than one hour's drill or exercise must be missed, and in cases where leave with pay is granted for a longer period absence must not be permitted from more than the drills or exercises of two complete days. Leave of absence will not be given for the first or last night of training to more than 10 per cent. of the number present.

Instructors. **209.** The leave granted to an instructor will not exceed 28 days in the year.

Leave to proceed abroad. **210.** An officer may not quit the United Kingdom without special permission. A brigade commander may grant permission to an officer under his command to proceed to countries in Europe, and to all British Colonies. Leave to visit other countries is to be obtained from the Army Council. The application must be submitted in time to reach the brigade commander or the War Office at least two weeks before the officer wishes to start.

When not granted. **211.** Leave will not be granted to visit countries where war is imminent or in progress.

V.—DUTIES IN AID OF THE CIVIL POWER.

Not to aid the civil power. **212.** Officers and soldiers of the Territorial Force are not liable to be called out in aid of the civil power as a military body in the preservation of peace.

Special constables. **213.** His Majesty's subjects are bound, in case of the existence of riots, to use all reasonable endeavours, according to the necessity of the occasion, to suppress and quell such riots. Soldiers of the Territorial Force are not exempted from this general obligation, and they may, in common with all other subjects of His Majesty, be required by the civil authority to act as special constables for such purposes. When so employed they will be armed with the ordinary constable's staff, and will not wear uniform.

Cases in which other weapons may be used **214.** In cases of serious and dangerous riots and disturbances, the civil authority may require His Majesty's subjects generally, including soldiers of the Territorial Force, to arm themselves with and use other weapons suitable to the occasion ; and such other weapons may be used accordingly by soldiers of the Territorial Force, according to the necessity of the case.

Defence of storehouses and armouries. **215.** In the event of an attack upon their storehouses or armouries, soldiers of the Territorial Force may combine and avail themselves of their organization to resist it, and may use arms if the necessity of the occasion requires it.

VI.—GUARDS OF HONOUR, SALUTES, AND MILITARY FUNERALS.

Guards of honour and escorts. **216.** A guard of honour or escort may be provided for a member of the Royal Family, or for the Lieutenant of the county, or for the President of the Association, on arrival in the neighbourhood of the headquarters of a unit, provided the officers and men volunteer for the duty. They will not, however, receive any remuneration unless specially sanctioned by the War Office. If an escort or guard of honour is furnished, a report will be made to the general officer commanding the division. In no other case will any body of soldiers of the Territorial Force take part in any public procession or ceremony, or form a guard of honour, without the special authority of the general officer commanding-in-chief.

217. No salute will be fired by artillery without authority from the general officer commanding-in-chief, who will only sanction the application on condition that no expense is caused to the public. The salute will be fired with service guns and ammunition under the orders of the officer commanding, and will be in strict accordance with the rules laid down for salutes in Field and Garrison Artillery Training. Artillery salutes.

218. When the Lieutenant, or President of the Association, is present in uniform at a review, field day, or inspection consisting only of units of the Territorial Force belonging to the county of which he is Lieutenant, or of whose Association he is President, he will be entitled to the salute on coming to the ground and at the march past, irrespectively of the locality in which the parade is held; but the military command will be exclusively in the hands of the officer in command, who will give the order for the salute, and march past at the head of the troops. Salutes at reviews, &c.

219. When any unit of artillery or engineers, or army service corps, having its headquarters in a town in which troops are quartered, has— Guards of honour, artillery salutes, &c.

(*a*) Furnished a guard of honour or escort;
(*b*) Obtained authority through the prescribed channel to furnish a guard of honour or escort;
(*c*) Obtained authority to take part in a public procession or ceremony (under paragraph 216);
(*d*) Obtained authority (under paragraph 217) to fire a salute;

the commanding officer will report the fact to the officer commanding the troops.

220. Military funerals may be accorded to deceased officers and soldiers of the Territorial Force who at the time of their death were on the active list of their unit, and who are to be buried within the district in which the headquarters are situated. The salutes and attendance of troops, which will be confined to the Territorial Force, are not to exceed those laid down in the King's Regulations for officers and soldiers of the regular army. All necessary arrangements will be made regimentally, and no expense will be borne by the public. Military funerals.

VII.—DUTIES AND EMPLOYMENTS.

221. Brigade commanders and commanding officers are responsible that the number of officers and men required for garrison or regimental guards, fatigues and other duties and employments is reduced to the lowest possible limit. The practice of excusing men going on or coming off guards or other duties from attending parades is prohibited. Responsibility of brigadiers, &c.

222. The captain and subaltern of the day or week, and all orderly serjeants and corporals will attend all parades. The Parades, attendance at.

quartermaster, assisted by the regimental police, will take general charge of and be responsible for the conduct and safe custody of the camp whenever a unit is absent from its lines.

Guards, employment of. **223.** Brigade and regimental guards should be sparingly employed, and may generally be dispensed with between reveille and retreat, their duties being taken by an effective system of police supervision. In any case, during the day parades, regimental guards will be reduced as far as possible.

Picquets. **224.** Picquets will be in the ranks unless specially required, and canteens will be closed during all parades.

Orderly room. **225.** Orderly room should be held at any convenient time of the day which does not interfere with instruction.

Brigade and regimental employ. **226.** *Brigade and Regimental Employ.*—The numbers given below will not be exceeded—

Brigade office	1 clerk and 1 orderly.
Officers' mess	1 non-commissioned officer and 4 men.*
Serjeants' mess	1 non-commissioned officer and 3 men.*
Cooks	1 non-commissioned officer and 1 or 2 men per company, according to strength.
Orderlies	2 (including postmen).
Regimental police....	1 non-commissioned officer and 3 men.
Assistant clerk (orderly room)	1 man } Not above the rank of lance-corporal.
Assistant clerk (quartermaster's office)	1 man } Not above the rank of lance-corporal.
Storeman	1 man } Only allowed if pioneers are not available.
Butcher	1 man } Only allowed if pioneers are not available.
Wash-houses and latrines	2 men } Only allowed if pioneers are not available.
Brigade canteen	1 non-commissioned officer and 6 men.*
Regimental canteen	} 1 non-commissioned officer and 3 men.*
Coffee shop....	} 1 non-commissioned officer and 3 men.*
Recreation room	} 1 non-commissioned officer and 3 men.*

Exemption from parades. **227.** The following non-commissioned officers and men only may be exempted from attending parades :—

Brigade.

Brigade office	Clerk and orderly.
Brigade canteen	2 men.*
Grooms to staff officers	All.

Regimental.

Officers' servants	{ 1 per field officer, 1 per company } from morning parades only.
Officers' mess	1 non-commissioned officer and 1 man.*

* Only allowed if these institutions are established under regimental arrangements and not under a contract or tenant system.

Serjeants' mess	1 non-commissioned officer and 1 man.*
Cooks	1 man per company or band.
Wash-houses and latrines	2 men.
Canteen	2 men.*
Coffee shop....	
Recreation room	
Police	1 non-commissioned officer and 3 men.
Grooms to mounted officers	All.
Staff - serjeants, except R.A.M.C.	All.

228. Reveille will be sounded daily at 5 a.m., and retreat beaten at 7 p.m., tattoo at 9.30 p.m. At a brigade camp retreat and tattoo will be beaten once a week by the massed fifers, drummers, buglers, and pipers of each battalion. Reveille and tattoo.

229. Brigade and regimental fatigues will be carried out in the early morning or in the evening, and will be limited as follows :— Fatigues.

Cleaning lines. (Pioneers to assist if necessary.)
Officers' mess, Serjeants' mess, Canteens, Coffee shop *.
Recreation room or tent.
Kitchens (all cleaning up to be done by the cooks).
Rations for sick (as required, but not to exempt from any parade or duty).
Guardroom or tent (to be done by the guard).

Rations should, if possible, be issued in the early morning, and drawn by the serjeant cook and cooks.

230. General officers commanding-in-chief will make all arrangements that may be necessary in connection with reviews or field days. Reviews and field days.

SECTION 5.—QUALIFICATION OF OFFICERS FOR PROMOTION, &c.

9 / Gen. No. / 380

242. An officer, unless he has qualified in the corresponding arm of the Regular Forces, Militia, Imperial Yeomanry, Volunteers, or the Territorial Force, within 3 years prior to his appointment or re-appointment to the Territorial Force, will be required to qualify as follows :— Examinations.

(*a*) *Second-lieutenant before promotion to the rank of lieutenant and within* 2 *years of his first appointment*—to pass the examination for Certificate A—*vide* Appendix 4—unless he

* See note on previous page.

already holds certificate A laid down for the branch of the service in which he is serving.*

(*b*) *Lieutenant before promotion to the rank of captain*—to pass the examination for Certificate B—*vide* Appendix 4—unless he already holds certificate B laid down for the branch of the service in which he is serving.*

(*c*) *Captain before promotion to the rank of major*—to pass an oral and practical examination in accordance with Appendix 4.

(*d*) *Major before promotion to the rank of lieutenant-colonel, or appointment to the command of a unit*—to undergo a practical or written examination—*vide* Appendix 4—and obtain a satisfactory certificate.

Obligatory courses. **243.** The courses of instruction which must be undergone by officers before promotion are laid down in Appendix 6.

GENERAL INSTRUCTIONS.

Exemptions. **244.** An officer who has passed an examination in military subjects as laid down in paragraph 257, and is thereby entitled to the letter (q) against his name in the Army List, will be exempt from passing the written part of the examinations required in Appendix 4, before promotion to the rank of lieutenant or captain, respectively.

Appointed direct. **245.** An officer, not already qualified under paragraph 242, who is appointed direct to the rank of lieutenant or captain, will be required to qualify under paragraph 242 (*a*) or (*b*), within one year of his appointment.

Transfer. **246.** An officer transferred from another branch of the service will be required, before promotion to higher rank, to qualify as laid down for the branch which he joins.

Procedure, subalterns. **247.** Examinations for Certificates A and B will be carried out periodically under arrangements made by the general officer commanding-in-chief. Papers for the written portion will be set and corrected by officers deputed by the General Staff of commands.

An officer will, except in very special circumstances, be examined in the command to which he belongs.

For the subjects of the examination, see Appendix 4.

Standard. **248.** To qualify, a candidate must obtain ·4 of the marks allotted to each written paper or practical subject, and ·6 of the aggregate marks allotted to the compulsory portion of the whole examination (written and practical).

Failure in one paper. **249.** A candidate who fails in one written paper or in one practical subject only, but obtains ·6 in the remainder of the compulsory examination, will be required to undergo re-examination in that paper or subject only. At his re-examination he must obtain ·6 of the marks allotted.

More than one paper. **250.** A candidate who fails in more than one paper or subject, or in the aggregate, must undergo the whole examination again.

* An officer who is in possession of a certificate, obtained in the Officers' Training Corps, which does not cover all the subjects required for the branch of the Service to which he belongs, will only be required to qualify in such subjects or sub-heads as will complete the certificate for the branch of the Service to which he belongs.

251. A candidate who fails at his first examination for either Certificate A or B, will not be allowed to present himself for re-examination until a period of three months from his first examination has elapsed. Re-examination.

252. The syllabus for the guidance of boards conducting examinations for promotion to the rank of major and lieutenant-colonel, is given in Appendix 4. Captains and majors.

253. Examinations for promotion to the rank of major or lieutenant-colonel will be held under arrangements made by the general officer commanding-in-chief. The president of a board of examination will be a regular officer not under the rank of major, and, if possible, not below the rank of lieutenant-colonel. Examination arrangements.

254. The result of all examinations, and qualifications for promotion, will be recorded by the general officer commanding-in-chief, who, when forwarding recommendations for promotion, will in each case attach a certificate to the effect that the officer is fully qualified. Qualifications will also be noted in an officer's record. Examination results.

255. A record will be kept by commanders of divisions and mounted brigades showing all courses and examinations undergone by officers under their command. Record

256. The case of any officer who is prevented from complying with paragraph 242 within the prescribed period of two years, will be specially considered by the general officer commanding-in-chief, who may authorise any reasonable extension (not exceeding twelve months) of the period during which such officer may obtain the necessary qualifications. Extension of time.

VOLUNTARY EXAMINATIONS.

(A)—In Military Subjects.

257. Officers, except medical officers, may present themselves for examination in the sub-heads of subject (*d*), specified in Appendix XI, King's Regulations, at the same time as officers of the regular forces, and under the conditions laid down in that Appendix, except that the sub-heads may be taken up separately. Officers of artillery may also present themselves for examination in "Artillery," and army service corps officers in "Army Service Corps" subjects; specially modified papers, based on King's Regulations Appendix XI (*e*), Artillery, (*g*) Army Service Corps, will be set. A candidate will only be examined in the armament of his unit. The qualifications as to eligibility for examination stated in the King's Regulations for officers of the regular forces will not be required. Examination in (*d*) and (*e*).

The sub-heads of subject (*d*) are as follows:—

(i.) Military engineering, tactics, and map reading, field sketching, and reconnaissance.
(ii.) Military law;
(iii.) Administration, organization and equipment;
(iv.) Military history.

A medical officer may present himself for examination in (*d*) (ii). An officer who, in any sub-head, obtains ·75 of the marks will receive a special certificate in that sub-head.

258. A field officer or captain will be examined in subject (*d*) on Papers.

the papers set for captains of the regular army ; a subaltern on those set for lieutenants of the regular army.

Distinguishing letters in Army List. **259.** When an officer has passed in all the sub-heads of subject (*d*), and if an artillery officer, in "Artillery," and if an army service corps officer, in subject "G" also, the fact will be shown against his name in the Army List by the letter (Q) if he was examined on captains' papers ; and by the letter (q) if he was examined as a subaltern.

Procedure. **260.** The general officer commanding-in-chief will forward the names of candidates for examination in subject (*d*) to the War Office on A.F. E 621, not later than the 7th April and 7th October in each year. An officer will, except in special cases, attend the examination in the command to which his unit belongs. For the examination in "Artillery," the general officer commanding-in-chief will forward the names of candidates to the War Office on A.F. E 644, stating the armament of each candidate's unit, not later than the 1st March and 1st September in each year.

(B)—In Foreign Languages.

Foreign languages. **261.** Officers will be allowed to present themselves for examination in the foreign languages mentioned in "Regulations relating to the Study of Foreign Languages," under the same conditions as those laid down for officers of the regular forces. They will not be eligible, however, if they pass, for any pecuniary reward.

SECTION 6.—TRAINING AND COURSES OF INSTRUCTION.

1.—GENERAL SYSTEM OF TRAINING.

Responsibility for training. **271.** General officers commanding-in-chief will be responsible to the Army Council for the efficiency of the Territorial Force within their commands. To cover the expenses of training, certain sums will be allotted to them.

Under the general officer commanding-in-chief, the command and training of the Territorial Force will be entrusted to divisional, mounted brigade, and coast defence commanders.

Annual schemes for training. **272.** Divisional, mounted brigade, and coast defence commanders will draw up annually a programme of training for the Territorial Force under their command (A.F. E 656), which will be submitted not later than the 1st January for the approval of the general officer commanding-in-chief. General officers commanding-in-chief will forward to the War Office A.F. E 656 by 1st February, for the approval of the Army Council.

System. **273.** In drawing up schemes for the training of the Territorial Force it will be necessary to consider the circumstances of each particular unit, and to arrange an elastic system such as will adapt the means of instruction to the special conditions of every case.

274. In the limited time available for the training of the Territorial Force in peace it is not to be expected that, as a whole, it can be trained up to the standard of the regular troops. The training should therefore be directed towards laying the foundation on which more extended training can be based, and should be confined wholly to such elements as are essential to success in war. It should aim at :— **Scope of training.**

(*a*) Producing an efficient body of officers and non-commissioned officers to serve both as instructors and leaders.

(*b*) Thoroughly instructing the rank and file, at first individually, and then in small tactical units.

275. The training should be systematic and progressive, and be carried out according to the instructions contained in the various training manuals. In applying these, however, commanders must remember that, the period of training being very much more limited than in the case of regulars, they must exercise discretion in confining the instruction to absolute essentials. **Training, systematic and progressive.**

276. The success of the training will depend on the standard of military knowledge amongst the officers and non-commissioned officers, and on their ability to instruct their men intelligently. Special efforts will therefore be required to assist them in qualifying themselves as efficient instructors. For this purpose periodical courses of instruction will be held by cavalry regiments, artillery training brigades, engineer units, infantry training centres, and army service corps companies. **Instruction of officers and non-commissioned officers.**

277. An adjutant and a permanent staff will be attached to every unit, or group of units, of the Territorial Force. They will be employed to train the recruits before they are finally passed on to their squadron, battery, or company commanders, and to assist generally the commanding and other officers in establishing an effective system of training. The presence of the permanent staff, however, will in no way relieve squadron, battery, or company commanders from the full responsibility for the training and efficiency of their respective commands. **Duties of permanent staff with regard to training.**

2. TRAINING OF RECRUITS.

278. At all headquarters, as well as at detachment centres, arrangements will be made for the training of recruits under the permanent staff or specially qualified instructors throughout the year. **Training requirements, recruits.**

Recruits should be encouraged to carry out their training as early as possible in the year, as it is desirable that they should have completed it before attending the annual training in camp.

The number of drills which the recruits of the various arms will be required to carry out is given in Appendix 6.

279. An officer or soldier will be excused his recruits' course of musketry if he has completed a recruits' course of musketry in the Royal Navy, Regular Army, Royal Marines, Militia, Special Reserve, Imperial Yeomanry, Volunteers, Royal Irish Constabulary, or the permanent forces of a colony. **Those excused recruits' course of musketry.**

Those excused recruits' drills.

280. An officer or soldier will be excused his recruit drills if he has served (as an officer or in the ranks respectively) for two months in his own arm of the service in any of the forces specified in paragraph 279, or has served for two years as an efficient in his own arm of the service in the Junior or Senior Division of the Officers' Training Corps.

Initial course for officers during first two years of service.

281. In addition to the training requirements during the first year of service given in Appendix 6, an officer may be attached during the first two years of his service to a regular unit, training centre, or school, for an initial course of instruction. Information regarding the duration of the initial course and the unit or school at which it may be carried out is given in paragraph 328. If the initial course is completed within his first year of service, an officer may be excused half of the recruit drills required from him.

In the case of artillery officers a general officer commanding-in-chief may authorise the initial course being extended to three months, which may be performed a fortnight at a time.

Drills prior to 1st November to count.

282. A recruit who joins after the annual training in camp may be allowed to count any attendances at recruits' drill or musketry performed prior to the 1st of November towards the requirements demanded from a recruit in his first year.

Electric light engineer.

283. An electric light engineer will not be deemed "trained" unless he possesses a competent practical knowledge in one of the following branches :—

(*a*) Electrical work of defence electric lights.
(*b*) Engine driving for defence electric lights.
(*c*) Telephone work in fortresses.

3. ANNUAL TRAINING.

(i) *General Instructions.*

284. Annual training will consist of :—

(*a*) Drills.
(*b*) Musketry.
(*c*) Annual training in camp.

Power to excuse units from camp training.

285. A general officer commanding-in-chief may, in exceptional circumstances, excuse a unit from carrying out any portion of the annual training in camp.

Training with unit other than own unit.

286. An officer or soldier, other than a recruit, may be allowed to carry out any portion of his drills, musketry, or training in camp with another unit of the same arm of the service, provided the written consent of the two commanding officers is obtained ; a certificate from the adjutant of the unit to which he has been attached being accepted as a voucher for the amount of training performed.

Training when absent in a colony.

287. An officer or soldier residing temporarily in a British colony or in Egypt, may, with the approval of the local commander of the forces, be allowed to be attached to a regular or local corps, for not more than two years in succession, for the purpose of carrying out any portion of his training required by Appendix 6. Such training will count as annual training, except for the purpose of pay and other emoluments.

(ii) *Drills.*

288. The number of "drills" which officers and soldiers of the Territorial Force of the various arms of the service will be required to carry out is given in Appendix 6. Number of drills.

A drill will consist of one hour's actual instruction. Any number of drills up to 3 may be performed in one day. Definition of a drill.

289. Training performed at drills should be of an elementary character and consist of individual or troop, section, or company training. The men should, as far as possible, be trained under their own officers. Nature of training at drill.

290. The drills may be performed at any time throughout the year outside the period of annual training in camp; but as they are best suited to afford elementary instruction, men should be encouraged to perform as many as possible prior to the annual training in camp. This will enable full advantage to be taken of the more extended training during camp and admit of a progressive system of training being adhered to. Unless a certain number of drills are performed prior to annual training in camp, pay cannot be drawn for such training in camp (*see* Appendix 6). Season at which drills should be performed.

291. An officer or non-commissioned officer may be allowed to count attendance at war games and lectures, as drills, up to a maximum of 5 drills. Lectures, &c., to count as drills.

A non-commissioned officer or private may be allowed to count attendance at physical training as drills (at the rate of 3 physical drills of 1 hour for 1 drill), up to a maximum of 5 drills.

292. In order to qualify for travelling grants under paragraph 624 a battery or company drill should consist of at least the following :— Minimum attendance at drills.

Artillery (Horse, Field, Mountain, and Heavy)	1 officer,	2 N.C.Os. and	12 privates.
Engineers (other than electric light) ...	1 "	3 " "	20 "
Infantry	1 "	4 " "	20 "
Army Service Corps ...	1 "	3 " "	15 "
Field Ambulance ...	1 "	3 " "	12 "

A battalion drill for which travelling allowance can be claimed, should consist of at least 4 companies, of which one half of the combatant officers and 25 per cent. of the men should be present.

293. Attendances at church parade, funerals, guards of honour, or on street duty, will not count towards the number of annual drills required under Appendix 6. Church parades, &c., not to count as drills.

294. In the case of yeomanry, squadrons may be assembled on the three days preceding the annual training in camp, and attendance on those days will be equivalent to the ten drills required under Appendix 6. These days will not be allowed to count as annual training in camp for the purpose of pay or emoluments. Yeomanry drills prior to camp.

(iii) *Musketry.*

295. Pending the issue of revised courses of musketry for the Territorial Force, yeomanry will fire the course of musketry as laid Course of musketry.

down in Musketry Regulations (Provisional), 1903; engineer field companies and infantry will fire the course laid down in Volunteer Regulations, 1901, Appendix VIII. (1901 edition), or that laid down in Musketry Regulations (Provisional), 1903. Engineer field companies will fire a course of musketry only when approved by the general officer commanding the Territorial Division.

The following, when once fully trained, may be excused musketry:—Bandmasters, regimental staff-serjeants, bandsmen, pioneers, trumpeters, buglers, drummers, and men of machine-gun sections.

In camp. **296.** The musketry course will not be fired during the annual training in camp unless special permission for doing so has been obtained from the general officer commanding-in-chief.

Ranges. **297.** When government ranges are available they may be used for musketry practice, with the approval of the general officer commanding concerned.

Attendance at musketry. **298.** During the firing of the annual course of musketry an officer of the unit, preferably one of the squadron or company concerned, should, if possible, be present. The adjutant should frequently visit the range, or ranges, and a non-commissioned officer of the permanent staff will always be present during practice.

(iv) *Annual Training in Camp.*

Duration of annual training in camp. **299.** Every officer and soldier of the Territorial Force will be required to carry out "annual training in camp" for a period of not less than 8, or more than 15, days (in the case of yeomanry not more than 18 days), and may be called out once or oftener for this purpose. Attendance at a hospital or other selected institution (for Royal Army Medical Corps), in defence works or at manœuvres may count as annual training in camp.

Camping of units of garrison artillery. **300.** Units of garrison artillery specially allotted to defended ports should be detailed to carry out their annual training in camp at the works of defence to which they are allotted on mobilization.

Electric light engineers. **301.** Electric light engineers will carry out their annual training in camp in the works of defence to which they are allotted on mobilization. If necessary, the general officer commanding-in-chief in whose command they may be, will arrange with the commander of the coast defences to which they are allotted on mobilization, as to the dates and places at which the annual training in camp is to be carried out.

Period and selection of camps. **302.** Camps will be held between 1st May and 30th September. Garrison artillery or other units which carry out their training in camp in works of defence, hospitals, &c., and not in the field, may, however, hold their camps at any convenient season of the year. Camps will be held only at places where works of defence, modern armament, ranges, or ground for field training are available, according to the branch of the service. As gun practice will be carried out during annual training in camp, artillery brigades should encamp at some place where practice is possible.

303. The date and place of formation of camps will be arranged by the divisional, mounted brigade, or coast defence commander. As a general rule, camps should be arranged by brigades when possible, though camps for single units may be held when necessary. Camps—arrangements for.

304. A day's training in camp will consist of not less than 6 hours' work, or if the day be Sunday, of not less than 6 hours' military duty. When officers and soldiers of medical units carry out their "annual training in camp" in a hospital or other selected institution, a day will consist of not less than 3 hours' work. Definition of a day's training.

Days of arrival at, and departure from, camp will count as days of training. In the case of units or individuals carrying out their annual training in camp in broken periods, not more than 2 days in all for assembling at, and departure from, camp will count as days of training.

305. Camps may be formed composed of details from two or more units, for the purpose of the annual training in camp of officers and soldiers who, in the opinion of their commanding officer, have reasonable cause for non-attendance at annual training in camp with their own unit. Provisional camps.

306. Before the commencement of annual training in camp, the non-commissioned officers of the permanent staff will be assembled at the headquarters of the unit for at least one week's special instruction under the adjutant. Instruction of permanent staff.

307. Under instructions received from the divisional, mounted brigade, or coast defence commander, an officer commanding a unit may exempt an officer or soldier from annual training in camp who, at the National Rifle Association Meeting during that year, has fired the complete course in the Grand Aggregate, in the Rapid Firing Aggregate, and in each of the competitions included in these aggregates. Attendance at N.R.A. meeting.

308. The training carried out in camp should be of a progressive nature and more advanced than that carried out during drills, as much time as possible being devoted to squadron, battery, and company training. Advantage should be taken of the time in camp to exercise the men chiefly in field operations. Nature of training.

Wet days should be utilised for the purpose of imparting theoretical instruction.

309. On arrival in camp commanding officers will furnish the medical officers in charge of units with a list of men reported temporarily unfit for the training in the previous year, showing, in each case, the cause of disability. Men temporarily unfit.

310. Non-commissioned officers and soldiers who, on joining, are found to be permanently unfit, will be discharged and sent to their homes. Those temporarily unfit, but likely to become available for part of the training, will be admitted into a military hospital when one is available, or will be treated in quarters; otherwise they will be sent to their homes. If, however, a man is found, on joining, to be suffering from an infectious disease, he will be temporarily detained and isolated; and the medical officer of health for the district will at once be informed, with a view to the man's transfer to the local hospital for infectious diseases. Disposal of.

311. On arrival at the place of assembly, or on arrival in camp, all horses will be inspected by a board of officers as to their health and Inspection of horses.

fitness for military duty; the board will be assisted by a veterinary officer. On the last day of training, the horses will again be similarly inspected, and a certificate filed as to the condition of the horses.

Service of notices. **312.** Notices to officers and soldiers to attend for annual training will be sent to their residences by post on A.F. E 654.

Publication of notices. **313.** Public notices will be sent to the constabulary and police in the United Kingdom, and also to the overseers of the poor in Scotland, for the purpose of being affixed on or near church doors, &c. These notices will be deemed sufficient intimation, notwithstanding any failure in the transmission or receipt of the notices sent by post; and any men not appearing at the time and place appointed in such public notice will be liable to be dealt with as absentees.

4. INSPECTION AND EFFICIENCY.

(i) *Inspection.*

Nature of inspection. **314.** Each unit will be inspected annually, under arrangements made by the divisional, mounted brigade, or coast defence commander. This inspection will be directed towards ascertaining:—

(*a*) Whether the unit is efficient in training, discipline, and interior economy.

(*b*) Whether the arms, clothing, and equipment are sufficient and in good order, and whether the books and records are properly kept.

The inspection of the unit as a whole will be carried out during the annual training in camp. It will usually take the form of a tactical exercise in the field, except in the case of engineer, army service corps, and medical units, which will be inspected in their technical duties. That portion of the inspection which refers to books and records may take place at any time throughout the year which may be convenient.

Inspection reports. **315.** The inspection report on a unit (A.F. E 657) will be so framed as to afford complete information regarding the efficiency and preparedness for war in all respects of the unit as a whole, and the capacity of the officers to act as instructors and leaders. Inspection reports will be forwarded in duplicate to the general officer commanding-in-chief, who will forward one copy to the War Office for the information of the Army Council. In this report will be included a statement whether the inspecting officer does or does not recommend the withholding of any portion of the establishment grant (paragraphs 608 to 611).

(ii) *Efficiency.*

Efficiency qualifications. **316.** In classing an officer or soldier as efficient for the purpose of earning certain financial grants, a divisional, mounted brigade, or coast defence commander will consider whether the annual training requirements set forth in Appendix 6 have been duly carried out during the year. He may in special cases class an individual as efficient who has not fully complied with these requirements, provided that he is satisfied that the necessary standard of efficiency has been attained, and similarly, he may classify an individual as non-efficient who has performed the training if he thinks fit.

317. The efficiency of the unit as a whole will be determined by the report of the inspecting officer at the annual inspection (paragraph 315). Efficiency of unit as a whole.

5. INSTRUCTION IN SPECIAL DUTIES.

(i) *Method of Training in Special Duties.*

318. In every unit a sufficient number of men will be trained to supply the machine gun sections, 1st line transport drivers, signallers, stretcher bearers, layers, range-takers, telephonists, saddlers, wheelers, cold shoers, fitters and other artificers, required by territorial force establishments. Training of specialists.

319. The men should be trained in their particular duties as far as possible during the drills performed throughout the year, so as to be able to carry them out during their annual training in camp. The general officer commanding-in-chief may authorise their attachment to a regular or training unit in lieu of annual training in camp. In particular duties.

(ii) *Signalling.*

320. Classes for instruction in signalling will be formed in each unit. The instruction will be carried out either by the adjutant or by an officer who is in possession of a signalling certificate from the Commandant, School of Signalling. The number of signallers required by territorial force establishments will be trained. Signalling classes.

321. Every facility will be given to officers and non-commissioned officers to attend a school of signalling in order to qualify for the appointment of instructor or assistant instructor. Qualifying as instructor or assistant instructor.

In special cases, where this attendance is impossible, the instruction will be carried out by the adjutant or other qualified officer.

Application will be made to the general officer commanding-in-chief for the candidates to be examined when they are sufficiently prepared. A regular officer in possession of an instructor's certificate of signalling will be detailed to carry out the examination, the necessary tests being forwarded on application by the Commandant, School of Signalling, to whom the results will be returned direct for checking, and who alone is empowered to issue certificates to successful candidates and to authorise the wearing of badges.

322. The annual inspection in signalling will be carried out in accordance with the "Training Manual—Signalling," under arrangements to be made between general officers commanding and the Commandant, School of Signalling, Aldershot. At least six months should elapse between each inspection. Not more than one inspection will be held in each year. Annual inspection.

The results of inspections must be received at the School of Signalling as soon as possible after the 31st October.

(iii) *Stretcher Drill.*

323. Classes for the instruction in stretcher drill as laid down in the King's Regulations will be held under regimental arrangements, for the purpose of training the stretcher bearers required by territorial force establishments and such others as it may be thought desirable to train in this duty. Those qualified will obtain a certificate of proficiency on A.F. E 596. Stretcher drill.

(iv) *Gymnastics and Fencing.*

Military gymnasia may be used.

324. Officers and soldiers will be permitted to receive instruction in gymnastics and fencing in the military gymnasia, when the gymnasia are not required for the regular classes, provided that they obtain the approval of the general or other officer commanding at the station, and that they comply with the following conditions :—

(*a*) Application for permission to attend will be made through the officer commanding the unit to which the applicant belongs.

(*b*) Those who are desirous of receiving instruction in fencing will supply their own fencing materials, and all will provide themselves with gymnastic belts and shoes.

(v) *Machine Gun Sections*

Machine gun section.

325. A machine gun section will be trained in each yeomanry regiment and infantry battalion. The numbers trained should not be less than :—

1 officer.
2 serjeants.
1 corporal (infantry).
10 privates (yeomanry).
16 „ (infantry).

The instruction will be carried out as laid down in Appendix to Training Manuals, Chapter VI.

Machine gun officer.

326. An officer, unless he has already done so, selected to command a machine gun section, will attend a course of instruction in machine gun duties at a school of musketry.

(vi) *Scouting.*

Scouts.

327. In each yeomanry regiment and infantry battalion courses of instruction for the training of scouts will be held. The numbers to be trained and the system of training will be in accordance with the instructions contained in Cavalry Training and Infantry Training.

The number of yeomanry scouts for whom badges will be allowed is as follows :—

1 serjeant scout.
8 1st class scouts.
16 2nd class scouts (4 per squadron).

6. COURSES OF INSTRUCTION.

Courses of instruction. **328.** The following courses of instruction for officers and non-commissioned officers will be held. Only those referred to in Appendix 6 are obligatory :—

—	Unit.	Rank of those attending.	Nature of Course.	Where held.	Duration of Course.
I.	Yeomanry ...	(*a*) Officers during first 2 years of service.	Initial course.	Regular unit.	1 month, or 2 periods of 2 weeks.
		(*b*) Officers within 2 years of promotion to major.	A course.	Regular unit.	14 days.
		(*c*) Officers and N.C.Os.	Musketry course.	School of Musketry, Hythe.	21 days, those selected for machine gun course 16 additional days.
		(*d*) Officers.	Cavalry Officers' Pioneer Course.	School of Military Engineering, Chatham.	1 month.
		(*e*) Officers.	Veterinary course.	Veterinary School, Aldershot.	1 month.
		(*f*) Officers holding certificates of field rank.	Cavalry course.	Cavalry School, Netheravon.	2 weeks.
		(*g*) Officers and N.C.Os.	Signalling course.	School of Signalling, Bulford or Strensall.	1 month.
		(*h*) 1 N.C.O. per unit to qualify as acting armourer.	Small arms course.	Royal Small Arms Factory.	1 month.
II.	Mounted Brigade and Divisional Artillery (Horse, field, mountain, and heavy).	(*a*) Officers during first 2 years of service.	Initial course.	Training brigade.	From 1 to 3 months, which may be performed in periods of 2 weeks (*see* para. 281.)
		(*b*) Officers before promotion to captain.	A course.	Training brigade.	14 days.
		(*c*) Officers before promotion to major.	Gun practice.	At a regular practice camp.	14 days.
		(*d*) N.C.Os. before promotion to serjeant,	A course.	Training brigade.	1 month.

—	Unit.	Rank of those attending.	Nature of Course.	Where held.	Duration of Course.
II.	Mounted Brigade, &c.—*cont.*	(*e*) Officers and N.C.Os.	Signalling course.	School of Signalling, Bulford or Strensall.	1 month.
		(*f*) Officers.	Veterinary course.	Veterinary School, Aldershot.	14 days.
III.	Garrison Artillery (Coast Defence heavy batteries and Coast Defence companies).	(*a*) Officers during first 2 years of service.	Initial course.	*Coast Defence Companies.*—In the Coast Defences to which allotted for war. Where this cannot be arranged, in one of the Coast Defence commands in which Schools of Instruction in Gunnery are established. *Heavy Batteries.*—Lydd.	From 1 to 3 months, which may be performed in periods of 2 weeks.
		(*b*) Officers before promotion to captain.	A course.	As at (*a*).	14 days.
		(*c*) Officers before promotion to major.	Gun practice.	As at (*a*).	14 days.
		(*d*) N.C.Os. before promotion to serjeant.	A course.	As at (*a*).	1 month.
		(*e*) Officers and N.C.Os.	Signalling course.	School of Signalling, Bulford or Strensall.	1 month.
IV.	Engineers ...	(*a*) Officers of all units during first 2 years of service.	Initial course.	Regular unit or R.E. School.	1 month, or 2 periods of 2 weeks.
		(*b*) Officers and N.C.Os. other than electric light engineers.	Engineering course.	School of Military Engineering, Chatham.	1 month.
		(*c*) Electric light officers once during their service; 10 per cent. of N.C.Os. and sappers of electric light engineers. (*See* para. 334.)	Electric light course.	School of Electric Lighting, Portsmouth or Plymouth.	2 months.

IV.	Engineers—*contd.*	(*d*) Electric light officers who are members or associate members of the Institute of Electrical Engineers.	Examination course.	School of Electric Lighting. Portsmouth or Plymouth.	14 days. Officers to join the school the day before the examination begins (see para. 335).
		(*e*) Officers (field companies).	Musketry course.	School of Musketry, Hythe.	21 days.
		(*f*) Officers (field companies).	Field course.	Regular unit or R.E. School.	1 month.
		(*g*) Officers and N.C.Os.	Signalling course.	School of Signalling, Bulford or Strensall.	1 month.
		(*h*) 1 N.C.O.	Small arms course.	Royal Small Arms Factory.	—
V.	Infantry ...	(*a*) Officers during first 2 years of service.	Initial course.	Training centre.	1 month, or 2 periods of 2 weeks.
		(*b*) Officers and N.C.Os.	Signalling course.	School of Signalling, Bulford or Strensall.	1 month.
		(*c*) Officers and N.C.Os.	Musketry course.	School of Musketry, Hythe.	21 days, those selected for machine gun course 16 additional days.
		(*d*) 1 N.C.O. to qualify as acting armourer.	Small arms course.	Royal Small Arms Factory.	1 month.
VI.	Army Service Corps.	(*a*) Officers during first 2 years of service.	Initial course.	Regular A.S.C. unit.	15 days.
		(*b*) Officers and Transport N.C.Os. before promotion to captain and serjeant respectively.	Transport course.	Transport Depôt Company or nearest A.S.C. Transport Company.	15 days.
		(*c*) Officers and Supply N.C.Os. before promotion to captain and serjeant respectively.	Supply course.	A.S.C. Training Establishment, Aldershot, or at a Supply Office at an A.S.C. Headquarter Station.	15 days.
		(*d*) Officers and N.C.Os.	Mechanical transport course.	A.S.C. Training Establishment, Aldershot.	—

—	Unit.	Rank of those attending.	Nature of Course.	Where held.	Duration of Course.
VI.	Army Service Corps—*cont.*	(*e*) Officers.	Veterinary course.	Aldershot, or with nearest regular unit to which a veterinary officer is attached.	14 days.
VII.	Medical units	(*a*) Officers.	Initial course for officers who do not attend camp during their 1st year.	Territorial Force Medical School or selected military institution.	8 days.*
		(*b*) Officers.	Course.	Territorial Force Medical School or selected military institution.	8 days.*
		(*c*) N.C.Os. and privates.†	Alternative course.	Hospital, other selected institution, or Territorial Force Medical School.	8 days.*
		(*d*) Officers and N.C.Os. (transport section).	Transport course.	With nearest Regular A.S.C. Transport Company.	15 days.
VIII.	All arms ...	(*a*) Officers and N.C.Os.	Voluntary courses to be arranged by G.Os. C.-in-C.	With Regular units or at training centres.	14 days to 1 month.
		(*b*) 1 N.C.O. per unit to qualify as serjeant cook.	Course of cookery.	School of Cookery, Aldershot, or be attached to a regular unit with which there is a serjeant cook.	6 weeks.
		(*c*) Officers and N.C.Os.	Transport course.	A.S.C. Training Establishment, Aldershot, or A.S.C. Depôts, Woolwich or Manchester.	14 days.
		(*d*) Officers and N.C.Os.	Supply course.	A.S.C. Training Establishment, Aldershot.	14 days.

* Alternative to camp.

† In the place of camp, an alternative course for recruits may be taken at a Military Hospital. Subsequent courses as for N.C.Os.

329. The obligatory courses of instruction which officers and soldiers of the various arms will be required to attend are given in Appendix 6. At all courses an officer or soldier must obtain a satisfactory report to enable him to count the attendance. Obligatory courses.

330. The dates on which courses at army schools will commence each year, and their duration, will be published in Army Orders of December of the preceding year, and commandants of schools will notify general officers commanding-in-chief of the number of officers and soldiers who may be detailed from each command. Courses at local schools will be arranged locally and published in command orders. Dates of courses, &c.

Courses at training centres or other regular units will be held at such times as may be arranged by general officers commanding-in-chief.

331. An application to attend a school or course of instruction, (A.F. E 534 or E 513) must reach the commandant of the school, or the commanding officer of the unit concerned, at least fourteen days before the date of the commencement of the course. A commanding officer, before recommending an officer or soldier to attend a course of instruction, should satisfy himself that the applicant has been sufficiently prepared to enable him to take full advantage of the course. This preparatory training will be carried out regimentally by the adjutant, assisted by the permanent staff. Applications to attend.

332. The syllabus of instruction at a school may be obtained on application to the commandant, or, in the case of the Royal Small Arms Factory, to the superintendent. Syllabus.

333. Officers and non-commissioned officers may attend a full course in signalling of two months' duration, provided vacancies are available, or they may attend the special classes for the Territorial Forces only, of one month's duration. Applications to attend a course should be made as required (without waiting for notification of vacancies), and should be accompanied by the certificates required by paragraph 813, King's Regulations. School of signalling.

334. Before being allowed to attend the course of electric lighting (paragraph 328, iv (*c*)), an officer or soldier must undertake to remain for the whole period of two months. In the case of an officer he must be certified by his commanding officer to have sufficient electrical knowledge to enable him to derive benefit from his instruction. In the case of a non-commissioned officer or sapper he must be certified by his commanding officer to possess educational qualifications at least equal to those required for a second-class certificate of education, and to have either sufficient electrical knowledge, or sufficient mechanical knowledge, to enable him to derive benefit from the instruction at the course. Electric lighting course.

335. Electric light officers who are members or associate members of the Institute of Electrical Engineers, and who are unable to attend the examination course mentioned in paragraph 328, iv (*d*), may, with the approval of the general officer commanding-in-chief, be examined locally by the chief instructor or instructor of the school to which the station is affiliated. Examination in electric lighting.

336. The officer commanding a training centre or other regular unit with which an officer or soldier carries out a course, or the commandant of a school of instruction, will, at the end of each List of those qualified.

course, forward their reports (on Army Form E 535 and Army Form E 661 for officers and soldiers respectively) to the divisional, mounted brigade, or coast defence commander under whom the officer or soldier may be serving, who will publish in orders a list of those who have qualified and will forward the reports on them to the officers commanding units, in order that the entries may be made in the regimental records of service.

7.—ATTACHMENT TO REGULAR UNITS OR TRAINING CENTRES.

Voluntary attachment.

337. With the approval of the general officer commanding-in-chief, an officer or a non-commissioned officer may be attached to a regular unit or training centre of his own arm of the service for a period not exceeding one month annually. Application for such attachment should be made in the manner laid down in para. 331.

Period of.

338. Except in the case of a recruit officer, all periods of attachment of officers and non-commissioned officers to regular units, other than courses of instruction, should, if possible, take place during the training season, *i.e.*, between the 1st March and the 31st October.

Permanent staff.

339. Non-commissioned officers of the permanent staff will attend a course of instruction with their own arm of the service for not less than one month every four years.

Attachment of permanent staff.

340. Non-commissioned officers of the permanent staff may be attached for 14 days annually to the nearest training centre or regular battalion for a special course, which should be directed towards training them as instructors. Should they require instruction in the duties of recruiting, advantage should be taken of this period of attachment for training them in those duties, when means for doing so exist.

SECTION 7.—FINANCE.

A.—Personal Emoluments.

I.—INTRODUCTORY.

Rules are for peace.

353. This section contains the rules governing the issue of personal emoluments to members of the Territorial Force in time of peace. On mobilization their conditions of service will conform in all respects to those of the regular army and their emoluments will be governed by the Pay Warrant and the Allowance Regulations. Separation allowance will then be issued to the wives and families of all married non-commissioned officers and privates.

Yeomen rates of pay.

354. Yeomen who on transfer to the Territorial Force enlist to complete the unexpired portion of their Imperial Yeomanry engagement or re-engagement will be allowed to retain their existing rates and conditions of pay as laid down in the Imperial Yeomanry Regulations during the period of such enlistment.

Yeomen enrolled before the passing of the Militia and Yeomanry

Act of 1901, who have not elected to come under the terms of that Act, will be allowed to retain existing rates and conditions of pay for a period of one year from 31st March, 1908, if they enlist for that period.

355. Non-commissioned officers of yeomanry paid as such at the end of the 1907 training will be permitted to retain their existing rates and conditions of pay for three more trainings if they continue to serve as non-commissioned officers for so long, even if the engagement on which they are serving when their unit is transferred has expired before the end of the 1910 training and they have entered into a fresh engagement. N.C.Os. of yeomanry, rates.

356. Non-commissioned officers, and men of the yeomanry who elect to retain their existing rates will not be entitled to any additional emoluments under these regulations, and, as the existing rates of remuneration include messing and rations, 6*d.* per diem for ration allowance will be deducted from the pay when army rations are issued. The yeoman will, as at present, contribute by regimental arrangement to the extra cost of messing. Not entitled to additional emoluments.

357. Officers of Volunteers, who have not finally qualified for the outfit allowance, will not, in the event of their not continuing to serve as officers of the Territorial Force when the transfer takes place, be called on to refund any outfit allowance drawn under paras. 450 and 452 Volunteer Regulations. Outfit allowance.

II.—PAY AND ALLOWANCES.

A.—Permanent Staff.

1. *Adjutants.*

358. The pay and allowances of adjutants who are officers on the active list of the regular army will, except when otherwise provided in these Regulations, be at the rates laid down in the Pay Warrant and the Allowance Regulations. For the days of annual training in camp an allowance of 4*s.* a day to cover mess expenses will be admissible. Adjutants.

359. Officers of the Territorial Force or others not on the active list of the regular army appointed adjutants will receive a consolidated allowance at the rate of £100 a year, which is to cover all expenses except the repayment of travelling expenses under the rules applicable to adjutants generally. Whilst present at the annual training in camp of their brigade or unit they will receive in addition regimental pay and allowances, including armament, engineer, or corps pay where applicable, and the use of a horse, or horse allowance in lieu, at the rate prescribed for officers of the Territorial Force. Consolidated allowance.

360. An adjutant or acting adjutant (other than an officer receiving the consolidated allowance under para. 359) will be entitled to forage and stabling for one horse if actually kept. Forage and stabling.

361. An officer of the Territorial Force appointed to act as adjutant during a vacancy or during the absence of the adjutant on certified sick leave will receive the army pay of his rank or, if a quartermaster, of the substantive rank corresponding to his honorary rank, but not exceeding that of a captain. If acting as Acting during vacancy.

adjutant of a yeomanry unit he will receive additional pay at the rate of 5*s.* a day. Neither armament, engineer, nor corps pay will be admissible.

During leave of adjutant.

362. An officer acting as above, or during the temporary absence without allowances of an adjutant on leave or on duty, will be granted allowances at army rates for lodging, fuel and light, servant, and (if he necessarily uses a horse and the adjutant's horse is not left at the disposal of the commanding officer) forage and stabling.

2. *Instructors.*

Pay.

363. Non-commissioned officers of the regular forces (including Royal Marines) while serving on the permanent staff as serjeant instructors will receive pay, engineer pay, corps pay, service or proficiency pay, and additional pay at the rates and under the conditions laid down in the Pay Warrant.

Allowances.

364. The allowances of instructors serving on army engagement will be governed by the Allowance Regulations, but lodging allowance will not be admissible for non-commissioned officers of the permanent staff who are in occupation of quarters owned or rented by County Associations. In any case in which a non-commissioned officer provides his own furniture for such a quarter an allowance, as under, will be issuable, viz. :—

	per diem.
Married non-commissioned officer ...	1½*d.*
Unmarried non-commissioned officer	1*d.*

The allowance will be drawn monthly in arrear on A.F. P 1934.

Ration returns.

365. Ration returns (A.F. F 776) will be furnished by units to the local officer of the Army Service Corps for the issues in kind made to the permanent staff; and this officer will send to the adjutant certificates (A.F. F 743) of the total number of rations drawn, which should correspond with the totals shown in the ration return in the pay list.

Rations, and messing allowance.

366. During attendance at annual training in camp, instructors will be fully rationed, and the daily ration (or allowance in lieu) and usual messing allowance will be inadmissible for such periods. A messing allowance of 1*s.* a day for each instructor will instead be drawn under the conditions laid down in paragraph 396 by the officer commanding the unit.

Clothing allowance.

367. An allowance of 3*d.* a day will be granted to each non-commissioned officer of the permanent staff to cover the cost of provision and upkeep of clothing. They will not receive clothing in kind. Non-commissioned officers holding the appointment of acting serjeant-major will receive an additional allowance of 1*d.* a day. These allowances will include the provision, maintenance, and renewal of a greatcoat.

Inspection of arms.

368. A non-commissioned officer of the permanent staff in the Territorial Force holding a certificate of competency for the care of arms will receive annually 1*d.* for each rifle or carbine in possession of the unit and inspected by him. This payment will be based on the maximum number of arms in possession of the unit during the year, but will not be allowed in any year in which a government viewer may report the state of the arms to be unsatisfactory. It will be issued in arrear and charged in the April accounts, under the head of "Inspection and Repair of Arms," supported by the certificate of the commanding officer to the effect that the work has been satisfactorily performed, and showing the number of arms in possession of the unit during the previous year.

369. Instructors employed in recruiting for the regular forces will not receive any additional allowances, but only the usual rewards payable on obtaining recruits. Recruiting rewards.

370. The pay and allowances of the permanent staff will be issued, as far as practicable, weekly in arrear by the adjutant. Issue of pay.

371. Pensioners, discharged soldiers, and others employed as temporary drill instructors will receive pay at the rate of 2*s.* a day. The first charge for these allowances will be vouched by the authority of the general officer commanding-in-chief. Pensioners', &c., pay.

372. If an instructor, not serving on his army engagement, is appointed acting serjeant-major he will receive additional pay at the rate of 6*d.* a day. A certificate of the date of such acting appointment will accompany the first charge of this additional pay. Additional pay.

373. Pensioners and others employed as temporary instructors will receive allowances at the following rates :— Allowances.

In lieu of lodgings, fuel and light ...	4*d.*
„ clothing	3*d.*

B.—Divisional and Brigade Headquarters.

374. The pay and allowances of officers of the divisional or brigade headquaters, who are officers of the regular army on full pay, are governed by the Pay Warrant and the Allowance Regulations. When such officers are not in receipt of staff pay, acting staff pay will be drawn during the period of annual training in camp at the rates and under the conditions laid down in the Pay Warrant for corresponding appointments. Pay and allowances.

375. Officers of the Territorial Force and others, not being officers of the regular army on full pay, appointed to the headquarters of mounted or infantry brigades, or of divisional artillery will receive consolidated allowances at the rate of £150 a year for commanders, and £100 a year for brigade majors and staff officers. Whilst present at the annual training in camp of their brigade, &c., they will receive in addition acting staff pay (but not regimental pay) and the allowances of their rank, at the rates and under the conditions laid down in the Pay Warrant and the Allowance Regulations for officers holding similar appointments in the regular forces, except that horses will be provided under the conditions laid down for officers of the Territorial Force. The consolidated allowances will be payable quarterly, in arrear, on the last days of June, September, December, and March, and the acting staff pay at the termination of the period of camp training. Consolidated allowances.

These emoluments will be drawn in addition to any half or retired pay to which the recipient may be entitled, and will cover personal expenses and remuneration of every kind throughout the year, except travelling for officers when required to travel on duty, and for a horse when necessarily taken.

376. A retired officer appointed staff officer to the administrative medical officer of a Territorial Division will receive an inclusive Retired officer.

allowance of £100 per annum in addition to his retired pay, with travelling and field allowance when issuable. A horse and forage will be provided for annual training in camp under paragraphs 401 and 402.

C.—Regimental Officers and Men.

1. *General.*

Pay and allowances. **377.** Pay and allowances (including armament, engineer, or corps pay, additional pay, and working pay) will be drawn by officers, non-commissioned officers and men of the Territorial Force, at the rates and under the conditions laid down in the Pay Warrant and the Allowance Regulations, for officers, non-commissioned officers and men of corresponding rank in the same arm of the service in the regular forces, except where other rates or conditions are prescribed in these regulations.

They will be drawn only for the days of actual attendance at annual training in camp (including days of leave authorised with pay), at obligatory courses of instruction, and, if approved by the general officer commanding-in-chief, at staff rides, instructional tours, voluntary courses of instruction, or when specially called up for duty. They will in no case be drawn during attendance at drills, musketry, &c., performed for efficiency outside the period of annual training in camp, nor for attendance at the National Rifle Association meeting, nor for attendance under paragraph 218.

Conditional issue. **378.** The issue of pay and allowances during annual training in camp will (except in the case of officers supernumerary in their units or on the unattached list who are permitted to attend) depend upon fulfilment of the conditions laying down the number of drills to be performed before attending the annual training in camp. Exemption may be granted by the general officer commanding-in-chief when he considers that officers or men have been prevented by sickness or extraordinary circumstances from complying with these conditions.

In billets. **379.** Where units are necessarily billeted, payment for the billet will be made at statutory rates, and issue of rations, messing allowance, and forage, will not be admissible.

2. *Pay.*

Deviations from Pay Warrant. **380.** The following deviations will be made from the rates of pay laid down in the Pay Warrant.

(1) The pay of lieutenant-colonels in the following arms will be as follows:—

	£	s.	d.	
Yeomanry	1	1	6	a day.
Field Artillery				
Garrison Artillery	0	18	0	"
Mountain Artillery ...				
Infantry				

(2) Officers, non-commissioned officers, and men of transport sections of the Royal Army Medical Corps will be paid at the rates laid down in the Pay Warrant for the Army Service Corps.

(3) No increase of pay will be given for length of service in the Territorial Force.

(4) Armament pay will be confined to officers of Garrison Artillery companies.

(5) A second-lieutenant of Engineers will be granted engineer pay at the higher rate of 4*s.* a day, provided he has qualified for promotion in any one of the prescribed methods.

(6) Proficiency pay will not be issued to non-commissioned officers and men of the Territorial Force.

381. An equitation bounty of £1 will be paid at the end of the annual training in camp to each non-commissioned officer and man of the yeomanry who has been present for not less than 8 days at the training and is then certified to be proficient in equitation. *Equitation bounty.*

382. Pay will be issued to an officer while attending an obligatory course of instruction, provided he remains for a continuous period of one month (except when a shorter course is permitted by the regulations), and obtains a satisfactory report (on A.F. E 535) on completion of the whole course, or, in the case of a musketry course, is placed on the list of qualified officers. If obliged to leave the course in consequence of sickness duly certified, pay will be issued for the period of attendance. *Courses.*

383. In cases of failure to obtain the report referred to in paragraph 382, or where the officer has completed as a continuous period only one half of the month's course, pay will be admitted for the first fortnight on a certificate from the commandant or officer commanding the service battery, company, or depôt to which the officer is attached, that he has displayed all proper zeal and industry, and has profited by the course. *Failure to gain report*

384. The issue of pay to non-commissioned officers and men during authorised courses of instruction will be subject to a certificate that they have been punctual and attentive during the course, or, in the case of musketry courses, to inclusion in the list of qualified men. *N.C.Os. and men.*

385. In the case of single attendances with training centres or regular units, officers, non-commissioned officers, and men will be allowed pay for days on which attendances of not less than six (or, in the case of R.A.M.C., three) hours are made, provided the total of such pay, together with any allowances and travelling expenses admissible, does not exceed that admissible for a continuous course of equivalent duration, six (in the case of R.A.M.C., three) attendances of one hour counting as one day. No emoluments will be issued to an officer except on a certificate that all proper zeal and industry have been displayed, and issue will not be made for over 14 days unless he obtains the satisfactory report on A.F. E 535 at the end of the course. *Single attendances.*

386. The issue of pay during attendance at voluntary courses of instruction will be subject to the discretion of the general officer commanding-in-chief, who will state whether it will be admissible when sanctioning the attendance. *Voluntary courses.*

387. Pay due under paragraphs 382 to 386 will be issued by the adjutant of the regiment, and the charge will be vouched by a copy of the order for the officer or soldier to attend, (containing the *Issue.*

decision of the general officer commanding-in-chief regarding the admissibility of pay in the case of a voluntary course) a certificate showing the period of attendance, and in the case of an officer, A.F. E 534 duly completed, and a reference to the date of the district order notifying that the officer has received a satisfactory report. In the case of a soldier the certificate referred to in paragraph 384 will be attached.

3. *Allowances.*

Lodging.

388. For the period of attendance at annual training in camp an officer will be granted an allowance at one-half the army rate of lodging money to cover the expense of providing furniture.

Quarters, &c.

389. When attending a continuous course of instruction with pay, officers, who do not reside at the station where instruction is given, will, as far as possible, be assigned quarters. When this is done they will receive fuel in kind, and a money allowance in lieu of light at the army rates laid down in the Allowance Regulations, as well as the allowance at half the army rate of lodging money if the quarters are unfurnished. If quarters are not assigned, money allowances at army rates will be given in lieu of lodging, fuel, and light, on a certificate that quarters were not assigned, and that the officer did not reside at his usual place of abode during the period, but had to engage special lodgings.

Night of arrival.

390. Lodging allowance for the night of an officer's arrival at the station will be admissible when he necessarily proceeds there for the purpose of reporting himself at the school of instruction on the following morning.

Field allowance.

391. When, during annual training in camp, or instruction, officers are placed under canvas, they will be granted field allowance in addition to the allowance for providing furniture.

Mess expenses.

392. For each day an officer is entitled to pay under paragraph 377, he will be granted an allowance of 4*s.* in aid of mess expenses.

Servant allowance.

393. Officers of the Royal Engineers, Army Service Corps, Royal Army Medical Corps, Army Veterinary Service, and Army Ordnance Department, will be granted servant allowance at the rate of 1*s.* a day whilst under instruction at a school, if soldier servants are not available, but not during the annual training in camp.

Payment for furnished quarters.

394. When an officer in receipt of pay and allowances is assigned quarters which have been furnished at the public expense, in accordance with Barrack Schedules 1 or 2, or becomes a member of a mess which has been publicly furnished under Barrack Schedules 9, 10 and 11, he will be required to make the following payments :—

Field officers	2*d.* a day for quarters.
Other officers	1*d.* a day for quarters.
All officers	1*d.* a day for mess.

The payment will be made to the cashier of the command in which the quarters and messes are situated, and credited to the public in the account of the district accountant.

Rations.

395. During annual training in camp non-commissioned officers and men will be rationed as regular soldiers. When under instruction at an authorised course, non-commissioned officers and men will be entitled to rations in kind or the allowance in lieu at army rates.

396. A messing allowance at the rate of 1*s.* a day, in lieu of the allowance of 3*d.* paid to soldiers of the regular army, will be drawn, for each non-commissioned officer or man present at annual training in camp, by the officer commanding the unit to which he belongs. The allowance will be expended on improving the messing or adding to the comfort (either in money or kind) of the men in camp in any manner which the officer commanding considers desirable, provided that no preferential treatment is given to any individual, or rank, at the expense of others. The conditions governing the issue of the 3*d.* in the regular army, except as regards age, will apply to the issue of the 1*s.* to the commanding officer. Messing.

When a full field service ration of groceries and extras is issued at the public expense, the messing allowance will be 9*d.* instead of 1*s.*

Commanding officers will keep an account of their expenditure of the allowance in order that it may be audited if at any time required by the Army Council.

During instruction at an authorised course, for which pay is drawn, the 1*s.* allowance will be issued to the soldier.

397. Non-commissioned officers or men attending a course of instruction will be provided with quarters or tent or lodging money in lieu, if accommodation is not available. Lodging at courses.

398. Kit allowance will not be issued to non-commissioned officers and men of the Territorial Force. Kit.

399. Separation allowance will be issued for the benefit of the wives and families of all married non-commissioned officers (including the acting non-commissioned officers referred to in paragraph 5) of the Territorial Force for the periods for which they are in receipt of pay during the annual training in camp, and at authorised courses of instruction. Separation.

The allowance will be issued at the rates for soldiers not in public quarters, and subject generally to the conditions laid down in the Allowance Regulations. It will be claimed on A.F. E 668. For annual training in camp it will be paid regimentally through the company pay lists at the end of the training, and for courses of instruction through the permanent staff pay list at the end of the course, the charges being supported by A.F. E 668 in each case. Rates.

400. A non-commissioned officer holding a certificate of competency for the care of arms will receive 1*d.* yearly for each rifle or carbine in the possession of the unit and inspected by him. The allowance will be charged in the pay list of the permanent staff for the month of April and will be subject to the conditions laid down in para. 368; it will not be drawn in respect of arms for which an allowance is drawn under that paragraph. Inspection of arms.

4. *Provision of Horses and Forage.*

401. All officers (other than regular adjutants), non-commissioned officers, and men requiring to be mounted at annual training in camp, or other duty authorised by the general officer commanding-in-chief, will be entitled to the use of a horse provided by their County Association. Horse.

Forage. **402.** Forage, or the allowance in lieu, at such daily rates as are current at the time in the command, will be granted under the conditions laid down in the Allowance Regulations, for one horse each for mounted officers and men during annual training in camp, or other authorised duty, for which the employment of a horse has been sanctioned by the general officer commanding-in-chief.

Rates, forage. **403.** The rates of forage allowance are notified periodically in Army Orders.

D.—Miscellaneous Grants, &c.

1. *Outfit Grants.*

Outfit grant. **404.** Officers joining the Territorial Force who have not previously served in the militia, yeomanry or volunteers will be allowed on first appointment an outfit grant of £20, subject to the following conditions.

This necessary qualification must, unless the Army Council otherwise approve, be obtained within two years of appointment. In order to qualify for the grant, officers must pass the prescribed examination after instruction at a school, or after attachment with the regular forces of their own arm of the service, for the period prescribed for the various arms as initial courses in the Regulations.

If an officer has obtained Certificate B. in the Officers Training Corps, has qualified for the rank of captain in the regular army, or, in the case of an officer of artillery or infantry, has obtained the rank of lieutenant of the Royal Navy, he will not be required to undergo instruction to qualify for the grant.

Grant to officer transferred. **405.** The Army Council will be prepared to consider the claim of an officer transferred for the benefit of the public service to another unit, or re-appointed, including those with previous service in the militia, yeomanry or volunteer forces, to such portion of the grant as would not exceed his actual expenditure for the purchase or alteration of his new outfit. The grant will be subject to the conditions in paragraphs 404 and 406. No claims under this paragraph from officers who become supernumerary in their units or are placed on the unattached list of the Territorial Force on transfer can be considered until they are absorbed into the establishment of a unit.

Refund of outfit grant. **406.** An officer who, except by reason of ill-health, death, or such special circumstances as the Army Council may decide, fails—

(*a*) To serve three years from the date of his appointment, re-appointment, or transfer;

(*b*) To qualify three times as efficient within that period;

(*c*) To undergo the course of instruction (unless otherwise qualified) and obtain a satisfactory report within two years of appointment, or any extension of that period granted under paragraph 256,

will be required to refund the amount paid to him. If, however, the officer has satisfied condition (*c*), he will be allowed to retain a proportionate amount of the total grant admissible for each completed year of service during which he has made himself efficient.

407. Officers eligible under the Volunteer Regulations to qualify for the outfit grant, who have not received it, will be allowed to earn the grant under the above conditions, commissioned service in the volunteer force being allowed to reckon towards the three years. If they have received the first advance, the balance may be issued on their fulfilling the conditions in the Territorial Force. Officers who have received the full grant, but have not completed three years' efficient service on transfer from the Volunteer force, will not be required to refund the money if they serve and make themselves efficient for the remainder of the period in the new force. **Conditions of.**

408. Claims of officers, whose transfer to the Territorial Force necessitates an alteration of uniform, may be specially considered by the Army Council for such portion of the grant as will not exceed actual expenditure for the purchase or alteration of outfit. **Alteration of uniform.**

409. Previous efficient service in the commissioned ranks of the Officers Training Corps will count in reduction of the service required to earn the grant. **Previous service.**

410. The grants will be claimed on A.F. M 1408, those under paragraphs 405 and 408 being accompanied by a statement of the expenses incurred by the officer in altering or completing his outfit. **Claims.**

2. *Special Service Section.*

411. Members of the Special Service Section will receive an annual retaining fee of 10*s*. This sum will be issued at the annual training. **Retaining fee.**

412. When on special service they will receive the pay and allowances of the corresponding rank in the regular army for the arm of the service to which they belong. **Pay and allowances.**

413. In the event of their being killed, wounded, or disabled while on special service, pensions will be granted under the same conditions as if the Territorial Force were mobilized. **Pensions.**

3. *Gratuity on Embodiment.*

414. A gratuity of £5 will be issued to each officer, non-commissioned officer and man of the Territorial Force, joining his unit on embodiment. **Gratuity.**

415. In the case of officers and men of the Special Service Section the gratuity will be issued in the event of their being called out and employed under their agreement for special service, and will be paid as soon as possible after they report themselves for duty. **Issue of.**

4. *Payment of Civilian Medical Practitioners and Veterinary Surgeons.*

416. In regiments in which a medical officer or a veterinary officer is not present at the annual training in camp a civilian practitioner may be employed. **Civilian practitioners.**

417. A medical practitioner thus employed will be paid at the rates laid down in the Pay Warrant. When it is proposed to **Rates of pay.**

employ a civilian veterinary surgeon, the rates of remuneration will be arranged by the officer commanding the regiment, and submitted to the general officer commanding-in-chief of the command for approval, before any engagement is entered into.

Agreement. **418.** A civilian medical practitioner or civilian veterinary surgeon will be required before appointment to make an agreement accepting the rates.

5. *Allowance for Divine Service.*

Pay of officiating clergymen. **419.** The remuneration payable to officiating clergymen appointed to hold Divine service on Sunday mornings and on Good Friday, will be as follows, and will be reckoned upon the actual number of officers and men (of each particular denomination) borne on the strength at the annual training in camp :—

When the number amounts to 100 and upwards ...£1 1*s.* 0*d.*		For each day that Divine service is performed.
When the number amounts to 25, but is under 100... 10*s.* 6*d.*		

When the number falls short of 25, no remuneration will be granted.

Claims will be forwarded to the district accountant on A.F. O 1610.

6. *Attestation Fees, &c.*

Fee of magistrate's clerk. **420.** The fee of the magistrate's clerk on the attestation of a member of the Territorial Force, or on his re-enlistment or re-engagement, will be 1*s.* No fee will be payable in the case of an attestation or re-engagement made before a commissioned officer.

Rewards, apprehension of deserters. **421.** The payment of rewards for the apprehension of deserters on or during embodiment will be governed by the rules laid down in the Pay Warrant (Articles 1194-1197).

III.—TRAVELLING EXPENSES AND ALLOWANCES.

A.—Permanent Staff.

1. *Adjutants.*

Duties entitling to travelling expenses. **422.** Adjutants, or acting adjutants, on duties in connection with the Territorial Force, except on journeys for which a grant is made on their account to County Associations, will be entitled to their travelling expenses, subject to the rules laid down in the King's Regulations and the Allowance Regulations. An adjutant will not be entitled to a higher rate of travelling allowance than that of captain unless actually holding the regimental rank of major in the regular forces.

Horse hire, adjutants'. **423.** Charges under the Allowance Regulations for horse-hire, and for travelling expenses within 10 miles, will, in the case of adjutants who, with the sanction of the general officer commanding-in-chief, are exempted from keeping a horse, be made quarterly.

The amount admissible from the beginning of the financial year to the end of any quarter will not exceed the amount of the forage and stable allowance for the same period. Cases in which exceptional expenses have been incurred by adjutants who will vacate their appointment before the end of the financial year may be submitted for special consideration.

424. The officer acting as adjutant, if entitled to forage under paragraph 362, but not keeping a horse, will be allowed the sum actually and necessarily expended in horse-hire, as limited by the Allowance Regulations, for mounted duties, and in conveyance on duty to places at a distance not exceeding 10 miles from headquarters. Such sum, however, will not exceed the amount of forage and stable allowance for the period during which the officer acts as adjutant. When horse-hire is claimed for an acting adjutant, the name of the adjutant for whom he is acting will be shown in the claim. Horse hire, acting adjutant.

425. When an adjutant is allowed to live away from headquarters, no extra expense for travelling thereby incurred will be admissible as a charge against the public, nor will any charge be admissible on account of travelling between his residence and headquarters. Adjutant not living at head-quarters.

2. *Instructors.*

426. The travelling expenses and allowances of instructors serving on army engagement will be governed by the Allowance Regulations, except for journeys for which a grant is made on their account to County Associations. Travelling expenses will not be allowed for distances of less than two miles from squadron, battery, or company headquarters. Instructors.

427. Travelling expenses will be allowed, subject to paragraph 426 :—

(*a*) To an instructor necessarily sent away from the headquarters of his unit for instruction. When allowed.

(*b*) To an instructor proceeding to an outlying squadron, battery or company for quarterly inspection of arms.

(*c*) To an instructor sent to an outlying squadron, battery or company during the absence at the School of Musketry, or at a School of Instruction for Artillery, of the instructor posted thereto.

(*d*) To a pensioner serjeant-instructor when ordered to attend the School of Musketry, a School of Instruction for Artillery, or the Royal Small Arms Factory.

428. Travelling expenses will not be allowed to an instructor sent to an outlying squadron, battery or company during the absence on private affairs of the instructor posted thereto. When not allowed.

429. District routes will be issued for all journeys made by serjeant-instructors from and to their stations, except when they return on the same day. For periodical visits to an out-station, one route will suffice for a period not exceeding one month. District routes.

430. Travelling expenses will not be admissible for more than one visit a week to an outlying squadron, battery or company unless special authority from the general officer commanding-in-chief for more frequent visits has been obtained. Weekly visits.

B.—Divisional and Mounted and Infantry Brigade Headquarters.

Allowance regulations govern.

431. Travelling expenses and allowances for divisional headquarters and for mounted and infantry brigade headquarters will be governed by the Allowance Regulations, subject to the conditions in paragraphs 432 to 434.

For whom admissible.

432. Travelling expenses and allowances will be admitted for the headquarters of divisional artillery, for mounted and infantry brigade headquarters (other than those commanded by the officers commanding the regiments of Foot Guards), and for the divisional medical staffs (administrative medical officer and his staff officer), within a limit of £40 for each headquarters in a command for all duly authorised journeys.

The general officer commanding-in-chief of each command will be allotted a lump sum assessed at this rate for each headquarters of divisional artillery, for each mounted or infantry brigade, and for the divisional medical staff in his command, to cover travelling expenses for brigade headquarters for all duly authorised journeys, as follows :—

(*a*) Travelling expenses for the officers, and the daily rate of travelling allowance, when admissible, to and from the annual training in camp.

(*b*) Travelling expenses and allowances when selecting sites for camps.

(*c*) Travelling expenses and allowances for actual and necessary visits to units (including in special cases visits to company and detachment headquarters) during the non-training period, not exceeding four visits annually, of the brigade commander and brigade-major to the headquarters of each unit, with detention allowance for one night on each occasion when absolutely necessary.

(*d*) Travelling expenses and allowances for all duly ordered journeys other than the above (as, for instance, when a brigade commander is ordered to go to the headquarters of a command or district for consultation, or to the station to which his brigade is allotted on mobilization or to a rifle range), expenses in these cases to be only allowed on the special authority of the general officer commanding-in-chief, or on the authority of an officer delegated by him.

Allotment of.

433. An allotment from the lump sum, referred to in paragraph 432, will be made at the discretion of the general officer commanding-in-chief to each divisional artillery headquarters, to each mounted or infantry brigade, and to each divisional medical staff as the maximum to be allowed for travelling expenses and allowances. Charges will be governed by the Allowance Regulations, and vouched in the ordinary way. Brigade and divisional artillery commanders will receive travelling allowance, when admissible, at the rate laid down in paragraph 366, Allowance Regulations, for army officers, classes 1–6, and similarly brigade-majors will receive travelling allowance at the rate laid down for classes 7–14.

How calculated.

434. All travelling expenses will be calculated from the divisional artillery, brigade, and divisional medical staff headquarters respectively when within the area of the division or brigade, or, if no greater expense for this journey is involved, from the officers' residences within these areas. In cases where the commander or staff officer is permitted to live outside the area these expenses will be calculated as from some convenient centre (to be fixed by the Army Council) within the area.

C.—Regimental Officers and Men.

1. *Annual Training in Camp, Drills and Musketry.*

435. The cost of conveyance of units to and from annual training in camp, drills and musketry, will be borne by the County Association. No personal allowances or expenses will be given. Conveyance to training, &c.

436. No grant from public funds will be made for the conveyance of officers' chargers in excess of the number laid down in the territorial force establishments. Officers' chargers.

2. *Instruction.*

437. Officers and men joining an obligatory course of instruction for which pay is drawn will be allowed their travelling expenses and allowances at army rates, provided the cost is not greater than that from the headquarters of their squadron, battery or company to the nearest available place of instruction. Travelling expenses in connection with the same course will only be admitted once. If an officer or man is permitted for his own convenience to attend a school or course which is not the nearest available one, any extra expense caused thereby will not be admissible. Officers and men attending a course of instruction will not be entitled to travelling expenses for their horses unless they are required to be mounted, and it is certified that they could not be supplied with a public horse. Officers attending courses.

438. Officers and men who reside at their homes while attending an obligatory course at an evening school of instruction will be allowed their travelling expenses to and from daily, provided such expenses do not exceed the lodging, fuel and light allowances referred to in paragraph 389. Residing at home.

439. Officers and men making single attendances to complete an obligatory course of instruction with training battalions or regular units will be granted travelling allowances and expenses, provided the total emoluments drawn do not exceed those admissible for a course extending over an equivalent continuous period. Single attendances.

440. Travelling allowances and expenses to voluntary courses of instruction may be admitted as laid down in paragraphs 437 to 439, if the general officer commanding-in-chief so directs when sanctioning the attendance. Voluntary courses.

441. Musketry instructors will be allowed travelling expenses, under the conditions laid down in the Allowance Regulations, when required in the absence of the adjutant to visit the authorised rifle ranges of their units to superintend musketry practice. Musketry instructors.

442. Officers examined in musketry will, if successful, be allowed travelling expenses from the headquarters of the units, &c., to the nearest station where an examination is held, together with allowances at army rates. Musketry examination.

Examination in languages. **443.** Officers will be allowed their actual travelling expenses incurred in attending for examination as interpreters, provided they qualify as interpreters.

When not admissible. **444.** Travelling expenses will not be admissible—

(1) for candidates for commissions travelling to and from schools of instruction;

(2) for officers about to be examined in military subjects, proceeding to and from the places appointed.

For inspection of arms. **445.** A non-commissioned officer holding a certificate of competency for the care of arms will be allowed travelling expenses for journeys performed for the purpose of the quarterly inspection of arms.

Special military duty. **446.** Officers travelling on military duties specially authorised by the Army Council or the general officer commanding-in-chief may be granted travelling allowances and expenses in accordance with the Allowance Regulations.

Warrants. **447.** Officers travelling in Great Britain on duty of a nature which entitles them to travel at the public expense should be provided with a warrant from Army Book 205, which must be given up at the booking office in exchange for a ticket. The warrant will be endorsed as follows, and signed by the adjutant of the unit "Territorial Force officer travelling on military duty at the Government expense."

Non-commissioned officers and men so travelling should be provided with railway warrants by the adjutant of the unit, or by the officer who gives the certificate referred to in paragraph 384.

This paragraph does not apply to journeys to camp, drills, training, or to ranges, except in the case of the instructor of musketry.

D.—Claims.

Claims, general. **448.** All claims for travelling expenses not under route, or for horse-hire, will be made out on A.F. O 1771, and dealt with as laid down in the Allowance Regulations; if made by adjutants, claims will be sent on the last day of each quarter.

Adjutant's horse hire. **449.** Charges for the expenses referred to in paragraph 423 will be made on separate claims from those for the adjutants' other expenses. They will be supported by (1) receipts for the horse-hire; (2) a statement showing the amounts drawn under paragraph 422 in the previous quarter of the same financial year; and (3) a certificate that forage and stable allowances have not been, and will not be, drawn, or showing the number of days for which they have been drawn.

Serjeant instructors, railway warrants. **450.** Serjeant-instructors, when entitled to travelling expenses, will be furnished with railway warrants whenever practicable. The remainder of their travelling expenses will be charged in the accounts of the regimental accountant, vouched by the route for the journey. Claims for travelling expenses to an outlying battery or company will be supported by the commanding officer's certificate that no other instructor at the public expense was employed with the same squadron, battery, or company at the same time.

IV.—HOSPITAL TREATMENT, MEDICAL EXPENSES AND GRATUITIES.

1.—Permanent Staff.

451. Members of the permanent staff will not be entitled to the attendance of a military medical officer, but a weekly allowance of 2*d.* for each person will be granted in aid of medical attendance for them and their families. This allowance will be paid monthly or quarterly by the adjutant and charged in his accounts. The term "family" includes the wife and the legitimate children and stepchildren up to 14 years of age, and, in the case of the adjutant, one civilian servant also. **Medical attendance.**

452. Instructors serving on army engagement, and, in extreme cases which will be decided by the senior local military medical officer, other instructors, will be granted admission to military hospitals. The stoppage levied during the period of treatment in hospital will, in the case of men serving on army engagements, be at the rates and subject to the conditions prescribed in the Allowance Regulations, and in other cases at the rate of 1*s.* a day. **Admission to hospital.**

2.—Regimental Officers and Men.

453. Non-commissioned officers and men of the Territorial Force when out for annual training in camp may be admitted to a military hospital under the conditions laid down for the regular forces in the Regulations for the Army Medical Service. They will be entitled to draw pay up to the date of expiration of the period of training for which they are called up. **Admission to hospital.**

454. Hospital stoppages will be made from their pay during the period of their being in hospital at the rates and under the conditions laid down in the Allowance Regulations for soldiers of the regular forces, so long as they draw pay. **Hospital stoppages.**

455. Should a non-commissioned officer or man be detained in hospital beyond the expiration of the annual training in camp of his unit, no charge will be made for his subsistence for the period of such detention. **When not charged.**

456. An officer suffering from disability contracted in and through the performance of military duty will be entitled to free treatment in a military hospital, or to medical attendance or re-imbursement of medical expenses under the conditions laid down in the Regulations for the Army Medical Service for an officer of the regular forces. Should the injury sustained, though not of a permanent nature, be such as temporarily to disable him from pursuing his civil employment, pay at the rate issuable to officers of the corresponding rank of the same arm of the service in the regular forces may, at the discretion of the Army Council, be granted for a period not exceeding six months. **Treatment in hospital.**

457. A sum not exceeding 3*s.* 6*d.* a day may be granted for a period not exceeding six months to a non-commissioned officer or man who is injured in and through the performance of military duty and rendered incapable of resuming his trade or calling. The injury will be at once reported to the general officer commanding-in-chief, who will direct an officer of the Royal Army Medical Corps to report on the case. **Injury on duty, gratuity.**

The gratuity will be limited to the period during which the man is shown to have been unable to follow his occupation, and will not be issuable for the period when the man is in receipt of pay, or subsisted in a military hospital.

Illness gratuity.

458. The gratuity referred to in paragraph 457 may be paid under the same conditions to a non-commissioned officer or man who is incapacitated by illness, proved to the satisfaction of the Director-General, Army Medical Service, to have been contracted in and through the performance of military duty, but no claim will be allowed which is not preferred within 12 months of the termination of the military duty in question.

Medical attendance.

459. In cases where, although the non-commissioned officer or man is able to follow his trade or calling, medical attendance is necessary in consequence of injury or sickness, his actual medical expenses up to a maximum of 3*s.* 6*d.* a day may be repaid, provided that the Director-General, Army Medical Service, is satisfied that the disability was contracted in and through the performance of military duty.

Amount.

460. The total amount issued under paragraphs 457 to 459 will not in any case exceed that of a payment of 3*s.* 6*d.* a day for six months.

V.—ACCOUNTS.

1. Permanent Staff.

Funds obtained by Adjutant.

461. The adjutant will obtain the funds for the payment of the permanent staff from the cashier of the command in which the headquarters of the unit are situated. He will forward the indent not later than the 20th of the month.

Payments, account of.

462. All payments made by the adjutant will be accounted for monthly to the regimental accountant on A.F. N 1452. This pay list will be made out in duplicate and forwarded to the accountant not later than four days after the expiration of the month.

Pay list.

463. The pay list will be examined by the accountant, and his observations upon it, if any, will be forwarded to the adjutant, who will answer and return them to the accountant without delay.

2. Training Account.

Training funds.

464. Immediately before the annual training in camp of the unit, the adjutant will forward to the cashier of the command an indent for the sum required for the pay and allowances of the officers, non-commissioned officers, and men during the training.

Issue to officers.

465. The adjutant will issue the pay and allowances of the officers and charge the amount against the public in A.F. N 1450.

N.C.Os. and men.

466. He will issue to the officers commanding companies, etc., the sums required by them for the pay, etc., of the non-commissioned officers and men during the training, and the sums so received will be accounted for in A.F. N 1451. Any balance on a pay list at the termination of the training will be adjusted between the adjutant and officer commanding the company, &c., before the latter leaves the station.

467. Within ten days after the termination of the training, the adjutant will transmit to the regimental accountant, an account, in duplicate, on A.F. N 1450, accompanied by the usual vouchers and by the company pay lists on A.F. N 1451. Accounts.

468. The account will be examined by the accountant and dealt with as laid down in paragraph 463. Examination of.

3. Accounts on Mobilization.

469. On mobilization, units will remain in the payment of the regimental accountant in which their peace headquarters are situated. Their pay will be issued, and accounts rendered, in the manner laid down for regular troops in the field. Pay on mobilization.

B.—Training Grant of General Officer Commanding-in-Chief.

470. A general officer commanding-in-chief will be responsible for the training and instruction of the members of the Territorial Force within his command. G.O.C.-in-C. responsible.

471. To enable him to meet the cost of such training and instruction, he will be credited with a sum not exceeding an amount representing the following payments in respect of each officer, non-commissioned officer and man of the Territorial Force present (including members of the brigade staffs), for a minimum period of 8 days at the annual training in camp of his unit:— Grant credited to G.O.C.

(*a*) 15 days' pay at the rates laid down for the various ranks and arms of the Territorial Force, including corps, armament and engineer pay.

(*b*) Allowances for officers for 15 days at the rates admissible.

(*c*) Rations in kind or an allowance in lieu, as provided in paragraphs 479 and 480, for 15 days for each non-commissioned officer and man, including the permanent staff.

(*d*) Messing allowance at the rate of 1*s*. a day for 15 days for each non-commissioned officer and man, including the permanent staff.

(*e*) 15 days' separation allowance, at army rates, for families without quarters, for each married non-commissioned officer entitled to the allowance.

(*f*) Equitation bounty for yeomen entitled to it.

472. With the exception of the money allotted in accordance with paragraph 471 in respect of officers and men of the Royal Army Medical Corps, the sum thus arrived at will be placed at the disposal of the general officer commanding-in-chief, no portion being specifically allocated to the training of any particular arm or unit. He will defray from it all expenses in connection with the annual training in camp and instruction of the members of the Territorial Force raised within his command, with the exceptions detailed in paragraphs 475, 477, 478, and 483. Expenses to be met from grant.

Credit for R.A.M.C.

The sum credited to general officers commanding-in-chief in respect of officers and men of the Royal Army Medical Corps is reserved for the training of that arm, and no part thereof may be employed for other purposes. Subject, however, to this reservation and to any general direction given by the Director-General, Army Medical Service, this portion of the training grant will be expended at the discretion of the general officer commanding-in-chief, who is responsible for the tactical training of medical units, in the same manner as that allotted for the training of other arms.

Expenditure on annual camp, &c.

473. It will be the aim of the general officer commanding-in-chief to secure that every unit is present at annual camp for a minimum period of 8 days, and that officers and non-commissioned officers attend such courses of instruction as are obligatory, but, subject to this, expenditure within the prescribed limit may be incurred at his discretion upon additional periods in camp, instructional tours or staff rides, local manœuvres, voluntary courses of instruction, and such other services as he may deem desirable for the training of the members of the Territorial Force within his command, subject to the following :—

(1) Personal emoluments are only to be given subject to the conditions laid down in regulations.

(2) The emoluments of individuals as prescribed in regulations according to their rank and arm of the service are not to be varied.

(3) The general officer commanding-in-chief is given a free hand as to the objects on which he spends his grant. This does not relieve him from the necessity of observing the ordinary rules by which expenditure is regulated.

Charges payable.

474. The charge thus payable will include—

I.—The regulated pay and allowances of officers and men of the Territorial Force issuable for the period of actual attendance at annual training in camp and obligatory courses of instruction, and—when authorised by the general officer commanding-in-chief—at staff rides or instructional tours, and voluntary courses of instruction, together with the rations, messing, and separation allowance of the serjeant-instructors of the permanent staff at annual training in camp.

II.—General expenses—

(*a*) The expenses of camps, including the hiring of grounds, the laying on of water, sanitation, &c. ; also the towage of targets when War Department vessels are not available.

(*b*) All travelling to schools and courses of instruction and travelling in connection with instructional tours or staff rides.

(*c*) All general expenditure for such items as additional pay to the staff of schools formed solely for the instruction of the Territorial Force, and all charges in connection with such schools, and any extra expenditure due to the visits of detached sections of the training battalions for instructing territorial units and analogous services.

475. The cost of conveying officers, non-commissioned officers, and men, horses, wagons, cycles, guns, regimental stores and baggage to annual training in camp, and of all travelling in connection with battalion or company drills, gun practice or musketry, except during the period of annual training in camp, will be defrayed by the County Associations. Conveyance, &c., except to camp, paid by Associations.

476. Tents and camp equipment will be issued from store, and the cost of their conveyance to and from the place of annual training in camp will fall against the general officer commanding-in-chief's grant. Tents, &c.

477. The general officer commanding-in-chief will obtain horses, motors, wagons and cycles required for the annual training in camp, and for staff rides or instructional tours, from the County Associations of the units concerned. He may employ for 15 days horses and cycles corresponding to the number of mounted officers other than adjutants, non-commissioned officers and men with whose pay he is credited, including men of the Special Reserve supernumerary to territorial units who train with the territorial units, and similarly with motors, wagons and draught horses according to the proportion of units which come up for training. A larger number may be employed at his discretion for a shorter period, or a smaller number for a longer period, provided that the total number is not thereby exceeded. Horses, &c., from Associations.

He will not be credited with any money in respect of horses, motors, cycles or wagons.

478. The general officer commanding-in-chief may authorise the issue of forage for each horse employed, on the principle laid down in paragraph 477. When possible, forage in kind will be issued from store or under local existing contracts, or special contracts for the camps will be made. When this is impracticable, a forage allowance at the rate current in the command will be issued to the officer commanding the unit. The cost of the provision of forage will be allowed extra to the sum laid down in paragraph 471. Petrol for motors will be supplied by County Associations. Forage. Petrol.

479. The general officer commanding-in-chief will be responsible for rationing the troops during the annual training in camp. Rations will, wherever possible, be drawn under existing War Department contracts, and where no such contracts exist special contracts will be entered into. In any special case where this cannot be done, the ration allowance of 6*d.* per man will be paid to the officer commanding the unit. In the case of individuals or small bodies attending courses of instruction, where the ration cannot be issued in kind, the 6*d.* will be issued to the men direct. Rations.

The 1*s.* per day messing allowance for each man who attends the annual training in camp, or instruction, will be paid to the officer commanding the unit for the purpose of improving the messing of the men and will be administered at his discretion. In the case of individuals attending courses of instruction it will be paid to the men. Messing allowance.

480. The general officer commanding-in-chief will be credited with 15 days' rations in kind for each man who attends the annual Rations credited to G.O.C.-in-C.

training in camp for 8 days. Rations issued in kind will be deducted from the total with which the general officer commanding-in-chief is thus credited, and the balance will, for the purpose of assessing the general officer commanding-in-chief's grant, be converted into a cash credit at the rate of 6*d.* per ration unissued, which sum will be available for the general purposes of the training which he controls.

Assessment of camp expenses.

481. The sum available under paragraph 471 cannot be finally assessed by a general officer commanding-in-chief until the actual number of men camping for 8 days is known. He will, however, when considering the scheme of training for the year, be able to form an approximate estimate in the light of experience, and will base his arrangements accordingly. The exact sum will be ascertained when the number of campers is definitely known, and the balance beyond the amount spent in actual annual training in camp will be at his disposal for defraying the cost of courses of instruction, &c., during the winter months.

Camp sites.

482. Where War Department ground is not used for camping, the co-operation of the County Association should be secured with a view to obtaining the most suitable sites on advantageous terms.

Fuel, light, &c., by A.S.C.

483. The supply of fuel, light, and paillasse straw during training will be arranged for by the Army Service Corps, but will not be charged against the grant. Money allowances in lieu of issues in kind are not to be authorised except at schools of instruction.

"Annual training."

484. The term "annual training in camp" includes training in a fortress, and attendance at manœuvres.

Force when training entitled to pay and allowances laid down.

485. The fundamental principle laid down in Parliament is that when the Territorial Force is "training" it is entitled to the pay and allowances laid down. At other times it will be administered by the County Associations. It is equally a fundamental principle, therefore, that the public funds allotted to the general officer commanding-in-chief should be kept absolutely distinct from those administered by the Association.

SECTION 8.—EQUIPMENT.

Equipment.

496. The Regulations governing the issue of arms and equipment to the Territorial Force are laid down in the Regulations for the Equipment of the Army, Part III, Territorial Force.

SECTION 9.—UNIFORM.

I.—OFFICERS.

507. The only obligatory uniform for officers is service dress as authorised in the Dress Regulations for officers of the regular army. **Obligatory uniform.**

508. An authorized pattern of full dress for officers is laid down for each unit, but its provision is optional. **Full dress.**

509. Officers attending levees, courts, state balls, and ceremonies at which Royalty is present, and on the occasions mentioned in Table A, page 277, King's Regulations, must wear the authorized full dress. Full dress will not be worn by officers parading with their men, unless the latter are wearing full dress or walking out dress. **Full dress, when worn.**

510. Officers gazetted to the Unattached List of the Territorial Force will provide themselves with service dress only. When called up for training they will be permitted to dine at mess in plain clothes. **Unattached list.**

511. Officers appointed aides-de-camp to the King will wear regimental uniform with a silver aiguillette, or the uniform laid down in the Dress Regulations for aides-de-camp to the King appointed from the regular army, with the exception that silver will be substituted for gold in the aiguillette, embroidery, lace, buttons, cocked hat, sword knot, slings, and horse furniture. The waist-sash will be of gold and crimson silk net, with tassels of gold and crimson silk. The aiguillette will be worn with full dress uniform by these officers when doing duty with their units. **Aides-de-camp to the King.**

512. The special uniform prescribed for aides-de-camp to the King will only be worn when His Majesty is present in State, at levees, and when on duty as King's aide-de-camp at field days and other military ceremonies at which His Majesty is present.

513. An aide-de-camp to the King, who is also a Lord Lieutenant or Deputy-Lieutenant of a county, will not wear the aide-de-camp's aiguillette with his Lord Lieutenant's or Deputy-Lieutenant's uniform.

514. An officer appointed Honorary Physician or Honorary Surgeon to the King will wear on State occasions, in addition to the shoulder belt and pouch, a silver aiguillette as for an aide-de-camp to the King, on the right shoulder under the shoulder cord which forms part of his uniform. **Honorary Physician and Honorary Surgeon to the King.**

515. Officers appointed to the staff of the army will wear regimental uniform with the special distinctions laid down for staff officers (see Dress Regulations), silver being substituted for gold, except for officers of units in which gold lace is worn. **Army staff.**

516. Commanders of brigades and commanders of royal artillery will wear the uniform laid down in the Dress Regulations for substantive colonels. Silver lace and white metal ornaments will be worn on all uniform and horse furniture by officers appointed from the Territorial Force. As an alternative, brigade commanders and commanders of royal artillery may wear the uniform in which they last served, with the badges of rank of colonel. **Brigade commander and C.R.A.**

Brigade major.

517. Brigade majors will wear the uniform in which they last served, with the staff distinctions prescribed for brigade majors of the regular forces, silver being substituted for gold on the aiguillette, cocked hat, forage cap, and gorget patches. The provision of the cocked hat and staff pantaloons for wear when the order of dress is "Staff in blue" is optional.

Administrative medical officer.

518. Administrative medical officers will wear the uniform prescribed for colonels of the Army Medical Service, silver being substituted for gold, or the uniform in which they last served, with the badges of rank of colonel. They will not wear the aiguillette or other staff distinctions.

Staff captains, R.A.

519. Staff captains for royal artillery will wear the uniform in which they last served, without aiguillette or staff distinctions.

Service dress, commanders of brigades, &c.

520. In service dress, commanders of brigades, commanders and staff captains, royal artillery, and administrative medical officers, will wear the blue serge frock described in paragraph 739, Dress Regulations, but without gorget patches; pantaloons or overalls as in full dress. Drab service dress may be worn in camp and at manœuvres.

Letters on shoulder straps.

521. Retired officers appointed to the staff of the Territorial Force will wear the letter "R" on shoulder straps and shoulder cords below the badges of rank. Officers appointed from the Territorial Force will continue to wear the letter "T."

Rank badges and letter "T."

522. Badges of rank will be similar to those for the regular army, and will be worn in silver on gold shoulder cords, and in gold on silver shoulder cords. The letter "T" will be worn below the badges of rank on all shoulder cords and shoulder straps. In service dress the "T" in bronze will be worn on the collar of the jacket below the collar badge.

Badges of rank, retired officers.

523. Officers who have been permitted to retain their rank on retirement from the regular army, and army reserve officers, will, when serving in the Territorial Force, wear the badges of their army rank, should such rank be higher than their rank in the Territorial Force.

Full dress uniform, silver lace.

524. Except in the cases of corps for which special uniforms have been sanctioned, and which join the Territorial Force as complete units of the same arm, full dress uniform will, as far as possible, conform to that of corresponding units of the regular forces, silver lace and white metal buttons and ornaments being substituted for gold lace and gilt metal. Existing yeomanry regiments wearing gold lace and gilt buttons are permitted to retain these distinctions.

Gold lace.

525. Units that desire for any special reason to obtain permission to wear gold lace and gilt ornaments must submit applications through County Associations for consideration. Each case will be considered on its merits.

Cord and lace.

526. The cord and lace of officers of infantry clothed in green or grey will be of the same pattern and applied in the same form as that on the tunic of rifle regiments of the regular forces. Units clothed in green will wear black cord and lace; units clothed in grey, cord and lace of silver or other authorized material.

Belts.

527. Officers of infantry units clothed in scarlet will in review order wear the web sword belt with silver laced slings, and the crimson waist-sash. In units clothed in grey or green they will

wear black or brown belts of rifle pattern, with pouch belt of the same colour; the flap of the pouch will be edged with $\frac{3}{4}$-inch silver lace, and may, if desired, bear the regimental badge in white metal.

528. Mounted officers will wear steel spurs. **Spurs.**

529. Forage caps will be of the universal pattern. For yeomanry the bands and welts of the colour of the facings. For other services, as in the regular army. Peaks for field officers embroidered with silver embroidery; in units wearing gold lace, gold embroidery. Highland kilted and Scottish trewed regiments will wear the glengarry cap. **Forage caps.**

530. Swords and scabbards will be of the pattern prescribed for corresponding units of the regular army, sword knots of gold or silver lace or brown or black leather, according to the belts. **Swords.**

531. The universal pattern "Sam Browne" belt in brown leather is to be worn with the service dress by all units. **"Sam Browne" belt.**

532. The wearing of mixed uniform, *i.e.*, service dress jackets with coloured trousers or trews, or *vice versâ*, is forbidden. **Mixed uniform forbidden.**

533. Units may adopt a mess dress similar in design to that approved for corresponding units of the regular forces; the provision of this dress is optional to the individual officer. **Mess dress.**

534. A serge frock, blue, green, or grey, according to the colour of the full dress uniform, similar to that authorized for officers of the regular army, may be worn as an undress garment. Buttons, regimental pattern; badges of rank in metal; no collar badges. This garment must not be worn on duty, or when parading with troops. Its provision is optional. **Serge frock.**

535. Officers of the Territorial Force are not required to provide themselves with the uniform frock coat. **Frock coat.**

536. Horse furniture will be of universal pattern as laid down for the regular army, with white metal fittings; brass or gilt fittings in the case of units wearing gold lace. Throat ornaments will not be worn. Lamb-skins, leopard-skins, and saddle cloths are not compulsory. **Saddlery.**

537. The instructions in para. 553 in regard to badges also apply to the badges worn by officers. **Badges.**

538. No deviation from authorized patterns of uniform is permitted, and no new patterns of uniform, badges, or horse furniture are to be introduced without previous submission to the War Office for approval. **Changes in pattern.**

539. Officers retiring with permission to wear uniform are entitled to wear the uniform in which they last served, with the letters "T.R." on the shoulder straps or shoulder cords below the badges of rank. **Retired officers.**

II.—NON-COMMISSIONED OFFICERS AND MEN.

540. An annual grant for each efficient non-commissioned officer and man is sanctioned for the maintenance of clothing and equipment, and will be paid to the County Association. **Annual grant.**

Service dress compulsory.

541. The provision of service dress is compulsory. The cost of service dress, and the maintenance of equipment constitute the first charges against the grant.

Details of service dress.

542. Service dress will consist of :—

Mounted Services.

Jacket.	Drab serge mixture, universal pattern.
Pantaloons.	Drab bedford cord.
Headdress.	Service dress cap of universal pattern. Units in possession of a slouch hat may continue to wear it in place of, or in addition to, the cap.
Putties,	Drab.
or	
Leggings.	Brown leather.
Spurs.	Hunting pattern, brown straps.
Greatcoat.	Drab, universal pattern (see paragraph 545).

Dismounted Services.

Jacket.	Drab serge mixture, universal pattern.
Trousers or Knicker-bockers.	Drab mixture.
Headdress.	Service dress cap, universal pattern. For Highland kilted and Scottish trewed regiments the glengarry cap.
Putties.	Drab, universal pattern. Scottish units wearing the kilt, drab spats.
Greatcoat.	Drab, universal pattern (see paragraph 545).

Cyclist battalions.

543. Cyclist battalions may adopt drab stockings and spats instead of putties, and a drab waterproof cape in place of, or in addition to, the greatcoat.

Fatigue clothing.

544. Where considered necessary, fatigue clothing may be provided for use in stables by mounted men.

Greatcoats.

545. Units in possession of cloaks or greatcoats other than those of service dress pattern may be permitted to retain them until worn out, but no further supplies of obsolete pattern are to be purchased.

Scale of uniform.

546. Two suits of uniform will be provided for each man, one of which must be service dress (see para. 542). The other may be as described in para. 547, and be used as an undress or "walking-out" uniform.

"Walking-out" dress.

547. Undress or "walking-out" dress will consist of tunic or frock, trousers or trews, forage or glengarry cap. Highland units previously authorized to wear the kilt may retain the kilt, sporran, and white spats instead of trousers or trews.

Sashes and girdles.

548. A sash will be worn by serjeants of infantry clothed in scarlet, and girdles by all ranks in the case of units wearing tunics, and similarly dressed to units of the regular army which wear them. Girdles are not to be worn with frocks.

Expenditure of grant.

549. No portion of the Government grant is to be expended on the provision and upkeep of any articles other than those detailed as forming part of the service dress or undress uniform, as defined in paras. 542, 543, 544, and 547. No other articles may be worn without the sanction of the County Association, subject to the provision of para. 550.

550. No deviation from authorized patterns of uniform is permitted, and no articles of clothing or badges, whether provided from the Government grant or from private funds, will be introduced without War Office approval. Application for authority to adopt new uniform or to effect any change will be submitted, accompanied by samples, or, in the case of badges, by sketches, and it should be stated whether funds are available to meet the expense. Patterns, after approval, will be sealed and returned to the units for record. **Changes in patterns.**

551. The wearing of mixed uniform, *i.e.*, service dress jackets, with coloured trousers or trews, or *vice versâ*, is forbidden. **Mixed uniform.**

552. The designations of the unit in black or white metal will be worn on the shoulder straps of tunics and serge frocks, and in black or gilding metal on service dress jackets and greatcoats. In the shoulder strap title the letter "T" will be placed above the name of the unit (see Appendix 16). Brass or gilding metal titles will be worn on tunics and serge frocks by units having permission to wear gold lace. **Metal titles.**

553. Honours worn by units of the regular army will not be worn by corresponding units of the Territorial Force, and the word "Ubique" will be omitted from all badges and appointments worn by royal artillery and royal engineers. With these exceptions the distinctive badges are common to both forces. In the "walking-out" uniform they will be entirely in white metal or bronze, except where special permission has been given for the adoption of gold lace and gilt ornaments, see para. 525. **Badges.**

554. No gold lace, gilt, gilding metal, or brass ornament will be worn with "walking-out" uniform except in yeomanry units permitted to retain gold lace, and in such other units as receive special permission to adopt gold lace and gilt ornaments. Gilding metal buttons will be worn with service dress except by units clothed in green, who will wear the black "rifle" button. Cap badges worn in service dress will be as worn in the regular army, subject to the mission of honours provided for in para. 553. **Gilt ornaments.**

555. Chevrons and badges of rank will, in design, correspond with those worn in the regular army. **Chevrons.**

556. Non-commissioned officers of units clothed in scarlet, grey, or blue, will wear chevrons of silver lace or of other material as may be authorized. In the Royal Engineers and in the Royal Army Medical Corps chevrons will be made up on blue cloth; Army Service Corps on white cloth; in other units clothed in blue or scarlet, on scarlet cloth. In units clothed in green, non-commissioned officers will wear light green chevrons made up on cloth the colour of the garment. Chevrons with the service dress will be of worsted material; badges will be of metal or embroidery as in the regular army. **Lace and embroidery.**

557. Men who have been returned as efficient four times may wear on the right forearm a star made of silk or worsted. The four returns of efficiency need not be in consecutive years, nor in the same unit. An additional star may be worn for every further **Efficiency star.**

aggregate of four years. A non-commissioned officer or man who has become entitled to wear a star or stars, and is returned as non-efficient in an annual return of his unit, may continue to wear such star or stars.

Previous efficient service in the yeomanry or volunteers shall count towards the award of this badge.

Geneva Cross. **558.** Medical units will wear the Geneva Cross as worn by regulars. For non-commissioned officers the edging will be silver embroidery instead of gold, and for buglers and privates white instead of yellow.

Badges, skill-at-arms. **559.** Badges for skill-at-arms, signalling, &c., will be of similar design, and worn in a corresponding manner to those of the regular forces, except that in all cases (other than as provided for in para. 554) silver embroidery will be substituted for gold embroidery, and white metal for gold. They will be awarded under the conditions governing the competitions for the several badges.

Unauthorized badges. **560.** No badges other than those above laid down may be worn.

Uniform on discharge. **561.** Non-commissioned officers who have served 10 years and upwards in and above the rank of serjeant, and who are allowed to retain their rank on discharge, may wear their uniform with the letter "R" in white metal or bronze above the chevrons on the right arm. They will provide the uniform at their own expense. This privilege does not extend to regular non-commissioned officers employed on the permanent staff.

Sale of old uniforms. **562.** Worn out uniform will be disposed of under arrangements made under the direct instructions of County Associations. The conditions of sale will provide that the purchaser shall not, either directly or indirectly, dispose of any tunics, frocks, jackets, trousers, or headdresses, as garments, unless they have first been so altered that they cannot be recognised as having been used as uniform of the Territorial Force.

Supply of materials, &c. **563.** Materials, cut-out unmade uniforms, badges, and headdresses as used by the regular forces may be obtained from the Royal Army Clothing Department at the rates quoted in the Priced Vocabulary of Clothing and Necessaries, if of the description authorized for wear by the Territorial Force. The supply of other articles and the making-up of the materials must be arranged locally.

Payment for. **564.** The articles demanded will be supplied on payment, which should be made on receipt of the necessary receivable order from the War Office, or if preferred their value will be deducted from the balance of the grant due to the Association on the following 1st November. In special cases the value may, with the sanction of the Army Council, be deducted in three yearly instalments.

Uniform parades. **565.** Uniform will be worn at all parades, except that company parades, parades under serjeant-instructors, and musketry may, with the authority of the officer commanding, be carried out in plain clothes.

Uniform abroad. **566.** Non-commissioned officers and men when attending banquets, receptions, or rifle meetings in foreign countries, will not wear uniform unless specially authorized by the Army Council.

III.—PERMANENT STAFF.

567. Non-commissioned officers appointed to the permanent staff of the Territorial Force will retain all personal clothing in their possession at date of transfer. **Personal clothing.**

568. The uniform to be worn by non-commissioned officers of the permanent staff will be that of the unit with which doing duty, and will be obtained on payment from the stores of the unit. **Uniform.**

569. Chevrons and badges will be worn as under, and will be of the pattern worn in the unit. **Chevrons and badges.**

Acting serjeant-major ...	Four bar chevrons and crown on right forearm.
Squadron S.M. instructor Battery S.M. instructor ... Company S.M. instructor Colour-serjeant instructor Staff-serjeant instructor	Three bar chevrons and crossed rifles and crown on right arm above the elbow.
Serjeant-instructor ...	Three bar chevrons and crossed rifles on right arm above the elbow.

Crossed rifles will not be worn unless the non-commissioned officer is in possession of a School of Musketry certificate.

In the Royal Artillery, Royal Engineers and Royal Army Medical Corps, a gun, grenade, or Geneva Cross will be worn in addition.

With service dress, badges and chevrons will be worn on both arms.

SECTION 10.—CORRESPONDENCE, FORMS AND BOOKS.

1.—CORRESPONDENCE.

580. A diagram showing the channels of correspondence emanating from units of the Territorial Force, and a statement showing, in the case of various subjects of correspondence, the officer with whom final responsibility rests and the channels through which correspondence passes to him from units or Associations, are given in Appendices 9 and 10. **Channels of.**

581. Correspondence emanating from units on subjects connected with command and training will be sent by unit commanders to the officers responsible for their command and training, viz. :—By units of yeomanry to the territorial mounted brigade commander; by units allotted to infantry brigades, and infantry and cyclist battalions attached to the territorial division, to infantry brigade commanders; by units, except cavalry, allotted to divisional troops to divisional troop commanders; by army troops attached to territorial divisions, and by medical units allotted to divisions, to the general officer commanding the division; and by units allotted to coast defences to the coast defence commander. **Correspondence of units. Command and training.**

582. Such correspondence will thereafter proceed by the channels laid down in the King's Regulations, with the exception of such **Procedure.**

correspondence relating to the training of medical units as cannot be decided by the divisional general or his subordinates. This correspondence will pass direct from the divisional general to the Director General of Army Medical Services.

Responsibility of officers.

583. The attention of regular officers holding intermediate positions in the chain of command should be directed to the ruling of para. 1841 King's Regulations, that they will not, unless in exceptional circumstances, refer to superior authority matters which they have power to decide themselves. It is of importance that no unnecessary work in connection with the Territorial Force should fall upon the general officer commanding-in-chief. All appointment, &c., of the permanent staff should, for instance, be made by the officer in charge of records concerned and the unit commander, unless a disciplinary question is involved, in which case the final decision must rest with the general officer commanding-in-chief.

Channel for correspondence.

584. Communications from general officers commanding divisions, officers commanding mounted brigades, or coast defence commanders, to county associations, whether addressed to the chairman or the secretary, should not be made through the medium of a staff officer. Conversely, communications from county associations will not be addressed to a staff officer, but to the general or other officer commanding, as the case may be. The same rule should be followed in communications with general officers commanding-in-chief, except on financial questions and questions of civil administration, when the correspondence may be addressed to the officer concerned.

Finance and civil administration.

The correspondence of units on questions of finance and civil administration will in all cases be addressed direct to the secretary of the county association.

Correspondence of County Associations.

585. In order to secure the harmonious administration of the Territorial Force it is obvious that the closest possible co-operation should exist between the county associations and the regular military authorities. It is, therefore, highly desirable that in any case of doubtful responsibility reference should be made to the divisional general (or the territorial mounted brigade commanders, or the coast defence commanders in cases where the yeomanry or units allotted to coast defence respectively are concerned) before a decision is given by the county association, and that these officers should be kept fully informed of every action taken by the county association which affects their duties.

New services.

586. In submitting a proposal for new services, or for services in connection with training or command, to the War Office, the county association will invariably enclose the remarks of the divisional general, mounted brigade commander, or coast defence commander upon it.

With military authorities.

587. The correspondence of the county association with the military authorities will always be sent to the divisional general, or to the mounted brigade commander, or coast defence commander, if these officers are primarily concerned.

With War Office.

588. The correspondence of the county associations with the War Office will be sent direct. Claims for grants and applications for payments, and routine matter connected therewith, will go to the chief accountant of the command for action.

9 / Gen. No. / 818

2.—REPORTS AND RETURNS.

589. Reports and returns will be rendered as shown in the following schedule :—

Return.	Army Form.	Rendered by.	To whom sent.	When due.
		(i.) *Returns of personnel.*		
Annual return ...	E. 568	Commanding officer	War Office direct ...	Oct. 8th.
Quarterly return	E. 548	Commanding officer	War Office direct, one copy; and County Association direct, one copy	Jan. 8th, Apl. 8th, July 8th, Oct. 8th.
Adjutant's quarterly return and diary	E. 540	Adjutant through commanding officer	Mounted Brigade commander, Divisional commander (through Brigade commander), or Coast Defence commander	Jan. 8th, Apl. 8th, July 8th, Oct. 8th.
State	B. 229	... ...	General officer commanding-in-chief direct	As required.
		(ii.) *Examination.*		
Officers for examination in Military Law and duties in the field before promotion	E. 621	Commanding officer through general officer commanding-in-chief	War Office	7th Apl. and 7th Oct.
Officers desirous of being examined in artillery	E. 644	Commanding officer through general officer commanding-in-chief	War Office	1st March and 1st Sept.
		(iii.) *Musketry, Artillery, Small Arms, &c.*		
Annual musketry return	B. 187	Commanding officer (two copies)	Officer commanding Mounted Brigade, Division, or Coast Defence; of which one copy to be transmitted to Commandant, School of Musketry	As soon as possible after 31st Oct., but not later than 30th Nov.
Annual Reports of Artillery Practice :—				
(i) Units belonging to Mounted Brigades and Divisions	B. 274 or B. 274A	Commanding officer (two copies)	Officer commanding Mounted Brigade or Division, of which one copy to be transmitted to Chief Instructor, Horse and Field School of Gunnery	On completion of practice.

Return.	Army Form.	Rendered by.	To whom sent.	When due.
(iii.) *Musketry, Artillery, Small Arms, &c.*—continued.				
Annual Reports of Artillery Practice—*cont.* (ii) Coast artillery units allotted fixed armament	B. 269	Commanding officer through coast defence commander	Commandant, School of Gunnery	On completion of practice.
(iii) Coast artillery units allotted to land front armament	B. 274A	Commanding officer through coast defence commander	Commandant, School of Gunnery	On completion of practice.
Annual return of small arm ammunition on charge	G.814A	Commanding officer	Chief ordnance officer of command	15th Sept.
Return of small arms in possession	G.893A	Commanding officer	Chief ordnance officer of command	15th Sept.
Annual return of the armament of artillery batteries and companies	E. 545	Officer commanding Mounted Brigade, Division, or Coast Defences	War Office	1st April.
Annual return of the armament of artillery batteries and companies—Amendments	G. 1086	Officer commanding Mounted Brigade, Division, or Coast Defences	War Office	1st Oct.
Annual return of guns and carriages	E. 522	Commanding officer of Artillery units not allotted to Coast Defence: through general officer commanding Mounted Brigade or Division	War Office	1st Oct.
Annual inspection of signallers	B. 225	Commanding officer	Inspecting officer ...	At inspection.

3.—ARMY FORMS, BOOKS, AND MILITARY PUBLICATIONS.

Indents. **590.** A list of the army forms and books supplied without payment is given in Army Form L 1366. Indents will be made annually, on the 1st October in each year, direct to the War Office. Supplementary indents for army forms and books will be made on Army Form L 1350.

Indents and payment. **591.** Indents for army forms and books on payment will be made on Army Form L 1370. The amount due will be paid to a cashier of the army accounts department, and his receipt obtained on the form before it is sent to the War Office. Direct payments to the War Office will not be accepted.

592. The following will be in possession of every unit, and will be produced at the annual inspection :— *Military publications supplied gratuitously.*

Territorial Force Regulations.
King's Regulations.
Pay Warrant
The Army Act.
Allowance Regulations.
Clothing Regulations.
Training Manual (for arm of service).
Combined Training.
Musketry Regulations.
Priced Vocabulary of Stores.
Equipment Regulations (Part III.)

593. Under the regulations for the issue of military books and maps one copy of any publication included in the list may be purchased at the price promulgated by Army Orders. Applications will be made on Army Form L 1372, and will be countersigned by the commanding officer. *Military publications on payment.*

PART II.

COUNTY ASSOCIATIONS.

Introductory.

Responsibility of. **600.** A County Association will be responsible for the administration of the units of the Territorial Force within its county area at all times other than when called up for annual training in camp, when embodied, or on actual military service.

Duties. **601.** It will be required to provide the necessary men, to clothe them, to find the necessary drill halls, headquarters, armouries, magazines, store houses, &c., to provide saddlery for their horses, and the ranges for their instruction in shooting, and to arrange for their attendance at drills, &c., outside the annual training in camp. It will also provide horses, cycles, and wagons for the annual training in camp of its units as required by the general officer commanding-in-chief, and for necessary exercises outside the period of annual training in camp, and will be responsible for the conveyance of troops to and from the place of annual camp.

It will also arrange for the distribution of separation and other allowances provided by the War Office to the wives and families of members of the Territorial Force when embodied or called out on actual military service.

Training. **602.** For the training of the Force, the general officer commanding-in-chief will be responsible, and the Association will not be financially concerned therewith.

Cadet corps. **603.** Cadet corps and battalions will, for the present, be administered as now by the War Office, and do not come within the jurisdiction of the Associations.

Regulation of income. **604.** The income of an Association from public funds will be regulated by the Army Council, on the principle of payment by results; but the Association will itself administer and conduct its expenditure, subject only to audit by a professional accountant, and to the rendering of an annual statement of accounts for the information of the Army Council.

Grants. **605.** To enable an Association to meet the necessary expenditure connected with the exercise and discharge of its powers and duties, grants will be made from Army funds, as detailed in Sections I. and II.

The services which these grants cover are detailed in paragraphs 669 and 670.

606. In the event of the Army Council being satisfied that any unit or portion thereof has not proved itself efficient in any year, or that irregularities have occurred in its administration, they may withhold from the Association such proportion of the grants in respect of such unit as they may think fit. Grants may be withheld.

SECTION 1.—GRANTS FOR WHICH ANNUAL ESTIMATES ARE REQUIRED.

607. The grants will be made under the following heads:— Heads of grants.

A.—Establishment grants.

B.—Clothing and personal equipment grant, and grant for upkeep of harness and saddlery.

C.—Travelling grants for drills, &c., outside the training period.

D.—Grants for rent, for structural repairs, for repayment of principal and interest on loans for land and buildings, and for payment of feu and other duties.

A.—*Establishment Grants.*

608. To meet the general expenses of administration in respect of each unit of the Territorial Force, a grant will be made at the following annual rates to the County Association under whose administrative control it is placed. Administration expenses.

For each—	£
Headquarters of a Mounted or Infantry Brigade or of Divisional Artillery ...	50
Administrative medical office of a division	25
Yeomanry squadron...	95
Horse Artillery battery with Mounted Brigade Ammunition column	195
Field Artillery battery	120
Field Artillery Ammunition column ...	155
Field Artillery (Howitzer) battery	115
Field Artillery (Howitzer) Ammunition column	80
Heavy Artillery battery and Ammunition column	200
Heavy Artillery battery for Coast Defences	115
Royal Garrison Artillery company ...	65
Mountain battery	175
Mountain Artillery Brigade Ammunition column	120
Field company, Royal Engineers	180
Wireless Telegraph company	60
Divisional Telegraph company	35
Cable Telegraph company	125
Air-Line Telegraph company	240

For each—	£
Balloon company	55
Railway battalion	445
Royal Engineer company for Works ...	80
Royal Engineer company for Electric Lights. (The establishment varies with the particular defences) ...	Special rates according to establishment.
Infantry company	100
Cyclist company of a Cyclist battalion ...	55
Mounted Brigade Transport and Supply column	100
Divisional Transport and Supply column ... No. 1 company	185
Divisional Transport and Supply column ... Other company	80
Mounted Brigade Field Ambulance ...	95
Field Ambulance	195
General Hospital	40
Sanitary company	85
Medical details	Special rates according to establishment in each county.

Grants at special rates may be allotted for any engineer units temporarily retained in addition to those provided in the Draft Scheme.

The grant made for the headquarters of a Brigade, of Divisional Artillery, or of a Medical Office, will cover the cost of any office accommodation or clerical assistance necessary, as well as that of postage, stationery, &c.

Provision of horses.

609. To enable an Association to provide the necessary horses for the instruction of mounted men, and to meet expenses incidental to hiring horses and such vehicles as are not issued by the War Department, for such units as may require them at times other than that of the annual training in camp, grants will be made, subject to the conditions prescribed below, at the following rates :—

For each	£
Yeomanry regiment...	150
Horse Artillery battery with Mounted Brigade Ammunition column	205
Field Artillery battery	130
Field Artillery Ammunition column ...	75
Field Artillery (Howitzer) battery... ...	120
Field Artillery (Howitzer) Ammunition column	25
Heavy Artillery Battery with Ammunition column	140
Heavy Artillery battery for Coast Defences	115
Mountain battery	80
Mountain Artillery Brigade Ammunition column	75

For each—

		£
Field company, Royal Engineers ...	...	60
Wireless Telegraph company	... ...	35
Divisional Telegraph company	... ...	25
Cable Telegraph company ...	... ...	70
Air-Line Telegraph company	... ...	105
Balloon company ...	... ...	40
Mounted Brigade Transport and Supply column ...	... ...	50
Divisional Transport and Supply column	No. 1 company	115
	Other company	40
Mounted Brigade Field Ambulance	...	55
Field Ambulance ...	... ...	60

The payment of this grant will be subject to a certificate from the general officer commanding-in-chief, in respect of each unit, to the effect that a reasonable standard of efficiency in mounted duties and drills has been attained. Certificate.

The guns and vehicles are only to be taken out for drill purposes, at annual training in camp, for practice at the range, or for duly authorised attendance at reviews and field days.

The grants will cover the cost of insuring or forming an insurance fund for the horses against loss of any kind during or resulting from military duty in peace, other than that for which compensation is provided in paragraph 660, and of providing any veterinary attendance that may be necessary.

Should Government horses be used a deduction in the grant may be made at the discretion of the Army Council.

610. In very exceptional cases, where it can be proved to the satisfaction of the Army Council that the grants under paragraphs 608 and 609 are insufficient to meet the necessary expenses of an Association, an increased amount may be approved. Increase of.

611. A County Association will be allowed a sum of 1*s.* for the medical examination of each recruit who joins the Territorial Force within its county area. The grant will be calculated on the number of recruits enlisted during the year ended on the 31st October. Medical examination, fee.

B.—*Clothing and Equipment Grant and Grant for Upkeep of Harness and Saddlery.*

612. To meet the cost of upkeep and replacement of the clothing and personal equipment of the men of the Territorial Force under its administrative control, a grant will be made annually to each County Association at the rate of £1 3*s.* for each efficient non-commissioned officer (exclusive of those on the permanent staff) or man. This grant allows for a small annual payment by the Association to men who provide themselves with serviceable boots at annual training in camp, to compensate for the extra wear due to their military service. Clothing and equipment.

613. An initial grant will be paid for the provision of clothing for each non-commissioned officer or man raised in excess of the numbers Clothing, initial grant.

for whom payment has already been made, up to the limit of the total authorised establishment for each Association. The numbers transferred from the Imperial Yeomanry and Volunteers to an Association, who continue to serve as members of the Territorial Force, will be considered as having already earned the initial grant, in view of the special grant to be given on the transfer taking place to compensate for the wear taken out of the articles transferred to an Association. Separate regulations will be issued as to this special grant. The initial grants will be at the following rates :—

	£	s.	d.
Clothing, mounted men	4	8	0
,, dismounted men	3	15	0

Equipment, initial grant.

614. An initial grant will be made for the provision of personal equipment under the same conditions as the clothing grant, at the following rate per man :—

	£	s.	d.
Yeomanry	0	17	6
Royal Artillery	0	12	6
Royal Engineers (dismounted) ...	0	14	0
,, (mounted)	0	12	0
Infantry...	1	0	0
Army Service Corps (dismounted) ...	0	12	6
,, ,, (mounted) ...	0	12	0
Royal Army Medical Corps	0	9	0

The grant may be made by an issue in kind, or partly in kind and partly in money, at the option of the Army Council.

Uniform.

615. Where a unit wears full dress in lieu of the ordinary walking-out suit, the extra cost of provision and replacement will not be admissible as a charge against the public funds of the Association.

Saddlery.

616. To meet the cost of cleaning, preservation, repair, and replacement of saddlery, an annual grant will be made at the rate of 8*s.* 4*d.* for each efficient officer, non-commissioned officer or man, of the Territorial Force required to be mounted for annual training in camp, including permanent staff other than the adjutant.

A further grant will be made for the upkeep and replacement of harness for draught horses, for which harness is issued for each unit, at the following rates :—

R.A. pole draught harness, neck collar pattern—	£	s.	d.
Per pair of wheel horses	1	13	9
,, lead horses	1	5	6
Packsaddlery	To be notified later		

Should it be decided to issue other kinds of harness the rates will be notified later.

All articles of harness or saddlery will be purchased from the Army Ordnance Department at prices to be fixed by the Army Council.

Saddlery, initial issue.

617. An initial issue of saddlery will be made for each mounted officer, non-commissioned officer or man in excess of the number for whom an issue has been previously made, or for whom provision has been made in kind, up to the limit of the authorised establishment. Non-commissioned officers and men transferred from the Imperial Yeomanry and Volunteers who continue to serve in the Territorial Force will be considered as having already earned the grant for the reasons given in paragraph 613.

618. An initial issue of harness will be made for the guns, ammunition, and such other wagons as may be approved, of units as they are formed. Units transferred to the Territorial Force will be treated under the same conditions as for saddlery in paragraph 617. Initial issue of harness.

619. The annual grants under paragraphs 612 and 616 will not be drawn for any year in respect of individuals or units for whom initial grants under paragraphs 613, 614, 617 and 618 or the special grant referred to in paragraphs 613 and 617 has been made during that year. Annual grants.

620. The grants under paragraphs 612 to 614, 616 and 617 will be made in respect of members of the Special Reserve borne supernumerary to units of the Territorial Force, and of the Regular Army Reserve similarly attached, under the same conditions as for men of the Territorial Force. Supernumeraries.

621. Provision will be made by the County Association by means of a sinking fund, or otherwise, for the periodic renewal of clothing, equipment, harness, saddlery, &c., and the auditor referred to in paragraph 682 will include in his report a reference to the steps taken in regard to this matter. Renewal fund for clothing.

622. The grant under paragraph 612 will be allowed for every non-commissioned officer or man who, during the year, enlists into the Royal Navy, Regular Forces, or Royal Marines, or who having enlisted for the Special Reserve passes into the Royal Navy, Regular Forces, or Royal Marines during or immediately on the conclusion of his drill in the Special Reserve on enlistment, provided he has completed the requirements of efficiency for the year or was returned as efficient in the year preceding that in which he so enlisted. Clothing and equipment grant.

623. The claim for the grants defined in paragraphs 612 and 616 will be supported by:— Claims.

(1) A certificate from the general officer commanding-in-chief, showing the number of efficients in each unit.

(2) A certificate signed by the officer commanding and the adjutant of each unit, and countersigned by the Association, that the unit is provided with clothing and equipment as detailed below; that the whole is in a condition of serviceability and completeness, and of the same pattern* throughout for each unit.

Clothing of the authorised pattern	For each non-commissioned officer and man two complete uniforms (one of which must be the regulation service dress*) with greatcoat.

* Except for units gradually changing over to Service dress, or changing their uniform and equipment during the transition stage.

Accoutrements ...	A complete set for each non-commissioned officer and man	As detailed in the Equipment Regulations, Part III.
Saddlery	A complete set for each mounted officer, non-commissioned officer, and man	
Harness of special War Department pattern for technical vehicles Packsaddlery... ...	In the authorised proportion for the unit	

C.—*Travelling Grants.*

Travelling grants.

624. Travelling grants will be given in aid of the expense of carrying out drills outside the period of annual training in camp at the rates to cover the return journey and under the conditions shown in Appendix 13, the mileage being calculated in each instance from the headquarters indicated, on the distance of the single journey, and the Association making its own arrangements with the railways or others concerned. Men supernumerary under paragraph 620 and serjeant-instructors of the permanent staff will earn these grants. The grants will only be given where actual expenditure on conveyance is necessarily incurred, and will not be admitted in respect of any attendance authorised by the general officer commanding-in-chief in connection with his training grant.

Increase of grant.

625. In the case of any units peculiarly situated as regards means of communication, want of railway facilities, &c., or in the case of the musketry practice grant, by reason of excessive distance from the range, the Army Council, on its being proved to their satisfaction that the expenses for travelling are necessarily much in excess of the regulated grant, and cannot be met from the funds at the disposal of the Association, may fix at their discretion a rate of travelling grant in excess of that laid down.

How calculated.

626. The grant will be calculated on the number of journeys performed during the year ended on the 31st October, but will be regarded as in aid of expenditure incurred by the Association during the 12 months ending on the following 31st March.

D.—*Grants for Rent, &c.*

Expenditure, land and buildings.

627. Expenditure in connection with the provision of such land and buildings, including ranges, as the Army Council consider necessary for the proper discharge of the functions of an Association. will be met by grants from army funds. In cases where the acquisition on lease, or orher agreement, of property as drill halls, headquarters of units, Association offices, gunsheds, ranges, riding schools, &c., has been sanctioned by the Army Council, the grants will be based on the actual net cost of rent. Where property is held by an

Association, subject to mortgage or loan, the grant will cover the payment of interest and repayment of principal.

628. The office accommodation and office furniture in accordance with Barrack Schedules for the general officers commanding the Territorial Divisions and their staffs will be provided by the War Office direct and not through the County Associations, unless no additional cost is thereby involved. Office accommodation

No claim will be admitted for office accommodation for Mounted Brigade, Divisional Artillery, or Infantry headquarters, or for the administrative medical officer of a division.

The cost of provision of Association offices will be met from this grant.

629. An Association will be responsible for keeping in structural and general repair all buildings which it holds with the approval of the Army Council, and for their general upkeep and maintenance. Repairs, responsibility for.

630. An annual grant calculated at 1 per cent. of the capital cost of all buildings, exclusive of the land which they cover, for the repair and upkeep of which it is liable, will be made to an Association to cover the cost of these services. In cases of considerable extraordinary damage by storm, lightning, &c., which cannot be met out of the 1 per cent. grant, the Army Council will consider applications for a special grant. Grant for.

631. The claims for payment will show in detail the properties held or rented, the rents payable, the sums due for sinking fund and interest, and also receipts from sub-letting. They will be supported by a certificate from the chief engineer of the command that the property concerned has been satisfactorily maintained, and is in an efficient state of repair. Where receipts are obtained from sub-letting of property not held on rental they will be taken in diminution of the total grant under this section. Details to be shown on claims.

632. Proposals for capital expenditure on land or buildings during the ensuing financial year (1st April to 31st March), will be submitted to the Army Council, together with an estimate of the cost, not later than 1st September in each year. Capital expenditure.

633. All proposals to acquire land, to purchase, erect, enlarge or alter buildings, to take premises on lease, feu or agreement, and all proposals to raise loans, whether from the Public Works Loan Commissioners or from private sources, for the purpose of meeting the capital cost of land, new buildings, &c., must be referred for the prior sanction of the Army Council. Cost of land, buildings, &c.

634. The procedure to be followed in such cases is laid down in Appendix 14. Procedure.

635. Property vested in or held by an Association may be let or sub-let in any manner consistent with its use by the Territorial Force for military purposes. Letting of property.

636. The property vested in an Association may not be alienated without the prior sanction of the Army Council; when such property is no longer required for military purposes an application for permission to dispose thereof by sale or otherwise will be made to the Army Council. The proceeds of any such sale will be paid over to the Army Council. Sale, &c.

Estimates and Payments.

Estimates. **637.** An Association will submit to the Army Council, not later than 1st December in each year, on Army Form M 1444, an estimate of the grants anticipated to be earned during the ensuing financial year (1st April to 31st March).

Heads. **638.** The estimate will be compiled under the four heads A, B, C, and D in paragraph 607.

The estimate for travelling (C) will be a forecast based on the number of journeys performed during the year ended the preceding 31st October, with any necessary modifications.

The estimate under (D) will show all charges for rent, repairs, &c., already approved by the Army Council, and all income derived from letting or sub-letting property.

Advances. **639.** An Association will be permitted after the 1st April to draw such advances as may be approved up to a maximum of three-fourths of the approved estimate. Application to be made on Army Forms 1544 and 1546.

Claiming of. **640.** The grants earned will be claimed on the succeeding 1st November (on Army Form 1545, showing the names, &c., of the units), the claim being supported by the certificates required under the terms laid down for each grant.

Balance-issue of. **641.** As soon as possible after the 1st November the actual sum due for the year will be assessed from the returns for 1st November, and the balance due will be issued to the Association before the close of the financial year.

SECTION 2.—GRANTS FOR SERVICES NOT INCLUDED IN THE ANNUAL ESTIMATES.

Provision of horses. **642.** An Association will receive a grant to enable it to provide the horses, other than those provided with the wagons, &c., under paragraph 643, indented for by the general officer commanding-in-chief for the period of annual training in camp, staff rides or instructional tours, at the following rates for each horse provided :—

When required for 15 days—£5.

When required for any other period—6*s*. 8*d*. for each day.

Associations will be required to satisfy a board of officers as to the soundness and fitness for military duty of the horses they provide before the commencement of the training.

Wagons, &c. **643.** A grant will be made at the rate of £1 a-day for each pair-horse wagon and horses, and 10*s*. for each single-horse wagon or cart with horse, provided by the Association for the general officer commanding-in-chief in accordance with the prescribed scale.

Services included. **644.** These grants will include, in addition to hiring charges, the cost of insurance against loss of any kind during or resulting from the annual training in camp, other than that for which compensation is provided in paragraph 660, and any veterinary attendance that may be necessary after its termination. In the case of draught horses for transport and other vehicles furnished by the Association, they will also include the provision of such harness as may be required. Payment at the rates in paragraph 642, and subject to the conditions as regards insurance and veterinary attendance, will be made by an Association to any officer or man who rides his own horse during annual training in camp.

645. A grant will be made at the rate of 35*s.* a day for each motor provided on the indent of the general officer commanding-in-chief as a transport vehicle of a cyclist battalion during the period of annual training in camp. This grant will cover all expenses, including wear and tear, cost of petrol, &c. Motors.

646. For the provision of cycles required by the general officer commanding-in-chief during annual training in camp, staff rides and instructional tours, a grant will be made at the rate of £1 for 15 days, or 1*s.* 4*d.* a day for other periods, for each cyclist required to be mounted. The grant will cover all claims for damage or repairs. Cycles.

647. The place of annual camp training for each unit will be indicated by the general officer commanding-in-chief. To cover the cost of conveyance of troops, horses, guns, cycles, stores, &c., to and from such place, grants will be paid to an Association, which will make its own arrangements with railways and others concerned. Conveyance to camp.

648. The grants in aid of expenses incurred in conveying officers, men, regimental stores and baggage to and from the place of annual camp will be made at the rate of 1*d.* a mile for each individual who travels to annual camp (including adjutants, serjeant-instructors, and officers supernumerary in their units or on the unattached list who are permitted to attend the annual training in camp), calculated on the distance from the headquarters of the squadron, battery, company, or recognised troop or section to which he belongs to the place of encampment (subject to paragraph 649), such grant to cover the return journey. Assessment of grant.

649. When Army Service Corps or regimental transport is provided, the grant will be calculated on the distance from the headquarters, indicated, to the detraining station of the unit near the place of encampment, instead of to the place of encampment itself. Calculation of.

650. The grant may not be drawn more than once in respect of any individual attending the annual training in camp. Should, however, more than one camp be authorised for a unit in any year, the grant may be drawn once for each camp which the individual attends. Drawn once.

651. The cost of travelling to courses of instruction, and travelling expenses in connection with staff rides or instructional tours, will be defrayed from the grant of the general officer commanding-in-chief, and will only be incurred under his authority. Travelling to courses, &c.

The cost of conveying camp equipment to and from the place of the annual camp will be defrayed from the grant of the general officer commanding-in-chief.

652. For the conveyance of guns and technical wagons, engineer and other technical stores and hired civilian transport, a grant will be made at the following rates per mile per ton conveyed on the Conveyance of guns.

distance from the headquarters at which they are kept, or the place of hiring, to the detraining station, such grant to cover the return journey:—

	s.	d.
Not exceeding 100 miles	0	4
Above 100 but not exceeding 150 miles ...	0	3½
Above 150 miles	0	3

Horses. **653.** For the conveyance of troop or draught horses a grant will be made at the rate of 2¼*d.* per mile for each horse conveyed, such grant to cover the return journey. In the case of horses brought by members of the Territorial Force, the allowance will be calculated on the distance from the headquarters of their squadrons, batteries, companies, or recognised troops or sections, to the detraining station near the place of encampment. In the case of hired horses the distance will be that from the place of hiring to the detraining station, provided the cost does not exceed that from the limits of the county area.

For officers' chargers the grant will in all cases be at the rate of 3*d.* per mile to allow for the provision of horse boxes.

The grant will not be made for more than one horse for each officer, except when more are allowed in the establishment tables.

Cycles. **654.** For the conveyance of cycles a grant at the following rates for each cycle will be made on a similar basis to the above:—

	s.	d.	
Not exceeding 25 miles	0	6	To cover the return journey.
Exceeding 25 but not exceeding 50 miles	1	0	
,, 50 ,, 75 ,,	1	6	
,, 75 ,, 100 ,,	2	0	
For each additional 50 miles or portion thereof	0	6	

No grant if under 10 miles. **655.** The grant for conveyance of guns, wagons, horses, and cycles will only be made provided the distance on which the mileage is reckoned is in excess of 10 miles.

How calculated. **656.** In all cases the mileage grant will be calculated on the most direct route available.

Increase of. **657.** In exceptional cases, where an Association can show that the total of the grants under paragraphs 648 to 656 in respect of all the units within its administrative control is insufficient to meet the necessary cost of travelling, a special grant may be made at the discretion of the Army Council.

Payment.

Claiming of. **658.** The grants under paragraphs 642 to 657 will be claimed immediately after the close of the training season on Army Form N. 1543, supported, in the case of the grants for provision of horses, wagons and cycles, by the original demand notes from the general officer commanding-in-chief.

Advances. **659.** An advance of funds may, if required, be issued to the extent of two-thirds of the amount which will probably become due.

SECTION 3.—MISCELLANEOUS.

1. *Compensation for Loss of Horses.*

660. Compensation for the loss through death, destruction, or fatal injury, of a horse provided in accordance with regulations by a County Association for an officer, non-commissioned officer or man of the Territorial Force, or for draught or transport purposes, will be granted up to the certified value, within a limit of £50, in cases where it is certified :— Horses, compensation for loss of.

(*a*) That the loss occurred as the direct result of the performance of military duty at annual training in camp, on the journey between place of assembly and place of encampment with a detachment under the command of an officer, or non-commissioned officer not below the rank of serjeant, or at authorised drills;

(*b*) That the horse was certified as sound and fit for military duty at the commencement of the training;

(*c*) That the loss was not the result of any fault or want of due care on the part of the rider or his agent;

(*d*) That the death or destruction is vouched by a certificate from a qualified veterinary surgeon. In the event of destruction, the injury must be certified as incurable.

Officers and men who bring their own horses will be entitled to compensation from the County Association under the same terms.

661. Compensation will not be granted for loss through an accident occurring in the execution of practices such as tent-pegging, lemon-cutting, tilting at rings, or the Loyd Lindsay Competition, unless an officer was present. When not granted.

No compensation will be granted for the temporary loss of an animal's services, or for deterioration in its value.

No claim will be entertained for repayment of veterinary expenses necessary after the termination of camp training.

662. An application for compensation will be forwarded to the general officer commanding-in-chief accompanied by the proceedings of a board of officers assembled to investigate the case, by the certificate referred to in paragraph 660, and by an estimate of the age and value of the horse certified by a veterinary surgeon and signed by the commanding officer, who will be held responsible that the estimate is just. The general officer commanding-in-chief will adjudicate on the claim, and his authority, with the above-mentioned documents, will be attached as a voucher to the charge. Applications for compensation.

2. *Fines, Rewards for Apprehension of Absentees, &c.*

663. Every sum payable by a man of the Territorial Force under the rules of the Association, and every fine recovered from him on prosecution before a court of summary jurisdiction, will be credited to the Public Funds of the Association of the county for which he was enlisted. Public funds of Association to get fines, &c.

Resignation, scale of payments.

664. An Association will, subject to the approval of the Army Council, frame a scale of payments to be made by men of the Territorial Force who wish to resign before the end of their current term of service. The payments must not in any case exceed £5, and should vary with the length of service uncompleted on the current engagement. No payment will be due from men leaving the force under the conditions stated in paragraph 622.

Fines.

665. All fines for offences are recoverable on prosecution before a court of summary jurisdiction. Any expenditure incurred in connection with their recovery will be defrayed from the funds of the Association.

Rewards.

666. An Association may pay out of the funds at its disposal such reward as it may think fit within a maximum limit of 10*s*., or 15*s*. in exceptional cases, to any person who may give such information as may lead to the conviction of a man who has committed one of the following offences:—

(*a*) Absence without leave from preliminary training or annual training.

(*b*) Improper enlistment or attempt to enlist in the Territorial Force while belonging to that force.

(*c*) Presenting himself for enlistment in the Territorial Force and denying his former service, or improperly serving in the Territorial Force after discharge for bad conduct or physical unfitness from the Royal Navy, Regular Forces (including the Royal Marines), or the Territorial Force.

In fixing the amount of the reward the Association will be guided by the circumstances of each individual case, and by the recommendation (if any) of the magistrate.

Mobilization.

667. To enable Associations to meet the cost of the equipment which they are required to provide on mobilization, a special grant will be made from army funds on the order to mobilize being given. The rates will be published later.

SECTION 4.—EXPENDITURE AND ADMINISTRATION OF FUNDS.

Grants are Association property.

668. All grants paid to an Association, whether in respect of units or individuals, are the property of the Association and not of any unit or individual.

Expenditure.

669. The grants paid to an Association under Item D of the Annual Estimate (Lands and Buildings: rent, repairs, &c.), may not be expended on any other object without the consent of the Army Council.

Services on which funds may be expended.

670. Subject to paragraph 669, the Public Funds of an Association may be expended at the discretion of the Association on any of the following approved services, but for no other purposes without the written consent of the Army Council. No part of it is specifically allocated to any particular purpose or unit; the allocation of grants among units, and, within the approved limits, the objects to which they are to be devoted, rest entirely in the discretion of the Association:—

The provision of fuel, light, cleaning, painting, whitewashing, &c., and miscellaneous expenditure for buildings, ranges, riding schools and drill grounds, &c., including payment of markers.

General administrative and orderly room expenses.
Insurance of arms.
Care, cleaning, &c., of arms.
Cost of supplying and maintaining clothing, other than for permanent staff and cadet corps or battalions, equipment and accoutrements, harness and saddlery, extra ammunition and engineer stores, if required, and horses.
Recruiting expenses and rewards for conviction of absentees, &c.
Postage and stationery. Band and prize expenses, within reasonable limits.
Miscellaneous expenditure, including travelling in connection with drill outside the annual training in camp, and to and from the annual training in camp.
Expenses of County Association organization, *e.g.*, salary of secretary, &c., office, travelling expenses of members to meetings where authorized by the Association, and contingent expenses.
Hiring horses, cycles and wagons during peace, and expenses in connection with the registration of horses for the Territorial Force on embodiment.
Insurance of horses, &c., in accordance with paras. 609 and 644.

No payment to officers or men of the Territorial Force for attendance at drills or musketry practice will be admitted against the public funds.

671. Payment may be made to members of the permanent staff for work not strictly within their duties, such as cleaning of arms and clerical assistance. Such payment must not, however, be given for ordinary duties, for which they receive remuneration as regular soldiers. **Payments to permanent staff.**

As the circumstances of the various units differ so widely, it is not possible to lay down a universal rate for such payment, but as a general rule the annual payment should not exceed £6 10*s.* per infantry company, or a proportional rate for units of other arms, with a further allowance of 6*d.* per day for one non-commissioned officer in each unit who acts as orderly-room clerk.

672. A schedule of such payments for each unit will be submitted to the Army Council for approval, and County Associations will be held responsible that no other payments either from the public or private funds of the Association are made to any instructor. **Payments to be reported.**

673. The salaries of the secretary and other paid officers of the Association, the fees of surveyors, and the fees of auditors appointed to audit the accounts, form a charge against its public funds. The remuneration will be fixed by the Association, subject to the approval of the Army Council. **Salaries to be approved.**

674. Associations will be indemnified against loss by fire on buildings, arms, government stores, and all Association property, kept in authorised buildings. If such property is retained by individuals or kept in unauthorised buildings, a charge for insurance will be admitted against an Association's public funds. **Loss by fire.**

The Association will, in any case, be held responsible for making good any loss of stores, arms, &c., not kept in authorised buildings.

Compensation claims. 675. Any claim for compensation, or other expenses, connected with damage committed by a unit or member of the Territorial Force at times other than the annual training in camp, may be met out of the funds of the Association, and recognised as a charge against the grants, unless it can be met by any policy of insurance or is attributable to the carelessness of an individual.

Money from private sources. 676. An Association is authorised to receive sums of money from private sources either for general or for specific purposes. When not received by it for a special purpose, such sums will be available for the purposes of any of its powers and duties.

Excess expenditure. 677. When any expenditure of an extraordinary character, or involving an excess on the grants received during the current year is contemplated, the sanction of the Army Council must first be obtained. In applying for this sanction the manner in which it is proposed to meet the liability must be clearly stated.

Deficit. 678. If, owing to unforeseen circumstances, the liabilities incurred by an Association during any year should exceed its grants from public funds and the deficit cannot be made good, every effort must be made to extinguish the debt before the close of the following financial year.

Liability of Association. 679. An Association as a whole will be subject to such liability as attaches to a corporate body, but the individual members will be under no pecuniary liability for any act properly done by them as members of the Association in carrying out the duties assigned to them by the constitution of the Association.

Delegation of duties. 680. An Association should delegate to commanding officers of units, as their agents, such powers of local administration, and should hand over to them such portions of the public grant, as they may deem advisable, but it will not thereby be in any way relieved of liability for the proper administration of all funds entrusted to it.

Responsibility for property. 681. Similarly, the responsibility of the Association for public property entrusted to it will remain unaffected, although commanding officers and others may be authorised to requisition, receive and hold such property on its behalf.

SECTION 5.—ACCOUNTS.

Grants paid to a bank. 682. The grants made to an Association will be paid into a bank to the account of the Association. These funds will be kept distinct from any private or regimental account, or from any account of funds arising from private subscriptions.

Cash book. 683. A cash book will be kept by the Association, in which will be recorded all sums received from the Government, and the full expenditure on the services specified in paragraph 670. All expenditure will be supported by the necessary vouchers.

Money from private sources. 684. An account of the receipt and expenditure of money received from private sources, either for general or specific purposes, will be kept on a suitable form and duly audited.

685. The accounts of an Association will be balanced on the 31st March in each year, and a statement on Army Form N. 1524 will be prepared by the Association as soon after that date as practicable. This statement will show— Accounts balanced yearly.

(1) The receipts from the Government, from fines, &c., during the year and, under the appropriate headings, the full expenditure on the authorised services.
(2) The total of the receipts from private sources.
(3) A balance statement showing the financial condition of the Association on the 31st March, with—
(4) An explanatory statement of the balances, together with certificates from the bankers, showing the actual state of the several banking accounts at the close of business on the 31st March.
(5) A statement of loans contracted for the benefit of the force.
(6) Statement of liabilities on the 31st March.
(7) Statement of assets showing the terms upon which the drill halls and ranges of the force are held, and the amount of money invested or placed on deposit.
(8) A schedule of payments to serjeant-instructors from Association funds.

686. The accounts will be audited by a professional auditor, appointed subject to the approval of the Army Council. The auditor will ascertain that the grants from public funds have been appropriated only to the approved purposes specified in paragraph 670, and that all charges are duly vouched. He will also ascertain that proper provision has been made, by sinking fund or otherwise, for the renewal of harness, saddlery, clothing and equipment. He will not be a person concerned in any way with keeping the accounts of the Association, nor will he be a member of it. The auditor must be a member either of an Institute or Society of Chartered Accountants in the United Kingdom or of the Incorporated Society of Accountants and Auditors. Auditor.

687. The statement of accounts indicated in paragraph 685 will be forwarded to the Army Council not later than 1st July in each year, together with the report of the auditor. Accounts sent to War Office.

688. The Army Council reserve the right to investigate the financial position and administration of an Association or to call for any vouchers relating to its public accounts. Investigation of position.

689. Should the Army Council, in consideration of the auditor's report, decide that a charge cannot be allowed against the public grants of an Association, the charge must be met from monies other than those voted by Parliament. Charges disallowed.

690. The fundamental principle laid down in Parliament is that when the Territorial Force is "training" it is entitled to the pay and allowances laid down by regulation. At other times it will be administered by the County Associations. It is equally a fundamental principle, therefore, that the public funds administered by the Association should be kept absolutely distinct from those allotted to the general officer commanding-in-chief. Force, when training, entitled to pay and allowances laid down.

APPENDICES.

APPENDIX 1.

THE TERRITORIAL AND RESERVE FORCES ACT, 1907.

(7 Edward VII., Cap. 9.)

An Act to provide for the reorganisation of His Majesty's military forces and for that purpose to authorise the establishment of County Associations, and the raising and maintenance of a Territorial Force, and for amending the Acts relating to the Reserve Forces. [2nd August 1907.]

PART I.

County Associations.

Establishment of associations.

I. (1.) For the purposes of the reorganisation under this Act of His Majesty's military forces other than the regulars and their reserves, and of the administration of those forces when so reorganised, and for such other purposes as are mentioned in this Act, an association may be established for any county in the United Kingdom, with such powers and duties in connection with the purposes aforesaid as may be conferred on it by or under this Act.

(2.) Associations shall be constituted, and the members thereof shall be appointed and hold office in accordance with schemes to be made by the Army Council.

(3.) Every such scheme shall provide—

(*a.*) For the date of the establishment of the association:

(*b.*) For the incorporation of the association by an appropriate name, with power to hold land for the purposes of this Act without licence in mortmain:

(*c.*) For constituting the lieutenant of the county, or failing him such other person as the Army Council may think fit, president of the association:

(*d.*) For the appointment of such number of officers representative of all arms and branches of the Territorial Force raised under this Act within the county (not being less than one-half of the whole number of the association) as may be specified in the scheme:

(*e.*) For the appointment by the Army Council, where it appears desirable, and after consultation with, and on the recommendation of, the authorities to be represented, of representatives of county and county borough councils and universities wholly or partly within the county:

(*f.*) For the appointment of such number of co-opted members as the scheme may prescribe, including, if thought desirable, representatives of the interests of employers and workmen:

(*g.*) For the appointment by the Army Council during the first three years after the passing of this Act, and subsequently for the election of a chairman and vice-chairman by the association, and for defining their powers and duties:

(*h.*) For the mode of appointment, term of office and rotation of members of the association, and the filling of casual vacancies:

(*i.*) For the appointment by the association, subject to the approval of the Army Council, of a secretary and other officers of the association, and the accountability of such officers, and for the provision of offices:

(*j.*) For the procedure to be adopted, including the appointment of committees and the delegation to committees of any of the powers or duties of the association:

(*k.*) For enabling such general officers of any part of His Majesty's forces, and not being members of the association, as may be specified in the scheme, or officers deputed by them, to attend the meetings of the association and to speak, but not to vote:

(*l.*) For dividing the county, where on account of its size or population it seems desirable to do so, into two or more parts, and for constituting sub-associations for the several parts, and for apportioning amongst the several sub-associations all or any of the powers and duties of the association, and regulating the relations of sub-associations to the association and to one another.

(4.) A scheme may contain any consequential, supplemental or transitory provisions which may appear to be necessary or proper for the purposes of the scheme, and also as respects any matter for which provision may be made by regulations under this Act and for which it appears desirable to make special provision affecting the association established by the scheme.

(5.) All schemes made in pursuance of this part of this Act shall be laid before both Houses of Parliament.

(6.) Until an Order in Council has been made under this Act for transferring to the Territorial Force the units of the Yeomanry and Volunteers of any county, references in this section to the Territorial Force shall as respects that county be construed as including references to the Yeomanry and Volunteers.

Powers and duties of associations.

II. (1.) It shall be the duty of an association when constituted to make itself acquainted with and conform to the plan of the Army Council for the organisation of the Territorial Force within the county and to ascertain the military resources and capabilities of the county, and to render advice and assistance to the Army Council and to such officers as the Army Council may direct, and an association shall have, exercise and discharge such powers and duties connected with the organisation and administration of His Majesty's military forces as may for the time being be transferred or assigned to it by order of His Majesty signified under the hand of a Secretary of State or, subject thereto, by regulations under this Act, but an association shall not have any powers of command or training over any part of His Majesty's military forces.

(2.) The powers and duties so transferred or assigned may include any powers conferred on or vested in His Majesty, and any powers or duties conferred or imposed on the Army Council or a Secretary of State, by statute or otherwise, and in particular respecting the following matters :—

(*a.*) The organisation of the units of the Territorial Force and their administration (including maintenance) at all times other than when they are called out for training or actual military service, or when embodied :

(*b.*) The recruiting for the Territorial Force both in peace and in war, and defining the limits of recruiting areas :

(*c.*) The provision and maintenance of rifle ranges, buildings, magazines and sites of camps for the Territorial Force :

(*d.*) Facilitating the provision of areas to be used for manœuvres :

(*e.*) Arranging with employers of labour as to holidays for training, and ascertaining the times of training best suited to the circumstances of civil life :

(*f.*) Establishing or assisting cadet battalions and corps and also rifle clubs, provided that no financial assistance out of money voted by Parliament shall be given by an association in respect of any person in a battalion or corps in a school in receipt of a parliamentary grant until such person has attained the age of sixteen :

(*g.*) The provision of horses for the peace requirements of the Territorial Force :

(*h.*) Providing accommodation for the safe custody of arms and equipment :

(*i.*) The supply of the requirements on mobilisation of the units of the Territorial Force within the county, in so far as those requirements are directed by the Army Council to be met locally, such requirements where practicable to be embodied in regulations which shall be issued to county associations from time to time, and on the first occasion not later than the first day of January, one thousand nine hundred and nine :

(*j.*) The payment of separation and other allowances to the families of men of the Territorial Force when embodied or called out on actual military service :

(*k.*) The registration in conjunction with the military authorities of horses for any of His Majesty's forces :

(*l.*) The care of reservists and discharged soldiers.

Expenses of association.

III. (1.) The Army Council shall pay to an association, out of money voted by Parliament for army services, such sums as, in the opinion of the Army Council, are required to meet the necessary expenditure connected with the exercise and discharge by the association of its powers and duties.

(2.) An association shall submit to the Army Council annually, at the prescribed time, and may submit at any other time for any special purpose, in the prescribed form and manner, a statement of its necessary requirements, and all payments to an association by the Army Council shall be made upon the basis of such statements in so far as they are approved by the Army Council.

(3.) Subject to regulations under this Act, all money so paid to an association shall be applicable to any of the purposes specified in the approved statements in accordance with which the money has been granted, but not otherwise except with the written consent of the Army Council:

Provided that nothing in this section shall be construed as enabling the Army Council to give their consent to the application of money to any purpose to which, apart from this section, it could not lawfully be applied, or to give their consent, without the authority of the Treasury, in any case in which, apart from this section, the authority of the Treasury would be required.

(4.) All other money received by an association (except such money, if any, as may be received by it for specified purposes) shall be available for the purposes of any of its powers and duties.

(5.) An association shall cause its accounts to be made up annually and audited in such manner as may be prescribed, and shall send copies of its accounts as audited, together with any report of the auditors thereon, to the Army Council.

(6.) Regulations made for the purposes of this section shall be subject to the consent of the Treasury.

(7.) The members of an association shall not be under any pecuniary liability for any act done by them in their capacity as members of such association in carrying out the provisions of this Act.

IV. (1.) Subject to the provisions of this Act, the Army Council may make regulations for carrying this Part of this Act into effect, and may by those regulations, amongst other things, provide for the following matters:— Regulations.

(*a.*) For regulating the manner in which powers are to be exercised and duties performed by associations, and for specifying the services to which money paid by the Army Council is to be applicable:

(*b.*) For authorising and regulating the acquisition by or on behalf of an association of land for the purposes of this Act and the disposal of any land so acquired:

(*c.*) For authorising and regulating the borrowing of money by an association:

(*d.*) For authorising the acceptance of any money or other property, and the taking over of any liability, by an association, and for regulating the administration of any money or property so acquired and the discharge of any liability so taken over:

(*e.*) For facilitating the co-operation of an association with any other association, or with any local authority or other body, and for providing by the constitution of joint committees or otherwise for co-operative action in the organisation and administration of divisions, brigades and other military bodies, and for the provision of assistance by one association to another:

(*f.*) For affiliating cadet corps and battalions, rifle clubs, and other bodies to the Territorial Force or any part thereof:

(*g.*) For or in respect of anything by this Part of this Act directed or authorised to be done or provided by regulations or to be done in the prescribed manner:

(*h.*) For the application for the purposes of this Part of this Act, as respects any matters to be dealt with by regulations, of any provision in any Act of Parliament dealing with the like matters, with the necessary modifications or adaptations, and in particular of any provisions as to the acquisition of land by or on behalf of volunteer corps.

(2.) All regulations made in pursuance of this Part of this Act shall be applicable to all associations, except in so far as may be otherwise provided by the regulations or by any scheme made under this Part of this Act.

(3.) All regulations made under this Part of this Act shall be laid before both Houses of Parliament as soon as may be after they are made.

Joint committees of associations.

V. (1.) Any county associations may from time to time join in appointing out of their respective bodies a joint committee for any purpose in respect of which they are jointly interested.

(2.) Any association appointing a joint committee under this subsection may delegate to it any power which such association might exercise for the purpose for which the committee is appointed.

(3.) Subject to the terms of delegation any such joint committee shall in respect of any matter delegated to it have the same power in all respects as the associations appointing it.

(4.) The costs of a joint committee shall be defrayed by the associations by whom it has been appointed, in such proportion as may be agreed between them, and the accounts of such joint committees and their officers shall for the purposes of the provisions of this Act be deemed to be accounts of the associations appointing them and of their officers.

PART II.

Territorial Force.

Raising and Maintenance of Force.

Raising and number of Territorial Force.

VI. It shall be lawful for His Majesty to raise and maintain a force, to be called the "Territorial Force," consisting of such number of men as may from time to time be provided by Parliament.

Government, Discipline, and Pay.

Government, discipline, and pay of Territorial Force.

VII. (1.) Subject to the provisions of this Part of this Act, it shall be lawful for His Majesty, by order signified under the hand of a Secretary of State, to make orders with respect to the government, discipline, and pay and allowances of the Territorial Force, and with respect to all other matters and things relating to the Territorial Force, including any matter by this Part of this Act authorised to be prescribed or expressed to be subject to orders or regulations.

(2.) The said orders may provide for the formation of men of the Territorial Force into regiments, battalions, or other military bodies, and for the formation of such regiments, battalions, or other military bodies into corps, either alone or jointly with any other part of His Majesty's forces, and for appointing, transferring, or attaching men of the Territorial Force to corps, and for posting, attaching, or otherwise dealing with such men within the corps; and may provide for the constitution of a permanent staff, including adjutants and staff sergeants who shall, except in special circumstances certified by the general officer commanding, be members of His Majesty's regular forces; and may regulate the appointment, rank, duties, and numbers of the officers and non-commissioned officers of the Territorial Force.

(3.) Subject to the provisions of any such order, the Army Council may make general or special regulations with respect to any matter with respect to which His Majesty may make orders under this section.

(4.) Provided that the said orders or regulations shall not—

(*a.*) Affect or extend the term for which, or the area within which, a man of the Territorial Force is liable under this Part of this Act to serve; or

(*b.*) Authorise a man of the Territorial Force when belonging to one corps to be transferred without his consent to another corps; or

(*c.*) When the corps of a man of the Territorial Force includes more than one unit authorise him when not embodied to be posted, without his consent, to any unit other than that to which he was posted on enlistment; or

(*d.*) When the corps of a man of the Territorial Force includes any battalion or other body of the regular forces, authorise him to be posted without his consent to that battalion or body.

(5.) Where a man of the Territorial Force was enlisted or re-engaged before the date of any order or regulation under this Part of this Act, nothing in such order or regulation shall render him liable without his consent to be appointed, transferred, or attached to any military body to which he could not without his consent have been appointed, transferred, or attached if the said order or regulation had not been made.

(6.) Orders and regulations under this section may provide for the formation of a reserve division of the Territorial Force, and may relax or dispense with any of the provisions of this Act relating to the training of the men of the Territorial Force so far as regards their application to men in the reserve division, and may, notwithstanding anything in this section, authorise a man in the reserve division to be transferred from one corps to another, so, however, that a man in the reserve division shall not, without his consent, be transferred to a corps of another arm.

(7.) All orders and general regulations made under this section shall be laid before both Houses of Parliament as soon as may be after they are made.

First appointments to lowest rank of officers of the Territorial Force.

VIII. Subject to any directions which may be given by His Majesty, first appointments to the lowest rank of officer in any unit of the Territorial Force shall be given to persons recommended by the president of the association for the county, if a person approved by His Majesty is recommended by the president for any such appointment within thirty days after notice of a vacancy for the appointment has been given to the president in the prescribed manner, provided he fulfils all the prescribed conditions as to age, physical fitness, and educational qualifications; and, where a unit comprises men of the Territorial Force of two or more counties, the recommendations for such appointments shall be made by the presidents of the associations for the respective counties in such rotation or otherwise as may be prescribed.

Enlistment, Service, Discharge.

Enlistment, term of service, and discharge.

IX. (1.) Subject to the provisions of this Part of this Act, all men of the Territorial Force shall be enlisted by such persons and in such manner and subject to such regulations as may be prescribed:

Provided that every man enlisted under this Part of this Act—

(*a.*) Shall be enlisted for a county for which an association has been established under this Act and shall be appointed to serve in such corps for that county or for an area comprising the whole or part of that county as he may select, and, if that corps comprises more than one unit within the county, shall be posted to such one of those units as he may select:

(*b.*) Shall be enlisted to serve for such a period as may be prescribed, not exceeding four years, reckoned from the date of his attestation:

(*c.*) May be re-engaged within twelve months before the end of his current term of service for such a period as may be prescribed not exceeding four years from the end of that term, and on re-engagement shall make the prescribed declaration before a justice of the peace or an officer, and so from time to time.

(2.) A man enlisted in the Territorial Force, until duly discharged in the prescribed manner, shall remain subject to this Part of this Act as a man of the Territorial Force.

(3.) Any man of the Territorial Force shall, except when a proclamation ordering the Army Reserve to be called out on permanent service is in force, be entitled to be discharged before the end of his current term of service on complying with the following conditions:—

(i.) Giving to his commanding officer three months' notice in writing, or such less notice as may be prescribed, of his desire to be discharged; and

(ii.) Paying for the use of the association for the county for which he was enlisted such sum as may be prescribed not exceeding five pounds; and

(iii.) Delivering up in good order, fair wear and tear only excepted, all arms, clothing, and appointments, being public property, issued to him, or, in cases where for any good and sufficient cause the delivery of the property aforesaid is impossible, on paying the value thereof:

Provided that it shall be lawful for the association for the county, or for any officer authorised by the association, in any case in which it appears that the reasons for which the discharge is claimed are of sufficient urgency or weight, to dispense either wholly or in part with all or any of the above conditions.

(4.) A man of the Territorial Force may be discharged by his commanding officer for disobedience to orders by him while doing any military duty, or for neglect of duty, or for misconduct by him as a man of the Territorial Force, or for other sufficient cause, the existence and sufficiency of such cause to be judged of by the commanding officer:

Provided that any man so discharged shall be entitled to appeal to the Army Council, who may give such directions in any such case as they may think just and proper.

(5.) Where the time at which a man of the Territorial Force would otherwise be entitled to be discharged occurs while a proclamation ordering the Army Reserve to be called out on permanent service is in force, he may be required to prolong his service for such further period, not exceeding twelve months, as the competent military authority may order.

Application of certain sections of the Army Act. 44 & 45 Vict., c. 58.

X. (1.) The following sections of the Army Act shall apply to the Territorial Force (that is to say):—

Section eighty (relating to the mode of enlistment and attestation);

Section ninety-six (relating to the claims of masters to apprentices);

Section ninety-eight (imposing a fine for unlawful recruiting);

Section ninety-nine (making recruits punishable for false answers);

So much of section one hundred as relates to the validity of attestation and enlistment or re-engagement;

Section one hundred and one (relating to the competent military authority); and

So much of section one hundred and sixty-three as relates to an attestation paper, or a copy thereof, or a declaration, being evidence.

And the said sections shall apply in like manner as if they were herein re-enacted, with the substitution—

(*a.*) Of "Territorial Force" for "regular forces," and of "man of the Territorial Force" for "soldier"; and

(*b.*) (In section one hundred) of "has not within three months claimed his discharge on any ground on which he is entitled under this subsection to do so" for "has received pay as a soldier of the regular forces during three months."

(2.) A recruit may be attested by any lieutenant or deputy-lieutenant of any county in the United Kingdom, or by an officer of the regular or Territorial forces, and the sections of the Army Act in this section mentioned, and also section thirty-three of the same Act, shall as applied to the Territorial Force be construed as if a justice of the peace in those sections included such lieutenant, deputy-lieutenant, or officer.

Enlistment of men discharged with disgrace from Army or Navy, or contrary to rules.

XI. (1.) If a person—

(*a.*) Having been discharged with disgrace from any part of His Majesty's forces, or having been dismissed with disgrace from the Navy, has afterwards enlisted in the Territorial Force without declaring the circumstances of his discharge or dismissal; or

(*b.*) Is concerned when subject to military law in the enlistment for service in the Territorial Force of any man, when he knows or has reasonable cause to believe such man to be so circumstanced that by enlisting he commits an offence against the Army Act or this Act; or

(*c.*) Wilfully contravenes when subject to military law any enactments, orders, or regulations which relate to the enlistment or attestation of men in the Territorial Force,

he shall be guilty of an offence, and shall, whether otherwise subject to military law or not, be liable to be tried by court martial, and on conviction to suffer such punishment as is imposed for the like offence by section thirty-two or thirty-four of the Army Act, as the case may be, and may be taken into military custody.

(2.) For the purpose of this section the expression "discharged with disgrace" means discharged with ignominy, discharged as incorrigible and worthless, or discharged for misconduct, or discharged on account of a conviction for felony or a sentence of penal servitude.

Enlistment into army reserve.

XII. If a man of the Territorial Force enlists into the army reserve without being discharged from the Territorial Force, the terms and conditions of his service whilst he remains in the army reserve shall be those applicable to him as a man belonging to the army reserve, and not those applicable to him as a man of the Territorial Force.

Area of service of Territorial Force.

XIII. (1.) Any part of the Territorial Force shall be liable to serve in any part of the United Kingdom, but no part of the

Territorial Force shall be carried or ordered to go out of the United Kingdom.

(2.) Provided that it shall be lawful for His Majesty, if he thinks fit, to accept the offer of any part or men of the Territorial Force, signified through their commanding officer, to subject themselves to the liability—

(*a.*) To serve in any place outside the United Kingdom ; or

(*b.*) To be called out for actual military service for purposes of defence at such places in the United Kingdom as may be specified in their agreement, whether the Territorial Force is embodied or not ;

and, upon any such offer being accepted, they shall be liable, whenever required during the period to which the offer extends, to serve or be called out accordingly.

(3.) A person shall not be compelled to make such an offer, or be subjected to such liability as aforesaid, except by his own consent, and a commanding officer shall not certify any voluntary offer previously to his having explained to every person making the offer that the offer is to be purely voluntary on his part.

Training.

XIV. (1.) Every man of the Territorial Force shall, by way of preliminary training, during the first year of his original enlistment— Preliminary training of recruits of Territorial Force.

(*a.*) If so provided by Order in Council, be trained at such places within the United Kingdom, at such times, and for such periods, not exceeding in the whole the number of days specified by the Order in Council, as may be prescribed, and may for that purpose be called out once or oftener ; and

(*b.*) Whether such an Order in Council has been made or not, attend the number of drills and fulfil the other conditions prescribed for a recruit of his arm or branch of the service.

(2.) The requirement to attend training and drills, and to fulfil conditions under this section, shall be in addition to the requirement to attend training and drills and to fulfil conditions for the purpose of annual training.

XV. (1.) Subject to the provisions of this section, every man of the Territorial Force shall, by way of annual training— Annual training.

(*a.*) Be trained for not less than eight nor more than fifteen, or in the case of the mounted branch eighteen, days in every year at such times and at such places in any part of the United Kingdom as may be prescribed, and may for that purpose be called out once or oftener in every year :

(*b.*) Attend the number of drills and fulfil the other conditions relating to training prescribed for his arm or branch of the service.

Provided that the requirements of this section may be dispensed with in whole or in part—

(i.) As respects any unit, by the prescribed general officer; and

(ii.) As respects an individual man, by his commanding officer subject to any general directions by the prescribed general officer.

(2.) His Majesty in Council may—

(*a.*) Order that the period of annual training in any year of all or any part of the Territorial Force be extended, but so that the whole period of annual training be not more than thirty days in any year; or

(*b.*) Order that the period of annual training in any year of all or any part of the Territorial Force be reduced to such time as His Majesty may seem fit; or

(*c.*) Order that in any year the annual training of all or any part of the Territorial Force be dispensed with.

(3.) Nothing in this section shall be construed as preventing a man, with his own consent, in addition to annual training, being called up for the purpose of duty or instruction in accordance with orders and regulations under this Part of this Act.

Laying of draft Orders in Council relating to training before Parliament.

XVI. Before any Order in Council is made under this Act providing for preliminary training or extending the period of annual training the draft thereof shall be laid before each House of Parliament for a period of not less than forty days during the Session of Parliament, and, if either of those Houses before the expiration of those forty days presents an address to His Majesty against the draft or any part thereof, no further proceedings shall be taken, without prejudice to the making of a new draft Order.

Embodiment.

Embodiment of Territorial Force.

XVII. (1.) Immediately upon and by virtue of the issue of a proclamation ordering the Army Reserve to be called out on permanent service, it shall be lawful for His Majesty to order the Army Council from time to time to give, and when given to revoke or vary, such directions as may seem necessary or proper for embodying all or any part of the Territorial Force, and in particular to make such special arrangements as they think proper with regard to units or individuals whose services may be required in other than a military capacity:

Provided that, where under any such proclamation directions have been issued for calling out all the men belonging to the first class of the Army Reserve, the Army Council shall, within one month after such directions have been issued, issue directions for embodying all the men belonging to the Territorial Force, unless an address has been presented to His Majesty by both Houses of Parliament praying that such directions as last aforesaid be not issued, and such directions shall not, unless the emergency so requires, be given until Parliament has had an opportunity of presenting such an address.

(2.) Whenever, in consequence of the calling out of the whole of the first class of the Army Reserve, directions are required under this section to be given for embodying the Territorial Force, if Parliament be then separated by such adjournment or prorogation as will not expire within ten days, a proclamation shall be issued for the meeting of Parliament within ten days, and Parliament shall accordingly meet and sit upon the day appointed by such proclamation, and shall continue to sit and act in like manner as if it had stood adjourned or prorogued to the same day.

(3.) Every order and all directions given under this section shall be obeyed as if enacted in this Act, and where such directions for the time being direct the embodiment of any part of the Territorial Force, every officer and man belonging to that part shall attend at the place and time fixed by those directions, and after that time shall be deemed to be embodied, and such officers and men are in this Act referred to as embodied or as the embodied part or parts of the Territorial Force.

Disembodying of Territorial Force.

XVIII. (1.) It shall be lawful for His Majesty by proclamation to order that the Territorial Force be disembodied, and thereupon the Army Council shall give such directions as may seem necessary or proper for carrying the said proclamation into effect.

(2.) Until any such proclamation of His Majesty has been issued the Army Council may from time to time, as they may think expedient for the public service, give such directions as may seem necessary or proper for disembodying any embodied part of the Territorial Force, and for embodying any part of the Territorial Force not embodied, whether previously disembodied or otherwise.

(3.) After the date fixed by the directions for the disembodiment of any part of the Territorial Force, the officers and men belonging to that part shall be in the position of officers and men of the Territorial Force not embodied.

Notices.

Service and publication of notices.

XIX. Notices required in pursuance of this Part of this Act or of the orders and regulations in force thereunder to be given to men of the Territorial Force shall be served or published in such manner as may be prescribed, and if so served or published, shall be deemed to be sufficient notice, and every constable and overseer shall, when so required by or on behalf of the Army Council, conform with the orders and regulations for the time being in force under this Part of this Act with respect to the publication and service of notices, and in default shall be liable on conviction under the Summary Jurisdiction Acts to a fine not exceeding twenty pounds.

Offences.

Punishment for failure to attend on

XX. (1.) Any man of the Territorial Force who without leave lawfully granted, or such sickness or other reasonable excuse as may be allowed in the prescribed manner, fails to appear at the embodiment. time and place appointed for assembling on embodiment, shall be guilty, according to the circumstances, of deserting within the meaning of section twelve, or of absenting himself without leave within the meaning of section fifteen, of the Army Act, and shall, whether otherwise subject to military law or not, be liable to be tried by court-martial, and convicted and punished accordingly, and may be taken into military custody.

(2.) Sections one hundred and fifty-three and one hundred and fifty-four of the Army Act shall apply with respect to deserters and desertion within the meaning of this section in like manner as they apply with respect to deserters and desertion within the meaning of those sections, and any person who, knowing any man of the Territorial Force to be a deserter within the meaning of this section or of the Army Act, employs or continues to employ him, shall be deemed to aid him in concealing himself within the meaning of the first-mentioned section.

(3.) Where a man of the Territorial Force commits the offence of desertion under this section the time which elapsed between the time of his committing the offence and the time of his apprehension or voluntary surrender shall not be taken into account in reckoning his service for the purpose of discharge.

Punishment for failure to fulfil training conditions.

XXI. Any man of the Territorial Force who without leave lawfully granted, or such sickness or other reasonable excuse as may be allowed in the prescribed manner, fails to appear at the time and place appointed for preliminary training, or for annual training, or fails to attend the number of drills and fulfil the other conditions relating to preliminary or annual training prescribed for his arm or branch of the service, shall be liable to forfeit to His Majesty a sum of money not exceeding five pounds recoverable on complaint to a court of summary jurisdiction by the prescribed officer, and any sums recovered by such officer shall be accounted for by him in the prescribed manner.

Wrongful sale, &c., of public property.

XXII. If any person designedly makes away with, sells or pawns, or wrongfully destroys or damages, or negligently loses anything issued to him as an officer or man of the Territorial Force, or wrongfully refuses or neglects to deliver up on demand anything issued to him as an officer or man of the Territorial Force, the value thereof shall be recoverable from him on complaint to a court of summary jurisdiction by the county association ; and he shall also, for any such offence of designedly making away with, selling or pawning, or wrongfully destroying as aforesaid, be liable on conviction under the Summary Jurisdiction Acts to a fine not exceeding five pounds.

Civil Rights and Exemptions.

Civil rights and exemptions.

XXIII. (1.) The acceptance of a commission as an officer of the Territorial Force shall not vacate the seat of any member returned to serve in Parliament.

(2.) An officer or man of the Territorial Force shall not be liable to any penalty or punishment for or on account of his absence during the time he is voting at any election of a member to serve in Parliament, or during the time he is going to or returning from such voting.

(3.) If a sheriff is an officer of the Territorial Force, then during embodiment he shall be discharged from personally performing the office of sheriff, and the under sheriff shall be answerable for the execution of the said office in the name of the high sheriff, and the security given by the under sheriff and his pledges to the high sheriff shall stand as a security to the King and to all persons whomsoever for the due performance of the office of sheriff during such time.

(4.) An officer or man of the Territorial Force shall not be compelled to serve as a peace officer or parish officer, and shall be exempt from serving on any jury, and a field officer of the Territorial Army shall not be required to serve in the office of high sheriff.

Legal Proceedings.

Trial of offences and application of penalties.

XXIV. (1.) Any offence under this Part of this Act, and any offence under the Army Act if committed by a man of the Territorial Force when not embodied, which is cognizable by a court-martial shall also be cognizable by a court of summary jurisdiction, and on conviction by such a court shall be punishable with imprisonment for a term not exceeding three months or with a fine not exceeding twenty pounds, or with both such imprisonment and fine, but nothing in this provision shall affect the liability of a person charged with any such offence to be taken into military custody.

(2.) Any offence which under this Part of this Act is punishable on conviction by court-martial, shall for all purposes of and incidental to the arrest, trial, and punishment of the offender, including the summary dealing with the case by his commanding officer, be deemed to be an offence under the Army Act, with this modification, that any reference in that Act to forfeiture and stoppages shall be construed to refer to such forfeitures and stoppages as may be prescribed.

(3.) Any offence which under this Part of this Act is punishable on conviction by a court of summary jurisdiction may be prosecuted, and any fine recoverable on such conviction may be recovered, in manner provided by sections one hundred and sixty-six, one hundred and sixty-seven, and one hundred and sixty-eight of the Army Act, in like manner as if those sections were herein re-enacted and in terms made applicable to this Part of this Act, subject to the following modification (namely)—

Every fine imposed under this Part of this Act on a man of the Territorial Force, or recovered on a prosecution instituted under this Part of this Act, shall, notwithstanding anything in any Act or charter or in the said sections to the contrary, be paid to the association of the county for which the man was enlisted.

(4.) Where a man of the Territorial Force is subject to military law and is illegally absent from his duty, a court of inquiry under section seventy-two of the Army Act may be assembled after the expiration of twenty-one days from the date of such absence, notwithstanding that the period during which he was subject to military law is less than twenty-one days or has expired before the expiration of twenty-one days

Supplemental provisions as to trial of.

XXV. (1.) A person charged with an offence which under this Part of this Act is cognizable both by a court-martial and by a court of summary jurisdiction shall not be liable to be tried both by a court-martial and by a court of summary jurisdiction, but may be tried by either of them, as may be prescribed:

Provided that a man who has been dealt with summarily by his commanding officer shall be deemed to have been tried by court-martial.

(2.) Proceedings against an offender before either a court-martial or his commanding officer, or a court of summary jurisdiction, in respect of an offence punishable under this Part of this Act, and alleged to have been committed by him when a man of the Territorial Force, may be instituted whether the term of his service in the Territorial Force has or has not expired, and may, notwithstanding anything in any other Act, be instituted at any time within two months after the time at which the offence becomes known to his commanding officer if the alleged offender is then apprehended, or, if he is not then apprehended, then within two months after the time at which he is apprehended.

(3.) Where an offender has on several occasions been guilty of desertion, fraudulent enlistment, or making a false answer, he may for the purposes of any proceedings against him be deemed to belong to any one or more of the corps to which he has been appointed or transferred as well as to the corps to which he properly belongs, and it shall be lawful to charge the offender with any number of the above-mentioned offences at the same time, whether they are offences within the meaning of the Army Act or offences within the meaning of this Part of this Act, and to give evidence of such offences against him, and, if he has been convicted of more than one offence, to punish him accordingly as if he had been previously convicted of any such offence.

Evidence.

XXVI. (1.) Section one hundred and sixty-four of the Army Act (which relates to evidence of the civil conviction or acquittal of a person subject to military law) shall apply to a man of the Territorial Force who is tried by a civil court, whether he is or is not at the time of such trial subject to military law.

(2.) Section one hundred and sixty-three of the Army Act (relating to evidence) shall apply to all proceedings under this Part of this Act.

Miscellaneous.

Exercise of powers vested in

XXVII. (1.) Any power or jurisdiction given to, and act or thing to be done by, to, or before any person holding any military office may, in relation to the Territorial Force, be exercised by or done by, to, or before any other person for the time being authorised in that behalf, according to the custom of the Service. holder of military office.

(2.) Where by this Part of this Act, or by any order or regulation in force under this Part of this Act, any order is authorised to be made by any military authority, such order may be signified by an order, instruction, or letter under the hand of any officer authorised to issue orders on behalf of such military authority, and an order, instruction, or letter purporting to be signed by any officer appearing therein to be so authorised shall be evidence of his being so authorised.

Application of enactments.

XXVIII. (1.) The Army Act shall apply to the Territorial Force and officers and men thereof in like manner as it applies to the Militia, and officers and men of the Militia, except that men of the Territorial Force shall, in addition, be subject to military law when called out on actual military service for purposes of defence, and shall be liable to dismissal as a punishment, and for that purpose the amendments contained in the First Schedule to this Act shall be made in the Army Act.

(2.) For the purpose of section one hundred and forty-three of the Army Act and of all other enactments relating to such duties, tolls, and ferries as are in that section mentioned, officers and men belonging to the Territorial Force, when going to or returning from any place at which they are required to attend, and for non-attendance at which they are liable to be punished, shall be deemed to be officers and soldiers of the regular forces on duty.

(3.) His Majesty may by Order in Council apply, with the necessary adaptations, to the Territorial Force or the officers or men belonging to that force any enactment relating to the Militia, Yeomanry, or Volunteers, other than enactments with respect to the raising, service, pay, discipline, or government of the Militia, Yeomanry, or Volunteers, and every such order in council shall be laid before both Houses of Parliament.

Transitory.

Transitory provisions.

XXIX. (1.) Where an association has been established under this Act for any county His Majesty may by Order in Council transfer to the Territorial Force such units of the Yeomanry and Volunteers or part thereof raised in the county as may be specified in the Order, and every such unit or part thereof shall from the date mentioned in the Order be deemed to have been lawfully formed under this Part of this Act as an unit of the Territorial Force as provided by the Order, and the provisions of this Part of this Act shall apply to it accordingly.

(2.) Every officer and man of an unit or part thereof mentioned in any such Order shall, from the date mentioned in that Order, be deemed to be an officer or man of the Territorial Force. Provided that nothing in this section or in any Order made thereunder shall, without his consent, affect the conditions or area of service of any person commissioned, enlisted, or enrolled before the passing of this Act.

(3.) An Order in Council under this section may provide—

(*a.*) For the application to officers and men who become subject thereto of the provisions of this Act as to conditions and area of service, and for the continuance of the application to officers and men who remain subject thereto of the provisions as to conditions and area of service previously in force as respects those officers and men:

(*b.*) For transferring to the association any property vested in a Secretary of State for the purposes of any unit to which the Order relates:

(*c.*) For transferring to the association any property belonging to or held for the benefit of any such unit so however that all property so transferred shall as from the date of the transfer be held by the association for the benefit in like manner of the corresponding unit of the Territorial Force or for such other purposes as the association, with the consent of such corresponding unit, to be ascertained in the prescribed manner, shall direct; and any question which may arise as to whether any property is transferred to an association, or as to the trusts or purposes upon or for which it is or ought to be held, shall be referred for the decision of a Secretary of State whose decision shall be final. The corresponding unit of the Territorial Force shall, in the event of any such transfer, become entitled, notwithstanding the terms of any trust, limitation, or condition affecting the property so transferred to the estate or interest in such property of the unit to the property of which the order relates; but, subject to this provision, the interest of any beneficiary other than such unit shall not, without the consent of such beneficiary, be affected. The order may, if it be deemed proper, having regard to the special circumstances of any case, provide for the appointment of special trustees to act together with or to the exclusion of the association in regard to any such property and such special trustees may be the existing trustees of such property:

(*d.*) For transferring to the association any liabilities of any such unit which the association is willing to assume, and providing for the discharge of any such liabilities which are not so transferred:

(*e.*) For transferring to the association any land or interest in land acquired by the council of a county or borough on behalf of any volunteer corps to which the order relates, and any outstanding liabilities of the council incurred in respect thereof, if the council and the association consent:

and may contain such supplemental, consequential, and incidental provisions as may appear necessary or proper for the purposes of the Order.

(4.) Every Order in Council made under this section shall be laid before both Houses of Parliament.

PART III.

Reserve Forces.

XXX. (1.) The power of enlisting men into the first class of the army reserve under the Reserve Forces Act, 1882, shall extend to the enlistment of men who have not served in His Majesty's regular forces, and men so enlisted who have not served in the regular forces are in this Part of this Act referred to as special reservists, and a special reservist may be re-engaged, and when re-engaged shall continue subject to the terms of service applicable to special reservists. Enlistment and terms of service of special reservists. 45 & 46 Vict., c. 48.

(2.) A special reservist may, in addition to being called out for annual training, be called out for a special course or special courses of training at such place or places within the United Kingdom at such time or times and for such period or periods, not exceeding in the whole six months, as may be prescribed, in like manner and subject to the like conditions as he may be called out for annual training, and may during any such course be attached to or trained with any body of His Majesty's forces.

(3.) Notwithstanding the provisions of section eleven of the Reserve Forces Act, 1882, any special reservists may be called out for annual training for such period or periods as may be prescribed by any order or regulations under the Reserve Forces Act, 1882.

(4.) Provided that where one of the conditions on which a man was enlisted or re-engaged is that he shall not be called out for training, whether special or annual, for a longer period than the period specified in his attestation paper, he shall not be liable under this section to be called out for any longer period.

(5.) Where a proclamation ordering the army reserve to be called out on permanent service has been issued, it shall be lawful for His Majesty at any time thereafter by proclamation to order that all special reservists shall cease to be so called out, and thereupon a Secretary of State shall give such directions as may seem necessary or proper for carrying the said proclamation into effect.

(6.) A special reservist who enlists into the regular forces shall upon such enlistment be deemed to be discharged from the army reserve.

XXXI. A Secretary of State may, by regulations under the Reserve Forces Act, 1882, authorise any special reservist having the qualfications prescribed by those regulations to agree in writing that, if the time when he would otherwise be entitled to be discharged occurs whilst he is called out on permanent service, he will continue to serve until the expiration of a period, whether definite or indefinite, Agreements as to extension of service.

specified in the agreement, and if any man who enters into such an agreement is so called out, he shall be liable to be detained in service for the period specified in his agreement in the same manner in all respects as if his term of service were still unexpired.

Liability of reservists to be called out.

XXXII. (1.) A special reservist shall, if he so agrees in writing, be liable during the whole of his service in the army reserve, or during such part of that service as he so agrees, to be called out on permanent service without such proclamation or communication to Parliament as is mentioned in section twelve of the Reserve Forces Act, 1882, and the calling out of men under this section shall not involve the meeting of Parliament as required by section thirteen of that Act:

Provided that—

(*a.*) The number of men so liable shall not at any one time exceed four thousand:

(*b.*) The power of calling out of men under this section shall not be exercised except when they are required for service outside the United Kingdom when warlike operations are in preparation or in progress:

(*c.*) Any agreement under this section may provide for the revocation thereof by such notice in writing as may be therein stated:

(*d.*) Any exercise of the power of calling out men under this section shall be reported to Parliament as soon as may be:

(*e.*) The number of men for the time being called out under this section shall not be reckoned in the number of the forces authorised by the Annual Army Act for the time being in force.

(2.) Six thousand shall be substituted for five thousand as the maximum number of men liable to be called out under section one of the Reserve Forces and Militia Act, 1898, and the liability to be called out under that section may, if so agreed, extend to the first two years of a man's service in the first class of the army reserve.

61 & 62 Vict., c. 9.

(3.) In paragraph (5) of section one hundred and seventy-six of the Army Act the words "under His Majesty's proclamation" shall be repealed.

Power to form battalions, &c., of reservists.

XXXIII. Orders and regulations under the Reserve Forces Act, 1882, may provide for the formation of special reservists into regiments, battalions, or other military bodies, and for the formation of such regiments, battalions, or other military bodies into corps, either alone or jointly with any other part of His Majesty's forces, and for appointing, transferring, or attaching special reservists to such corps, and for posting, attaching, or otherwise dealing with special reservists within such corps.

Transfer of Militia battalions to reserve.

XXXIV. (1.) His Majesty may by Order in Council transfer to the Army Reserve such battalions of the Militia as may be specified in the order, and every battalion so transferred shall from the date mentioned in the order be deemed to have been lawfully formed under this Part of this Act as a battalion of special reservists.

(2.) As from the said date every officer of any battalion so transferred shall be deemed to be an officer in the reserve of officers, and every man in such battalion shall be deemed to be a special reservist, and the order may contain such provisions as may seem necessary for applying the provisions of the Reserve Forces Acts, 1882 to 1906, as amended by this Act, to those officers and men:

Provided that, unless any officer or man in any battalion so transferred indicates his assent to such transfer certified by his commanding officer, nothing in the order shall affect his existing conditions of service.

(3.) All Orders in Council made under this section shall be laid before both Houses of Parliament.

XXXV. Subsection (4) of section six of the Reserve Forces Act, 1882, which makes a certificate purporting to be signed by an officer appointed to pay men belonging to the army reserve evidence in certain cases, shall, where a person other than an officer is appointed to pay men belonging to the army reserve, apply to certificates purporting to be signed by such person. Amendment of 45 & 46 Vict., c. 48, s. 6 (4).

XXXVI. The acceptance of a commission as an officer in the reserve of officers shall not vacate the seat of any member returned to serve in Parliament. Commissions in reserve of officers not to vacate seats in Parliament.

PART IV.

SUPPLEMENTAL.

XXXVII. (1.) Every Order in Council or scheme required by this Act to be laid before each House of Parliament shall be so laid within forty days next after it is made, if Parliament is then sitting, or, if not, within forty days after the commencement of the then next ensuing session; and, if an address is presented to His Majesty by either House of Parliament within the next subsequent forty days, praying that any such order or scheme may be annulled, His Majesty may thereupon by Order in Council annul the same, and the order or scheme so annulled shall thenceforth become void and of no effect, but without prejudice to the validity of any proceedings which may in the meantime have been taken under the same. Provisions as to orders, schemes and regulations.

(2.) All Orders in Council, orders, schemes, and regulations made under this Act may be varied or revoked by subsequent Orders in Council, orders, schemes, and regulations made in the like manner and subject to the like conditions.

XXXVIII. In this Act, unless the context otherwise requires— Definitions.

The expression "county" means a county or riding of a county for which a lieutenant is appointed, and includes the City of London; and each county of a city or county of a town mentioned in the first column of the Second Schedule to this Act shall be deemed to form part of the county set opposite thereto in the second column of that schedule;

The expression "man of the Territorial Force" includes a non-commissioned officer;

The expression "prescribed" means prescribed by orders or regulations;

Other expressions have the same meaning as in the Army Act.

Special provisions as to special places.

XXXIX. (1.) The Lord Warden of the Cinque Ports may ex-officio be a member of the association of the county of Kent or of the county of Sussex, or of both, as may be provided by schemes under this Act.

(2.) The Warden of the Stannaries may ex-officio be a member of the association of the county of Cornwall or of the county of Devon, or of both, as may be provided by schemes under this Act.

(3.) The Lord Mayor of the City of London shall ex-officio be president of the association of the City of London.

(4.) The Governor or Deputy Governor of the Isle of Wight shall ex-officio be a member of the association of the county of Southampton.

(5.) Nothing in this Act shall affect the raising and levying of the Trophy Tax as heretofore in the City of London, but the proceeds of the Tax so levied may be applied by His Majesty's Commissioners of Lieutenancy for the City of London, if the Royal London Militia Battalion is re-constituted as a battalion of the Army Reserve, for any purposes connected with that battalion, and may also, if His Majesty's Commissioners of Lieutenancy for the City of London in their discretion see fit, be applied for the purposes of any of the powers and duties of the association of the City of London under this Act.

Application to Scotland and the Isle of Man.

XL. (1.) In the application of this Act to Scotland the following modifications shall be made:—

(*a.*) This Act shall apply to a county of a city in like manner as to any other county: Provided that on the representation or with the consent of the corporation of any county of a city it shall be lawful for His Majesty, by order signified under the hand of a Secretary of State, at any time after the passing of this Act, to declare that such county of a city shall for the purposes of this Act be deemed to form part of the county set opposite thereto in the second column of the Third Schedule to this Act, and to provide for all matters which may appear necessary or proper for giving full effect to the order;

(*b.*) The expression "county borough council" means the town council of a royal, parliamentary, or police burgh with a population of or exceeding twenty thousand according to the census for the time being last taken;

(*c.*) The expression "land" includes heritages;

(*d.*) The expression "overseer" means an inspector of poor.

(2.) This Act shall apply to the Isle of Man as if it formed part of, and were included in the expression, the United Kingdom, subject to the following modifications:—

(*a.*) The Isle of Man shall be deemed to be a separate county;

(*b.*) References to the Governor of the Island shall be substituted for references to the lieutenant of a county;

(*c.*) References to a High Bailiff or two justices of the peace and to conviction by such a Bailiff or justices shall be substituted for references to a court of summary jurisdiction and to conviction under the Summary Jurisdiction Acts;

(*d.*) References to the Tynwald Court shall be substituted for references to Parliament in the section of this Act relating to civil rights and exemptions.

XLI. This Act may be cited as the Territorial and Reserve Forces Act, 1907, and so far as it relates to the reserve forces may be cited with the Reserve Forces Acts, 1882 to 1906, as the Reserve Forces Acts, 1882 to 1907. Short title.

SCHEDULES.

FIRST SCHEDULE.

Amendment of Army Act.

Section 28.

Section.	Amendment.
S. 13 (1) (*a*) and (*b*)..	After the word "Militia" there shall be inserted the words "or Territorial Force."
S. 115 (7)	After the word "Whenever" there shall be inserted the words "a proclamation ordering the Army Reserve to be called out on permanent service or"
S. 115 (8)	After the words "then if" there shall be inserted the words "a proclamation ordering the Army Reserve to be called out on permanent service or"
S. 175..	After paragraph (3) there shall be inserted the following paragraph:— "(3A) Officers of the Territorial Force other than members of the permanent staff."
S. 176	After paragraph (6) there shall be inserted the following paragraph:— "(6A) All non-commissioned officers and men belonging to the Territorial Force— "(*a*) When they are being trained or exercised, either alone or with any portion of the regular forces or otherwise; and "(*b*) When attached to or otherwise acting as part of or with any regular forces; and "(*c*) When embodied; and "(*d*) When called out for actual military service for purposes of defence in pursuance of any agreement."
S. 181 (4)	The words "the unit of the Territorial Force," shall be inserted after the words "officer commanding," where those words first occur, and the words "an unit of the Territorial Force," shall be inserted after those words where they secondly occur, and the words "Territorial Force," shall be inserted after the words "an officer, non-commissioned officer, or man of the."
S. 181 (4) (*a*).. ..	After the word "any" there shall be inserted the words "man of the Territorial Force or"

FIRST SCHEDULE—*continued.*

Section.	Amendment.
S. 181 (4) (*b*) and (*c*)	The word "Militia" shall be repealed in both places where that word occurs, and the words "of the Territorial Force or Militia" shall be inserted after the word "man" in both places where that word occurs.
S. 181 (6)	After the word "Volunteers" there shall be inserted the words "or the Territorial Force."
S. 190 (12)	After the word "means" there shall be inserted the words "the Territorial Force."

SECOND SCHEDULE.

Section 38.

Names of Cities and Towns.	County.
ENGLAND.	
County of the city of Chester	Chester.
County of the city of Exeter	Devon.
County of the town of Poole	Dorset.
County of the city of Gloucester	Gloucester.
County of the city of Bristol	Gloucester.
County of the city of Canterbury	Kent.
County of the city of Lincoln	Lincoln.
County of the city of Norwich	Norfolk.
County of the town of Newcastle-upon-Tyne ..	Northumberland.
Borough and town of Berwick-upon-Tweed ..	Northumberland.
County of the town of Nottingham	Nottingham.
County of the town of Southampton	Southampton.
County of the city of Lichfield	Stafford.
County of the city of Worcester	Worcester.
County of the city of York	West Riding of York.
County of the town of Kingston-upon-Hull ..	East Riding of York.
County of the town of Carmarthen	Carmarthen.
County of the town of Haverfordwest	Pembroke.
IRELAND.	
County of the city of Waterford	Waterford.
County of the town of Londonderry	Londonderry.

THIRD SCHEDULE.
Scotland.

Name of County of City.	County.
County of the city of Edinburgh	Edinburgh.
County of the city of Glasgow	Lanark.
County of the city of Dundee	Forfar.
County of the city of Aberdeen	Aberdeen.

APPENDIX 2.

MODEL SCHEME.

TERRITORIAL AND RESERVE FORCES ACT, 1907.

COUNTY OF________________

SCHEME MADE BY THE ARMY COUNCIL FOR THE ESTABLISHMENT AND CONSTITUTION OF AN ASSOCIATION FOR THE COUNTY OF UNDER THE TERRITORIAL AND RESERVE FORCES ACT, 1907.

1. For the purposes of the Territorial and Reserve Forces Act, 1907, there shall, as from the day of , 1907, be established an Association for the county of , and that Association (hereinafter referred to as "the Association") shall be called the Territorial Force Association of the county of . Establishment and name.

2. The Association shall be a body corporate by the name of the Territorial Force Association of the county of , with a common seal, and may sue and be sued and be described for all purposes by that name, and shall have power to acquire and hold land for the purposes of the Territorial and Reserve Forces Act, 1907, without licence in mortmain. Incorporation and power to hold land.

3. The Lord Lieutenant for the time being of the county of shall be President of the Association. President.

4. The Association shall first consist of the President, a chairman and vice-chairman appointed by the Army Council, and ordinary members. Not less than half of the whole number of the Association shall be military members; shall be representative members; and shall be co-opted members. Number of members.

After the term of office of the first appointed members of the Association has expired, the Association shall consist of the President and ordinary members. Not less than half of the whole number of the Association shall be military members; shall be representative members; and shall be co-opted members; and the Association shall from time to time elect a member of the Association to be chairman and another member to be vice-chairman.

5. The chairman and vice-chairman appointed by the Army Council shall hold office till the day of . Chairman and vice-chairman.

The chairman and vice-chairman first elected by the Association shall hold office until the day of , . The term of office of every chairman and vice-chairman subsequently elected shall be one year, but both the chairman and the vice-chairman shall be eligible for re-election.

On a casual vacancy occurring in the office of chairman or vice-chairman of the Association by reason of the death, resignation, or inability to act of the chairman or vice-chairman, or otherwise, the vacancy, if it occurs before the day of shall be filled by appointment by the Army Council, and if it occurs subsequently shall be filled by election by the Association, and the person appointed in the place of the vacating chairman or vice-chairman shall hold office until the time when the person in whose place he is appointed would have regularly gone out of office, and shall then go out of office, but he shall be eligible for re-election.

Provided that a chairman or vice-chairman whose term of office has expired by effluxion of time shall, if he is a member of the Association, hold office until his successor is appointed.

Appointment of military members.

6. The military members of the Association shall be appointed by the Army Council from amongst the officers of the Yeomanry and Volunteer forces of the county of until the Territorial Force is raised for that county, and afterwards from amongst the officers of that force. Provided that officers of those forces, whether retired or not, may be appointed if by virtue of their commissions or otherwise they are legally entitled to the style and rank of officers.

Appointment of representative members.

7. The representative members of the Association shall be appointed by the Army Council as follows:—

persons on the recommendation of the council of the county of ;

persons on the recommendation of the council of the county borough of ;

persons on the recommendation of the governing body of the University of .

Before recommending any person as a representative member of the Association, the council or other body entitled to make the recommendation shall consult with the Army Council.

Appointment of co-opted members.

8. The co-opted members of the Association shall be appointed by the Association, and the first co-opted members shall be appointed within one month of the establishment of the Association.

In every year in which all the ordinary members of the Association are newly appointed the first business at the first meeting of the Association shall be the appointment of the co-opted members; and the election of the chairman and vice-chairman shall take place at a subsequent meeting at which the co-opted members shall be entitled to vote. Provided that the year of office of every such chairman and vice-chairman shall be deemed to commence on the day on which the military and representative members come into office.

The co-opted members shall include persons representative of the interests of employers and persons representative of the interests of workmen in the county.

9. On the day of , and on the day of in every third year thereafter, all the members of the Association, other than the President, shall go out of office, and new appointments shall be made ; but a person going out of office may, if otherwise qualified, be re-appointed. Provided that, if by reason of any change in the forces raised in the county, the military members of the Association shall, in the opinion of the Army Council, cease to be fairly representative of all arms and branches of the Territorial Force raised within the county, the Army Council may at any time cancel the appointment of any military member of the Association, and appoint another member in his place as upon the occurrence of a casual vacancy in the Association. Term of office.

10. (*a*) If a member of the Association, other than the President— Vacation of office.

(i) is absent from meetings of the Association for more than six months consecutively, except for some reason approved by the Association ; or

(ii) is convicted, either summarily or on indictment, of any crime and sentenced to imprisonment with hard labour without the option of a fine, or to any greater punishment ; or

(iii) is adjudged bankrupt, or makes a composition or arrangement with his creditors ;

he shall vacate his office as a member of the Association.

(*b*) If a military member of the Association ceases to be legally entitled to the style and rank of an officer of the Yeomanry, Volunteer, or Territorial Forces, he shall vacate his office as a military member of the Association.

(*c*) A person shall be disqualified from being appointed or being a member of the Association if he holds any paid office under the Association, or is concerned in any bargain or contract entered into with the Association, or participates in the profit of any such bargain or contract or of any work done under the authority of the Association.

Provided that a person shall not be disqualified from being appointed or being a member of the Association by reason of being interested—

(i) in the sale or lease of any lands to the Association ; or

(ii) in any agreement as to compensation under the Military Manœuvres Act, 1897 ; or

(iii) in any newspaper in which any advertisement relating to the affairs of the Association is inserted ; or

(iv) in any contract with the Association as a shareholder in any joint stock company ; or

(v) in any bargain or contract which the Army Council may from time to time by general or special order permit an Association to make with a member thereof.

Provided that a member shall not vote at any meeting of the Association on any question in which he or such company is interested.

Provision as to casual vacancies.

11. (*a.*) On a casual vacancy occurring in the Association by reason of the death, resignation, disqualification, or absence of a member, or otherwise, another qualified person shall be appointed a member of the Association, by the authority and in the manner by and in which the member so vacating office was appointed.

A person so appointed to fill a casual vacancy shall hold office until the person in whose place he is appointed would have regularly gone out of office, and shall then go out of office, but he shall be eligible for re-election.

(*b.*) On a casual vacancy occurring in the Association the secretary of the Association shall forthwith give notice of the vacancy to the Army Council, and, if the member vacating office was a representative member, also to the council or body on whose recommendation he was appointed.

Persons to preside at meetings.

12. At every meeting of the Association the chairman, if present, shall preside. If the chairman is absent, the vice-chairman, if present, shall preside. If the chairman and vice-chairman are both absent, such member of the Association as the members then present choose shall preside:

Provided that the President of the Association, if present at a meeting of the Association, shall, if he so elects, be entitled to preside.

Quorum.

13. The quorum of the Association shall be one-fourth of the whole number of the Association.

Decision of questions by majority of votes.

14. Every question at a meeting of the Association shall be decided by a majority of votes of the members present and voting on that question, and, in the case of equality of votes, the person presiding at the meeting shall have a second or casting vote.

General Purposes Committee.

15. There shall be a general purposes committee of the Association consisting of the chairman and vice-chairman of the Association, and such other members as the Association may determine, and the chairman and vice-chairman of the Association shall be the chairman and vice-chairman of the general purposes committee.

All matters relating to the exercise by the Association of their powers (except such as may be referred to a special committee under this scheme) shall stand referred to the general purposes committee, and the Association before exercising any such powers shall, unless in their opinion the matter is urgent, receive and consider the report of the general purposes committee with respect to the matter in question, and may also delegate to the general purposes committee, with or without any conditions or restrictions, as they think fit, any of such powers, and shall so delegate any of such powers if so required by the Army Council.

No order for payment of any sum shall be made by the Association except in pursuance of a resolution of the Association passed on the recommendation of the general purposes committee, and no costs, debt, or liabilities exceeding fifty pounds shall be incurred except upon a resolution of the Association passed on an estimate submitted by the general purposes committee.

Committees, and delegation of powers.

16. The Association may appoint, out of their own body, such and so many other special committees, and consisting of such number of persons as they think fit, for any purposes which, in the opinion of the Association, would be better regulated and managed by means of special committees, and may, except as aforesaid,

delegate, with or without any conditions or restrictions, as they may think fit, any of their powers and duties to any committee of the Association so appointed.

17. The Association may make regulations as to the quorum, proceedings, and place of meeting of the general purposes or any special committee so appointed, but subject thereto, the quorum, proceedings, and place of meeting of the committee shall be such as the committee determine. **Regulations as to Committees.**

18. A minute of the proceedings of the Association, or of a committee thereof, signed at the same or the next ensuing meeting by a member of the Association describing himself as, or appearing to be, chairman of the meeting at which the minute is signed, shall be received in evidence without further proof, and until the contrary is found, every meeting in respect of the proceedings whereof a minute has been so made, shall be deemed to have been duly convened and held, and all the members of the meeting shall be deemed to have been duly qualified, and, where the proceedings are proceedings of a committee, the committee shall be deemed to have been duly constituted, and to have had power to deal with the matter referred to in the minutes. **Evidence of proceedings at meetings.**

19. No act or proceeding of the Association shall be questioned on account of any vacancy in their body or on account of the appointment of any member having been defective. **Proceedings not to be questioned on account of vacancies, &c.**

20. Subject to the provisions of this Scheme, the Association may regulate their own procedure. **Power to regulate procedure.**

21. The secretary of the Association shall be appointed by the Association subject to the approval of the Army Council, and the secretary shall not be moved from his office except with the consent of the Army Council, and the Association shall appoint another person (who may be a Bank) to be treasurer of the Association, and may appoint such other officers as, subject to the approval of the Army Council, they think necessary for the proper conduct of the business of the Association. **Appointment of officers.**

There shall be paid to every officer so appointed such salary, if any, as the Association think fit.

22. (*a*) Every officer appointed by the Association shall at such times during the continuance of his office, or within three months after his ceasing to hold it, and in such manner as the Association direct, deliver to the Association a true account in writing of all matters committed to his charge, and of his receipts and payments with vouchers, and shall at all times on the demand of the Association deliver up to them any book or document in his possession belonging to the Association. **Accountability of officers.**

(*b*) All moneys due from such officer shall be paid by him to the treasurer of the Association, or as the Association may direct.

(*c*) Every such officer shall, if required by the Association, give such security as the Association may direct for the due performance of his duties and for the due accounting for and payment of all moneys received by him, and the security shall be for such sum and shall be given in such manner and form, as the Association may from time to time order in the case of each office and the

Association may at any time require that the amount or nature of any such security be varied.

Power to acquire and provide offices.

23. The Association may, from time to time, for the purpose of any of their powers or duties, acquire, purchase, or take on lease or exchange any lands or any easements or rights, over or in land, and may acquire, hire, erect, and furnish such offices and other buildings as they may from time to time require.

Power to certain officers to attend and speak at meetings.

24. The following general officers, viz. :—

or any officer deputed by any of those officers, may attend any meeting of the Association and speak thereat, but no such general or other officer shall be entitled to vote at any meeting of the Association.

Short title.

25. This Scheme may be cited as the County Association Scheme, 1907.

By Command of the Army Council,

APPENDIX 3.

TABLES OF ESTABLISHMENTS.

EXPLANATORY NOTES.

A.—HEADQUARTERS.

DETAIL OF ADDITIONAL PERSONNEL.

The following is the detail of the additional personnel provided from other units :—

For Headquarters of Division :—

From Yeomanry.—1 Assistant Provost-Marshal, 10 M.M.P.
From Engineers.—3 printers, 2 litho-draughtsmen, 1 litho printer, 3 drivers for printing and litho sections.
From Infantry.—1 signalling officer, 7 signallers, 3 clerks, 1 cook, 28 bâtmen.

For Headquarters of Mounted Brigade :—

From Yeomanry.—1 signalling officer, 4 signallers, 10 M.M.P., 1 cook, 11 bâtmen.

For Headquarters of Infantry Brigade :—

From Yeomanry.—5 M.M.P.
From Infantry.—1 signalling officer, 4 signallers, 1 cook, 10 bâtmen.

For Headquarters of Divisional Artillery:—

From Artillery.—4 clerks and orderlies, 4 signallers, 1 cook, 9 bâtmen.

For Headquarters of Divisional Engineers:—

From Engineers.—1 engineer clerk, 1 sapper (orderly to M.O.), 1 driver (orderly to M.O.), 7 bâtmen.

All bâtmen will be fully armed and trained as soldiers.

In the Yeomanry the numbers given above are included in the Establishment of the regiments provided for Divisions. In other arms they will be supernumerary to the Establishment of selected units in peace, but will be administered in all respects by those units, and will, as a rule, only join the staff when the Division trains as a whole.

TRAINING.

The units to train the additional personnel of Artillery, Engineers, and Infantry will be selected by the G.O.C. the Division.

The A.S.C. drivers will be trained as follows:—

For the Headquarters Division, Divisional Artillery and Divisional Engineers.—By the Headquarters Company of the Divisional Transport and Supply Column.

For the Headquarters, Mounted Brigade.—By the Mounted Brigade T. and S. Column.

For the Headquarters, Infantry Brigade.—By the Company from which they are detached on mobilization.

ADDITIONAL NUMBERS ON MOBILIZATION.

The following numbers are not included in the Training Establishment, but will be found on mobilization either from supernumerary officers of Territorial units, or from the Reserve of Officers:—

For Headquarters of Division.—1 G.S. officer (2nd grade); 2 G.S. officers (3rd grade); 1 A.Q.M.G.; 2 A.D.C.s.

For Headquarters of Mounted Brigade, Infantry Brigade, and Divisional Artillery.—Each 1 A.D.C., 1 staff captain.

B.—HORSES AND VEHICLES ALLOWED FOR TRAINING.

When the number of men attending camp falls below the full establishment, the allowance of horses and vehicles allowed for training will be reduced proportionately.

HEAD

Headquarters.	G.O.C.	Colonel.	Lieut.-Col.	Gen. Staff Officer, 2nd or 3rd Grade.	Brigade-Major.	Staff Captain.	D.A.A. and Q.M.G.	Adjutant.	Total Officers.	Clerks.	Total, all ranks.	R.A.M.C. Administrative Medical Officer.	R.A.M.C. Staff Officer, R.A.M.C.	R.A.M.C. Medical Officer.
	Maintained in Peace as Staff or													
Headquarters of Division—														
Establishment (Personnel) ...	(b)1	...	...	(b)1	...	...	(b)1	...	3	(d)2	5	(f) 1	(c)1	...
Horses allowed for training ...	(a)	...	...	(a)	...	...	(a)	...	...	...	...	*1*	*1*	...
Headquarters of Mounted Brigade—														
Establishment (Personnel) ...	...	(c)1	...	...	(c)1	...	...	...	2	(c)1	3	...	...	...
Horses allowed for training ...	...	*2*	...	...	*1*	...	...	...	...	...	...	...	...	...
Headquarters of Infantry Brigade—														
Establishment (Personnel) ...	...	(c)1	...	...	(c)1	...	...	...	2	(e)1	3	...	...	...
Horses allowed for training ...	...	*2*	...	...	*1*	...	...	...	...	...	...	...	...	...
Headquarters of Infantry Group—														
Establishment (Personnel) ...	...	(c)1	...	...	(c)1	...	...	...	2	(e)1	3	...	...	...
Horses allowed for training ...	...	*2*	...	...	*1*	...	...	...	...	...	...	...	...	...
Headquarters of Divisional Artillery—														
Establishment (Personnel) ...	...	(c)1	...	...	(c)1	1	...	...	2	(e)1	3	...	...	...
Horses allowed for training ...	...	*2*	...	...	*1*	(a)	...	...	...	...	...	...	...	...
Headquarters of Divisional Engineers—														
Establishment (Personnel) ...	...	...	(f)1	...	...	...	...	(h)	1	...	1	...	...	(f) (g)2
Horses allowed for training ...	...	...	*1*	...	...	...	...	*1*	...	...	...	...	...	*1*

(a) Horses for these officers are not included in the training numbers, as they will be required all the year round and will be maintained by the officers, the expense being covered by their consolidated pay, as Regular Staff Officers.

(b) Regular officers on full pay.

(c) Regular officers not on full pay, or Territorial officers.

(d) Ex-soldiers.

(e) Yeomanry, Infantry, and Artillery, Territorial soldiers, respectively, with no extra emoluments.

]UARTERS.

with Headquarter units.											Additional personnel required on mobilization but borne supernumerary to establishment of selected units in peace. (*See explanatory notes.*)										
Attached.										Horses, officers' riding (including attached).	Yeomanry (not supernumerary).		Artillery.		Engineers.		Infantry.		A.S.C.	Total.	
R.A.M.C.			A.V.C.			Army Postal Service.		Total attached.													
Sanitary Officer.	Clerks, &c.	R.A.M.C. for water duties.	Administrative Veterinary Officer.	Veterinary Officer.	Clerk.	Officers.	Other ranks.	Officers.	Other ranks.		Officers.	Other ranks.	Officers.	Other ranks.	Officers.	Other ranks.	Officers.	Other ranks.	Drivers.	Officers.	Other ranks.
(*f*)1 *1*	(*k*)5 ...	(*k*)2 ...	(*f*)1 *1*	(*f*)1 *1*	(*k*)1 ...	... ...	(*k*)4 ...	5 ...	12 ...	... *5*	1 ...	10 ...	... ...	... ...	... ...	9 ...	1 ...	39 ...	(*j*)4 ...	2 ...	62 ...
... ...	... ...	... ...	... ...	... ...	... ...	... ...	(*k*)4 ...	... ...	4 ...	... *3*	1 ...	26 ...	... ...	... ...	... ...	... ...	... ...	... ...	1 ...	1 ...	27 ...
... ...	... ...	... ...	... ...	... ...	... ...	... ...	(*k*)4 ...	... ...	4 ...	... *3*	... ...	5 ...	... ...	... ...	... ...	... ...	1 ...	15 ...	(*j*)3 ...	1 ...	23 ...
... ...	... ...	... ...	... ...	... ...	... ...	... ...	... ...	... ...	... ...	... *3*	... ...	... ...	... ...	... ...	... ...	... ...	... ...	... ...	... ...	... ...	... ...
... ...	... ...	... ...	... ...	... ...	... ...	... ...	... ...	... ...	... ...	... *3*	... ...	... ...	... ...	18 ...	... ...	... ...	... ...	... ...	1 ...	... ...	19 ...
... ...	... ...	... ...	... ...	(*f*)1 *1*	... ...	... ...	... ...	3 ...	... ...	... *4*	... ...	... ...	... ...	... ...	... ...	10 ...	... ...	... ...	1 ...	... ...	11 ...

(*f*) Territorial officers.

(*g*) Two medical officers are included in the establishment to ensure that there shall always be one present at training, but only one will be trained with the unit in any year; on mobilization only one will be called up with the unit.

(*h*) The officer doing duty as adjutant to the group of 2 Field Companies and 1 Divisional Telegraph Company is also adjutant of the headquarters of Divisional Engineers and forms part of that unit.

(*j*) Includes a corporal.

(*k*) Territorial soldiers with no extra emoluments.

HONOURABLE ARTILLERY COMPANY OF LONDON.

Detail.	Headquarters.	Horse Artillery. 2 Batteries.	Horse Artillery. 2 Mounted Brigade Ammunition Columns.	Horse Artillery. Total.	Infantry. Headquarters.	Infantry. Machine Gun Section.	Infantry. 4 Companies.	Infantry. Total.	Total.
Lieut.-Colonel...	1	...	...	...	...	...	...	...	1
Majors	...	2	...	2	1	...	...	1	3
Captains	...	2	2	4	...	...	4	4	8
Subalterns	...	6	2	8	...	1	8	9	17
Quartermaster	1	...	...	...	...	...	...	...	1
Total officers ...	2	10	4	14	1	1	12	14	30
Acting serjeant-major ...	1	...	...	...	...	...	...	...	1
Quartermaster serjeant ...	...	...	...	...	1	...	...	1	1
Battery serjeant-majors ...	...	2	2	4	...	...	...	...	4
Battery quartermaster-serjt.	...	2	2	4	...	...	...	...	4
Orderly room clerk	...	...	...	...	1	...	...	1	1
Serjeant drummer	...	...	...	...	1	...	...	1	1
Pioneer serjeant	...	...	...	...	1	...	...	1	1
Serjeant cook	...	...	...	...	1	...	...	1	1
Transport serjeant	...	...	...	...	1	...	...	1	1
Signalling serjeant	...	...	...	...	1	...	...	1	1
Serjeant shoemaker	...	...	...	...	1	...	...	1	1
Armourer serjeant	...	...	...	...	1	...	...	1	1
Farrier serjeant	...	2	2	4	...	...	...	...	4
Colour serjeant	...	...	...	...	...	...	4	4	4
Serjeants	...	10	8	18	...	1	16	17	35
Total serjeants ...	1	16	14	30	9	1	20	30	61
Corporals	...	10	6	16	...	1	20	21	37
Bombardiers	...	18	8	26	...	...	...	...	26
Shoeing smiths	...	6(*a*)	4	10	...	...	...	...	10
Saddlers	...	4	4	8	...	...	...	...	8
Fitters or wheelers ...	...	6	4	10	...	...	...	...	10
Gunners	...	104	36	140	...	...	...	...	140
Drivers	...	96	48	144	5	2	8	15	159
Privates	...	...	...	...	...	12	400*	412	412
Orderlies for medical officer	...	4	...	4	2	...	...	2	6
Batmen...	3	28	6	34	2	1	12	15	52
Total rank and file ...	3	276	116	392	9	16	440	465	860
Trumpeters and buglers ...	...	4	2	6	...	...	8	8	14
Total all ranks	6	306	136	442	19	18	480	517	965
Attached:—									
Medical officers	...	4†	...	4†	2†	...	...	2†	6
Veterinary officers ...	...	2	...	2	...	...	...	...	2
Drivers, A.S.C. ...	...	6	8	14	3	...	...	3	17
R.A.M.C. for water duties	...		...	4	3	...	...	3	7

* Includes 1 pioneer, 4 signallers, and 2 stretcher bearers per company.

† 2 Medical officers are included for each Horse Artillery Battery and 2 for Infantry, to ensure one being present at training.

(*a*) Includes 2 corporals.

Permanent Staff:—

Horse Artillery—The same as for R.H.A., Territorial Force.

Infantry—2 Serjeant Instructors.

Horses and vehicles for annual training:—

Horse Artillery—The same as for R.H.A., Territorial Force.

Infantry—

Horses 7:
- 1 Major.
- 1 Transport Serjeant.
- 1 Medical Officer (attached).
- 2 for Machine Gun.
- 2 for G.S. Wagon.

Vehicles 2:
- 1 Machine Gun.
- 1 G.S. Wagon.

YEO

	Lieutenant-Colonel.	Majors.	Captains.	Lieutenants and 2nd Lieutenants.	Quarter-Master.	Total Officers.	Regimental-Serjeant-Major.	Regimental-Quarter-Master-Serjeant.	Squadron-Serjeant-Majors.	Squadron-Quarter-Master-Serjeants.	Farrier-Quarter-Master-Serjeant.	Saddler-Serjeant.	Farrier-Serjeants.
Squadron	...	1	1	3	...	5	...	...	1	1	...	...	1
Machine-Gun Section	...	...	...	1	...	1	...	...	...	...	...	...	...
Regiment	1	5	4	13(*a*)	1	25(*b*)	1	1	4	4	1	1	4
Horses allowed for annual training	*1*	5	*4*	*13*	*1*	...	*1*	*1*	*4*	*4*	*1*	...	*4*
Guns and vehicles allowed for annual training	...	...	...	...	...	...	...	...	...	...	...	...	...

* Two squadrons will have 84 privates only.

(*a*) 1 subaltern will act as machine-gun officer, 1 as signalling officer, and 1 as transport officer.

(*b*) The adjutant and serjeant-instructors (shown under P.S.) form part of the normal establishment of the regiment, and are included in these totals.

(*c*) Includes 1 for machine-gun, 1 for signalling, 1 for transport, 1 armourer-serjeant, and 1 serjeant-cook.

(*d*) May be serjeants or corporals, according to service. If a corporal, the total serjeants will be reduced and the corporals increased accordingly.

MANRY.

Serjeants.	Orderly-Room Clerks.	Trumpeters.	Corporals.	Shoeing-smiths.	Saddlers.	Privates.	Total other Ranks.	Total all Ranks.	Permanent Staff.		Attached.				Machine Gun.	2nd Line Regimental Transport Wagons.	Total Horses, including P.S. and attached.			
									Adjutant.	Serjeant-Instructors.	Medical Officer.	R.A.M.C. for Water Duties.	Veterinary Officer.	Drivers A.S.C. 2nd Line Transport.			Officers.	Riding.	Draught.	Pack for Machine-Gun.
5	...	2	6	4	1	85*	106	111	...	1	...	...	...	...	...	...	...	...	...	...
1	...	...	1	...	...	14	16	17	...	...	...	...	...	...	...	...	...	...	...	...
21 (c)	2(d)	8	25(e)	16	4	(k) 352	(b) 449	474(b)	1	5	2(h)	3(g)	1	7	...	...	...	...	...	...
19	...	*8*	*25*	*16*	*4*	*304*	...	...	...	*5*	*1*	...	*1*	...	*3*	*6*	*26(f)*	*396*	*6*	*3*
...	...	...	...	...	...	...	...	...	...	...	...	...	...	...	*1*	*3*	...	...	...	...

(*e*) Includes 1 for machine-gun section.
(*f*) Does not include the adjutant.
(*g*) Includes 1 corporal.
(*h*) Two medical officers are included to ensure that there shall always be one present at training; only one will be trained with the unit in any year.
(*k*) Includes 12 signallers.

Note.—Horses are not allowed for the following:—1 armourer-serjeant, 1 serjeant-cook, saddler-serjeant, 2 orderly-room clerks, 16 bandsmen, and 32 privates (8 per squadron).

ROYAL

ROYAL

l Units.	Majors.	Captains.	Lieutenants and 2nd Lieutenants.	Total Officers.	Battery-Serjeant-Major.	Battery-Quarter-Master-Serjeant.	Farrier-Serjeant.	Serjeants.	Trumpeters.	Shoeing-Smiths.	Saddlers.	Fitters or Wheelers.	Corporals.	Bombardiers.	Gunners.
Horse Artillery Battery with Mounted Brigade	1	1	3	5	1	1	1	5	2	3(*a*)	2	3(*b*)	5(*c*)	9(*c*)	52(*c*)
Horses allowed for annual training...	*1*	*1*	*3*	...	*1*	*1*	*1*	*4*	*2*	*2*	...	...		47(*i*)	
Guns and vehicles allowed for annual training	...	...	...	...	...	...	...	...	...	...	...	...	...	...	...
Mounted Brigade Ammunition Column—															
Headquarters	...	1	...	1	1	1	1	...	...	...	...	...	...	1(*h*)	2(*h*)
Section	...	...	1	1	...	...	...	4	1	2	2	2	3	3	16
Horses allowed for annual training	...	*1*	*1*	...	*1*	*1*	*1*	*2*	*1*	*1*	...	...	3	3	2
Vehicles allowed for annual training	...	...	...	...	...	...	...	...	...	...	...	...	...	...	...

(*a*) Includes 1 corporal.
(*b*) One wheeler takes the place of the armament artificer, who in the Field Army, is attached from the A.O. Corps.
(*c*) These combined ranks include 2 look-out men.
(*d*) Two men (one an acting bombardier) trained to the duties are placed under the orders of the medical officer. The gunner drives the cart for medical equipment.
(*e*) Fully trained and armed soldiers, and are available for duty in the ranks.
(*f*) The P.S. is that allotted to the battery and ammunition column.

ARTILLERY.

HORSE ARTILLERY.

Drivers.							Permanent Staff.		Attached.					Vehicles.				Total Horses, including P.S. and attached.			
																	2nd Line Regimental Transport.				
For Vehicles.	For Spare Horses.	Spare Drivers.	Orderlies for Medical Officer.	Bâtmen.	Total other Ranks.	Total all Ranks.	Adjutant.	Serjeant-Instructors.	Medical Officer.	R.A.M.C. for Water Duties.	Veterinary Officer.	A.S.C. Drivers for 2nd Line Transport.	Guns.	Ammunition Wagons.	Wagons for Ammunition.	S.A.A. Carts, or Hired Carts.	Wagons.	Officers.	Riding.	Draught.	Spare, Riding for Instructional Purposes.
36	8	4	2(d)	14(e)	148	153	1(f)	2(f)	2(g)	2	1	3	...	...	...	...	...	...	...	...	...
...	...	...	...	...	...	...	...	2	1	...	1	...	24	24	...	...	2	7(j)	60	50	...
...	...	...	...	...	...	...	...	...	...	...	...	...	4	4	...	...	1	...	...	...	...
...	...	...	...	2(e)	8	9	...	...	...	...	...	2	...	...	...	...	...	...	...	...	...
19	3	2	...	1(e)	58	59	...	...	...	...	...	2	...	...	...	...	...	...	...	...	...
...	...	...	...	...	...	...	...	...	...	...	...	...	...	...	16	4	2	2	15	22	6
...	...	...	...	...	...	...	...	...	...	...	...	...	...	...	4	2	1	...	...	...	...

(g) 2 medical officers are included in the establishment to ensure one being present at training. One only will train with the unit in any year. On mobilization only 1 will be called up with the unit.
(h Trained in signalling for communications.
(i) Composed as follows (including horse holders):—Detachment, 30; mounted orderly, 1; observing party, 6; signallers, 3; patrol, 3; coverers, 4. Total, 47.
Does not include the horse for the adjutant.

ROYAL

FIELD ARTIL

Units.	Lieutenant-Colonel.	Majors.	Captains.	Lieutenants and 2nd Lieutenants.	Orderly Officers.	Total Officers.	Serjeant-Major.	Battery-Serjeant-Major.	Battery-Quarter-Master-Serjeant.	Farrier-Serjeant.	Serjeants.	Trumpeters.	Shoeing-Smiths.	Saddlers.	Fitters or Wheelers.	Corporals.	Bombardier.	Gunners.
Field Artillery Brigade (3 batteries):—																		
Headquarters	1	...	...	...	1	3(*a*)	...(*b*)	...	...	...	...	1	...	...	1(*c*)	1(*d*)	2(*d*)	1(*b*)
Horses allowed for annual training	*1*	...	...	...	*1*	...	...	...	...	...	...	*1*	...	...	...	*1*	*1*	...
Vehicles allowed for annual training	...	...	...	...	...	...	...	...	...	...	...	...	...	...	...	...	...	...
For each Battery	...	1	1	3	...	5	...	1	1	1	5	2	3(*h*)	2	2	5(*i*)	9(*i*)	52(*i*)
Horses allowed for annual training	...	*1*	*1*	*3*	...	...	...	*1*	*1*	*1*	*4*	*2*	*1*	...	...		19 (*n*)	
Guns and vehicles allowed for annual training	...	...	...	...	...	...	...	...	...	...	...	...	...	...	...	...	...	...
Field Artillery Brigade:—																		
Ammunition Column	...	...	1	4	...	5	...	1	1	1	8	2	7(*h*)	3	3	9	9(*j*)	42(*j*)
Horses allowed for annual training	...	...	*1*	*2*	...	...	...	*1*	*1*	*1*	*4*	*2*	*2*	...	...	*3*	*3*	...
Vehicles allowed for annual training	...	...	...	...	...	...	...	...	...	...	...	...	...	...	...	...	...	...
Field Artillery (Howitzer) Brigade (2 batteries):—																		
Headquarters	1	...	...	...	1	3(*a*)	...(*b*)	...	...	...	...	1	...	...	1(*c*)	1(*d*)	2(*d*)	1(*b*)
Horses allowed for annual training	*1*	...	...	...	*1*	...	...	...	...	...	...	*1*	...	...	...	*1*	*1*	...
Vehicles allowed for annual training	...	...	...	...	...	...	...	...	...	...	...	...	...	...	...	...	...	...
For each Battery	...	1	1	3	...	5	...	1	1	1	5	2	3(*h*)	2	2	5(*i*)	9(*i*)	52(*i*)
Horses allowed for annual training	...	*1*	*1*	*3*	...	...	...	*1*	*1*	*1*	*4*	*2*	*1*	...	...		19 (*n*)	
Guns and Vehicles allowed for annual training	...	...	...	...	...	...	...	...	...	...	...	...	...	...	...	...	...	...
Field Artillery (Howitzer) Brigade:—																		
Ammunition Column	...	...	1	2	...	3	...	1	1	1	4	2	3(*h*)	2	2	4	5(*k*)	20(*k*)
Horses allowed for annual training	...	...	*1*	*2*	...	...	...	*1*	*1*	*1*	*2*	*2*	*1*	...	...	*2*	*3*	...
Vehicles allowed for annual training	...	...	...	...	...	...	...	...	...	...	...	...	...	...	...	...	...	...

(*a*) The adjutant (shown under P.S.) forms part of the normal establishment of the unit, and is included in these totals.

(*b*) An extra gunner to allow of the promotion of a serjeant-major on mobilization, to replace the acting-serjeant-major shown under P.S.

(*c*) Takes the place of the armament artificer, who in the Field Army is attached from the A.O. Corps.

(*d*) Provides 2 signallers, 2 range takers, 2 orderlies, and 3 horse-holders.

(*e*) Two men (one an acting bombardier) trained to the duties, are placed under the orders the medical officer. The gunner drives the cart for medical equipment.

Fully trained and armed soldiers, and are available for duty in the ranks.

(*g*) Two medical officers are included in the establishment to ensure one being present at training. One only will train with the unit in any year. On mobilization only one will be called up with the unit.

ARTILLERY—*continued.*

LERY UNITS.

Drivers.								Permanent Staff.			Attached.					Vehicles.					Total Horses, including P.S. and attached.			
For Vehicles.	For Spare Horses.	Spare Drivers.	Orderlies for Medical Officer.	Bâtmen.	Clerks.	Total other Ranks.	Total all Ranks.	Adjutant.	Acting-Serjeant-Major.	Serjeant-Instructor.	Medical Officer.	R.A.M.C. for Water Duties.	Veterinary Officer.	A.S.C. Drivers for 2nd Line Transport.	Guns.	Ammunition Wagons.	Wagons for Ammunition.	S.A.A. Carts or Hired Carts.	2nd Line Regimental Transport. Wagons.	2nd Line Regimental Transport. Carts.	Officers'.	Riding.	Draught.	Spare, Riding, for Instructional Purposes.
...	6(*d*)	...	2(*e*)	9(*f*)	1	24	27(*a*)	1(*a*)	1(*b*)	...	2(*g*)	4(*h*)	1	1	...	...	...	...	...	...	...	...	...	
...	...	...	...	...	...	...	...	...	*1*	...	*1*	...	*1*	...	...	...	...	...	...	*1*	4(*m*)	*4*	*1*	...
...	...	...	...	...	...	...	...	...	...	...	...	...	...	...	...	...	...	...	...	*1*	...	...	...	...
36	7	4	...	10(*f*)	...	140	145	...	...	2(*o*)	...	...	...	3	...	...	...	...	...	...	...	...	...	...
...	...	...	...	...	...	...	...	...	...	*2*	...	...	...	...	*24*	*16*	...	...	*2*	...	*5*	*31*	*42*	...
...	...	...	...	...	...	...	...	...	...	...	...	...	...	...	*4*	*4*	...	...	*1*	...	...	...	...	...
49	7	6	...	5(*f*)	...	153	158	...	...	...	...	...	...	5	...	...	...	...	...	...	...	...	...	...
...	...	...	...	...	...	...	...	...	...	...	...	...	...	...	...	...	*36*	*6*	*2*	...	*3*	*17*	*44*	*6*
...	...	...	...	...	...	...	...	...	...	...	...	...	...	...	...	...	*9*	*3*	*1*	...	...	...	...	...
...	6(*d*)	...	2(*e*)	9(*f*)	1	24	27(*a*)	1(*a*)	1(*b*)	...	2(*g*)	3(*h*)	1	1	...	...	...	...	...	...	...	...	...	...
...	...	...	...	...	...	...	...	...	*1*	...	*1*	...	*1*	...	...	...	...	...	...	*1*	4(*m*)	*4*	*1*	...
...	...	...	...	...	...	...	...	...	...	...	...	...	...	...	...	...	...	...	...	*1*	...	...	...	...
30	6	4	...	10(*f*)	...	133	138	...	...	2(*o*)	...	...	...	3	...	...	...	...	...	...	...	...	...	...
...	...	...	...	...	...	...	...	...	...	*2*	...	...	...	...	*24*	*16*	...	...	*2*	...	*5*	*31*	*42*	*5*
...	...	...	...	...	...	...	...	...	...	...	...	...	...	...	*4*	*4*	...	...	*1*	...	...	...	...	...
28	4	3	...	3(*f*)	...	83	86	...	...	...	...	...	...	4	...	...	...	...	...	...	...	...	...	...
...	...	...	...	...	...	...	...	...	...	...	...	...	...	...	...	*16*	*8*	...	*2*	...	*3*	*13*	*26*	*6*
...	...	...	...	...	...	...	...	...	...	...	...	...	...	...	...	*4*	*2*	...	*1*	...	...	...	...	...

(*h*) Includes 1 corporal.

(*i*) These combined ranks includes 2 look-out men.

(*j*) Includes 5 mounted bombardiers and 2 dismounted gunners trained in signalling for communications.

(*k*) Includes 1 bombardier and 2 gunners trained in signalling for communications.

(*m*) Does not include the horse for the adjutant.

(*n*) Composed as follows (including horse-holders):—Ground scouts, 2; mounted orderly, 1; observing party, 6; signallers, 3; patrol, 3; and coverers, 4.

(*o*) Includes Ammunition Column.

ROYAL

HEAVY AND MOUN

Units.	Lieutenant-Colonel.	Majors.	Captains.	Lieutenants and 2nd Lieutenants.	Orderly Officers.	Total Officers.	Serjeant-Major.	Battery Serjeant-Major.	Battery-Quarter-Master-Serjeant.	Farrier-Serjeant.	Serjeants.	Shoeing-Smiths.	Saddlers.	Fitters or Wheelers.	Trumpeters.	Corporals.	Bombardiers.	Gunners.
Heavy Artillery :—																		
Battery	(u)	1	1	3	...	5	...	1	1	1	6	3	2	2	2	6	6	72
Horses allowed for annual training ...	...	*1*	*1*	*3*	...	...	...	*1*	*1*	*1*	...	...	...	...	*2*	...	*8(b)*	...
Guns and vehicles allowed for annual training	...	...	...	...	...	...	...	...	...	...	...	...	...	...	...	...	...	...
Ammunition Column	...	...	...	1	...	1	...	...	...	...	1	1	1	2	...	1	2	18
Horses allowed for annual training ...	...	...	...	*1*	...	...	...	...	...	...	*1*	*1*	...	...	...	...	...	...
Vehicles allowed for annual training ...	...	...	...	...	...	...	...	...	...	...	...	...	...	...	...	...	...	...
Mountain Artillery Brigade :—																		
Headquarters	1	...	...	...	1	3(g)	(j)	...	...	...	...	...	...	1(e)	1	1(h)	2(h)	7(hj)
Horses allowed for annual training ...	*1*	...	...	...	*1*	...	...	...	...	...	...	...	...	...	*1*	...	...	...
Vehicles allowed for annual training ...	...	...	...	...	...	...	...	...	...	...	...	...	...	...	...	...	...	...
For each Battery	...	1	1	3	...	5	...	1	1	1	4	4(i)	3	3	2	4	4	64(q)
Horses allowed for annual training ...	...	*1*	*1*	*3*	...	...	...	*1*	*1*	*1*	...	*1*	...	...	*2*		*9(s)*	
Guns and vehicles allowed for annual training	...	...	...	...	...	...	...	...	...	...	...	...	...	...	...	...	...	...
Brigade Ammunition Column... ...	...	...	1	3	...	4	...	1	1	1	4	4(i)	3	3	2	4(n)	4(n)	36
Horses allowed for annual training ...	...	...	*1*	*2*	...	...	...	...	...	...	...	*1*	...	...	...	...	...	...
Vehicles allowed for annual training ...	...	...	...	...	...	...	...	...	...	...	...	...	...	...	...	...	...	...
Small-Arm Section Ammunition Column :—																		
Brigade Ammunition Column (*p*) ...	...	...	...	1	...	1	...	...	...	1	2	1	...	...	1	3	3(d)	18(d)
Horses allowed for annual training ...	...	...	...	*1*	...	...	...	...	...	*1*	...	*1*	...	...	*1*	...	...	...
Vehicles allowed for annual training ...	...	...	...	...	...	...	...	...	...	...	...	...	...	...	...	...	...	...

(*a*) These are gunners acting as drivers.
(*b*) For observation party.
(*c*) Does not include the horse for the adjutant.
(*d*) 3 bombardiers and 2 gunners trained in signalling for communications.
(*e*) Takes the place of the armament artificer, who in the Field Army is attached from the A.O. Corps.
(*f*) Fully armed and trained soldiers, and are available for duty in the ranks.
(*g*) The adjutant (shown under P.S.) forms part of the normal establishment of the unit, and is included in these totals.
(*h*) Provides for 2 signallers, 2 range takers, 2 orderlies, and 3 horse-holders.
(*i*) Includes 1 corporal.
(*j*) An extra gunner is included to allow of the promotion of a serjeant-major on mobilization to replace the acting-serjeant-major (shown under P.S.).
(*k*) 2 medical officers are included in the establishment to ensure one being present at training. One only will train with the unit in any year. On mobilization only one will be called up with the unit.

ARTILLERY—*continued.*

TAIN ARTILLERY UNITS.

Drivers. For Vehicles.	Drivers. For Spare Horses.	Drivers. Spare Drivers.	Orderlies for Medical Officer.	Batmen.	Clerks.	Total other Ranks.	Total all Ranks.	Permanent Staff. Adjutant.	Permanent Staff. Acting-Serjeant-Major.	Serjeant-Instructors.	Attached. Medical Officers.	Attached. R.A.M.C. for Water Duties.	Attached. Veterinary Officer.	Attached. A.S.C. Drivers for 2nd Line Transport.	Guns.	Vehicles. Ammunition Wagons.	Vehicles. Wagons for Ammunition.	Vehicles. S.A.A. Carts or Hired Carts.	Vehicles. 2nd Line Regimental Transport. Wagons.	Vehicles. 2nd Line Regimental Transport. Carts.	Total Horses, including P.S. and attached. Officers.	Total Horses. Riding.	Total Horses. Draught.	Total Horses. Spare, for Instructional Purposes.	Pack Mules or Ponies. Ordnance.	Pack Mules or Ponies. Baggage.
40(a)	7(a)	5(a)	...	6(f)	...	160	165	1(u)	(u)	2(t)	...	2	...	3	...	...	...	...	...	...	...	...	...	...	...	...
...	...	...	...	...	...	...	...	...	...	2	...	...	...	...	32	16	...	...	2	...	5(c)	15	50	...	...	...
...	...	...	...	...	...	...	...	...	...	...	...	...	...	...	4	4	...	...	1	...	...	...	...	...	...	...
16(a)	3(a)	2 (a)	...	1(f)	...	48	49	...	...	...	...	...	...	1	...	...	...	...	...	...	...	...	...	...	...	...
...	...	...	...	...	...	...	...	...	...	...	...	...	...	...	...	...	16	...	...	1	1	3	17	...	...	...
...	...	...	...	...	...	...	...	...	...	...	...	...	...	...	...	...	4	...	...	1	...	...	...	...	...	...
...	...	...	2(r)	9(f)	1	24	27(g)	1(g)	1(j)	...	2(k)	4(i)	1	2	...	...	...	...	...	...	...	...	...	...	...	...
...	...	...	...	...	...	...	...	...	...	...	1	...	1	...	...	...	...	...	...	1	4	1	1	...	...	...
...	...	...	...	...	...	...	...	...	...	...	...	...	...	...	...	...	...	...	...	1	...	...	...	...	...	...
94(m)	...	9 (a)	...	6(f)	...	200	205	...	...	2	...	...	...	5	...	...	...	...	...	...	...	...	...	...	...	...
...	...	...	...	...	...	...	...	...	...	2	...	...	...	...	...	...	...	...	2	...	5	17	2	...	32	...
...	...	...	...	...	...	...	...	...	...	...	...	...	...	...	4	...	...	...	1	...	...	...	...	...	...	...
52(a)	3(a)	6(a)	...	4(f)	...	128	132	...	...	(t)	...	...	...	3	...	...	...	...	...	...	...	...	...	...	...	...
...	...	...	...	...	...	...	...	...	...	...	...	...	...	...	...	...	24	...	2	...	3	10	26	...	12	...
...	...	...	...	...	...	...	...	...	...	...	...	...	...	...	...	...	6	...	1	...	...	...	...	...	...	...
25	4	3	...	1(f)	...	62	63	...	...	(p)	...	...	...	1	...	...	...	...	...	...	...	...	...	...	...	...
...	...	...	...	...	...	...	...	...	...	...	...	...	...	...	...	...	24	6	...	...	1	3	30	...	...	...
...	...	...	...	...	...	...	...	...	...	...	...	...	...	...	...	...	6	3	...	...	...	...	...	...	...	...

(*l*) This number includes 24 for mules, and 4 for spare mules.
(*m*) Gunners as drivers for pack mules.
(*n*) Includes 4 signallers.
(*p*) The P.S. allotted to the Mountain Artillery Brigade includes this unit.
(*q*) Composed as follows (including horse-holders):—Detachment, 52; signallers, 4; orderlies, 2; and spare, 10 per cent.
(*r*) Two men, one an acting bombardier, trained to the duties are placed under the orders of the medical officer. The gunner drives the cart for medical equipment.
(*s*) Signallers 3; range-takers 3; patrol 3.
(*t*) Includes Ammunition Column.
(*u*) The heavy artillery of the East and West Lancashire Divisions and of the 1st and 2nd London Divisions will have 1 lieut.-colonel, 1 adjutant, and 1 acting serjeant-major, to the two batteries and ammunition columns as a temporary measure.

ROYAL GARRISON ARTILLERY.

COAST DEFENCE UNITS.

	Major.	Captain.	Lieutenants and 2nd Lieutenants.	Total Officers.	Battery-Serjeant-Major.	Company-Serjeant-Major.	Battery-Quarter-Master-Serjeant.	Farrier-Serjeant.	Serjeants.	Trumpeters.	Corporals.	Bombardiers.	Shoeing-Smith.	Saddler.	Fitter or Wheeler	Gunners.	Drivers. For Vehicles.	Drivers. Spare.	Total other Ranks.	Total all Ranks.	Permanent Staff.	Guns.	G.S. Wagons for Ammunition.	Total Horses. Officers.	Total Horses. Riding.	Total Horses. Draught.
Half Company (Hebrides)	...	...	*1*	*1*	...	...	...	...	*4(b)*	...	...	...	...	...	...	*41(b)*	...	...	*45*	*46*	(*See* opposite page)	...	...	...	...	...
Garrison Company	...	1	2	3	...	1	...	...	3	2	4	2	...	...	...	65	...	...	77	80		...	...	...	...	...
Heavy Battery	1	1	3	5	1	...	1	1	6	2	8	4	1	1	1	65	24	10	125	130		...	...	...	...	...
Horses allowed for annual training ...	*1*	*1*	*3*	...	*1*	...	*1*	*1*	...	*2*	...	*1 (a)*	...	...	...	...	...	...	...	...		*32*	*16*	*5*	*6(a)*	*48*
Guns and vehicles allowed for annual training	...	...	...	...	...	...	...	...	...	...	...	...	...	...	...	...	...	...	...	...		*4*	*4*	...	...	...

(a) Includes 1 horse for orderly.
(b) Provides 4 sections, each consisting of 1 serjeant and 10 gunners. Also includes 1 bâtman.
(d) For Field Officers *see* next page.

Note.—An exact scale of medical personnel attached cannot be fixed. Approximate numbers have been shown for each District. Arrangements will be made according to local requirements.

ROYAL GARRISON ARTILLERY.

COAST DEFENCE UNITS
(Provisional).

Units.	Allotment.	Companies.	Heavy Batteries.	Officers extra to Company and Battery Establishment. Lieutenant-Colonel.	Major.	Permanent Staff. Adjutant.	*Serjeant-Instructors.
Orkney	Orkneys	7	...	1	2	1	2
North Scottish ...	Hebrides...	½	...	1	3	1	1
	Cromarty	1	...				1
	Aberdeen	2	...				1
	Tay	2	...				1
	Forth	2	...				1
Forth and Clyde ...	Edinburgh	4	...	1	2	1	2
		1	...				1
	Clyde	1	...				1
		2	...				1
Lancashire and Cheshire	Mersey	3	...	1	3	1	1
	,, ...	2	...				1
	Barrow	2	...				1
Glamorgan and Pembroke	Milford	4	...	2	3	2	2
	,, ...	4	...				2
	Swansea	1	...				1
	Cardiff and Barry ...	4	...				2
Tynemouth	Tyne	6	...	1	2	1	2
Durham	Sunderland	2	...	1	2	1	1
	,, ...	...	1				1
	Tees and Hartlepool ...	4	...				2
East Riding	Humber	4	...	...	1	1	2
Hants	Portsmouth	...	1	1	1	1	1
	,, ...	7	...				2
Dorset	Portland	3	...	...	1		1
Devon	Plymouth	...	2	1	1		2
	,, ...	4	...				2
Cornwall	Falmouth	5	...	1	1	1	2
	,, ...	...	2				2
Essex and Suffolk ...	Harwich	3	...	1	3	1	1
	,, ...	2	...				1
	Thames and Medway...	3	...				1
Sussex and Kent ...	Dover	5	...	1	2	1	2
	Newhaven	3	...				1
	Thames and Medway...	2	...				1
	Total	95½	6	13	27	14	49

* Acting Serjeant-Majors from within the numbers of Permanent Staff shown on this page will be allowed as follows :—

2 for Glamorgan and Pembroke R.G.A. ;

1 for all other groups, except Orkneys, Tynemouth, East Riding, and Dorset R.G.A.

ROYAL

FIELD

Units.		Majors.	Captains.	Lieutenants and 2nd Lieutenants.	Total Officers.	Company Serjeant-Major.	Company Quarter-Master Serjeant.	Serjeants.	Trumpeters and Buglers.	Corporals.	2nd Corporals.	Shoeing and Carriage-smith.	Sappers.
Field Company	M	1	1	4	6	...	1	1	1	1	1	1	...
	D	...	...	...	...	1	...	5	1	6	6	...	138(*i*)
Horses allowed for annual training ...		*1*	*1*	*4*	...	...	*1*	*1*	*1*	*1*	*1*	*1*	...
Vehicles " "		...	...	...	...	...	...	...	...	...	...	...	...
Divisional Telegraph Company ...	M	...	1	1	2	...	...	1	...	1	1	...	..
	D	...	...	...	...	...	...	...	...	...	1	...	21
Horses allowed for annual training ...		...	*1*	*1*	...	...	...	*1*	...	*1*	*1*	...	*4*
Vehicles " "		...	...	...	...	...	...	...	...	...	...	...	...

(*a*) The P.S. is that allowed for each group of 2 Field Companies and 1 Divisional Telegraph Company. The Officer doing duty as Adjutant to each divisional group of 2 Field Companies and 1 Divisional Telegraph Company is also adjutant of the Headquarters of Divisional Engineers.

(*b*) Does not include the horse for the adjutant (shown under P.S.).

(*c*) For the N.C.O's. (P.S.) shown under (*a*).

(*d*) Carrying 2 pontoons capable of constructing 15 yards of medium bridge.

ENGINEERS.

UNITS.

Drivers.							Permanent Staff.			Attached.		Vehicles.						Total Horses, including P.S. and Attached.			
												Wagons.									
For Vehicles.	For Spare Draught Horses.	For Pack Animals.	Spare.	Batmen.	Total Other Ranks.	Total All Ranks.	Adjutant.	Acting Serjeant Major.	Serjeant Instructors.	R.A.M.C. for Water Duties.	A.S.C. Drivers.	Cable.	Pontoon.	Trestle.	For Equipment, Balloons, &c.	Light Spring.	Carts, Tool, Double, R.E.	Officers.	Riding.	Draught.	
25	3	4	3	12 (h)	53	59	...	...	...	...	1	...	...	...	...	...	...	..	...	...	M
...	...	...	...	...	157	157	...	...	...	2	...	...	...	...	...	...	...	...	...	...	D
...	...	2	...	...	...	...	...	...	...	...	...	...	*8*	*4*	*2*	..	*8*	6(b)	*8*	*22*	
...	...	...	...	...	...	...	...	...	...	...	...	...	2(d)	*1* (e)	*1*	...	*4*	...	...	...	
							1(a)	1(a)	4(a)	...	...	...	...	...	...	...	...	...	3 (c)	...	
7	1	...	1	4 (h)	16	18	...	...	...	...	...	...	...	...	...	...	...	...	...	...	M
...	...	...	...	...	22	22	...	...	...	2	...	...	...	...	...	...	...	...	...	...	D
...	...	*1*	...	...	...	...	...	...	...	...	...	*8*	...	...	...	*4*	...	2(b)	*8*	*12*	
...	...	...	...	...	...	...	...	...	...	...	...	2(f)	...	...	...	2(g)	...	...	...	...	

(e) Carrying 2 trestles and 1 bay of superstructure capable of constructing 5 yards of medium bridge.

(f) Each carrying 8 miles of cable; 2 extra miles are carried in each of the light spring wagons.

(g) Pending issue of these vehicles forage carts will be utilised.

(h) Fully armed and trained soldiers, and available for duty in the ranks

(i) Of suitable trades.

Field

Units		Lieutenant-Colonel.	Majors.	Captains.	Lieutenants and 2nd Lieutenants.	Total Officers.	Company Serjeant-Major.	Company Quarter-Master-Serjeant.	Military Mechanists.	Farrier Serjeant.	Serjeants.	Trumpeters and Buglers.	Corporals.	Shoeing and Carriage-smith Corporals.	2nd Corporals.	Shoeing and Carriage-smiths.
Wireless Telegraph Company ...	M	1 (a)	...	1	2	4	...	...	...	...	1	...	1	...	1	...
	D	...	...	...	...	...	1	1	2	...	2	...	2	...	2	...
Horses allowed for annual training ...		*1*	...	*1*	*2*	...	...	...	...	...	*1*	...	*1*	...	*1*	...
Vehicles „ „ ...		...	...	...	...	...	...	...	...	...	...	...	...	...	...	...
Cable Telegraph Company ...	M	(a)	1	1	4	6	1	...	...	...	4	2	3	2	3	2
	D	...	...	...	...	...	...	1	...	...	...	...	3	...	4	...
Horses allowed for annual training ...		...	*1*	*1*	*4*	...	*1*	...	...	...	*2*	*1*	*2*	*1*	*2*	...
Vehicles „ „ ...		...	...	...	...	...	...	...	...	...	...	...	...	...	...	...
Air-Line Telegraph Company ...	M	(a)	1	2	4	7	1	...	...	1	6	2	4	1	4	4
	D	...	...	...	...	...	...	1	...	...	6	...	6	...	6	...
Horses allowed for annual training ...		...	*1*	*2*	*4*	...	*1*	...	...	*1*	*4*	*2*	*2*	...	*2*	...
Vehicles „ „ ...		...	...	...	...	...	...	...	...	...	...	...	...	...	...	...

(a) This officer commands the group of 3 companies (1 wireless, 1 cable, and 1 air-line). He will not be required in that capacity on mobilization.
(b) Fully armed and trained soldiers, and available for duty in the ranks.
(c) The P.S. is that allowed for each group of 3 companies (1 wireless, 1 cable, and 1 air-line), when units are not located together.
(d) For the N.C.Os. (P.S.) shown under (c).
(e) Does not include the horse for the adjutant shown under (c).

Units, R.E.—*continued.*

Sappers.	Drivers. For Vehicles.	Drivers. For Spare Draught Horses.	Drivers. Spare.	Batmen.	Total Other Ranks.	Total All Ranks.	Permanent Staff. Adjutant.	Permanent Staff. Acting Serjeant Major.	Permanent Staff. Serjeant Instructors.	Attached. R.A.M.C. for Water Duties.	Attached. A.S.C. Drivers.	Vehicles. Cable.	Vehicles. Wagons. Light Spring.	Vehicles. Wagons. Special.	Vehicles. Wagons. Air Line.	Total Horses, including P.S. and Attached. Officers.	Total Horses, including P.S. and Attached. Riding.	Total Horses, including P.S. and Attached. Draught.	
...	17	2	2	6(*b*)	30	34	...	...	...	...	1	...	...	...	...	...	...	...	M
26	...	...	...	...	36	36	...	...	...	2	...	...	...	...	...	...	...	...	D
...	...	*1*	...	...	...	...	...	...	...	...	...	...	*4*	*8*	...	*4* (*e*), (*i*)	*4*(*i*)	12 (*i*)	
...	...	...	...	...	...	...	...	...	...	...	...	...	*2*(*f*)	*2*	...	...	...	...	
...	27	3	3	12(*b*)	62	68	1 (*c*)	1(*c*)	5(*c*)	...	1	...	...	...	...	...	3 (*d*)	...	M
80	...	...	...	...	88	88	...	...	...	2	...	...	...	...	...	...	...	...	D
8	...	2	...	...	...	...	...	...	...	...	...	*16*	8	...	...	6 (*e*), (*k*)	*19*(*k*)	*24*(*k*)	
...	...	...	...	...	...	...	...	...	...	...	...	*1*(*g*)	*4*(*f*)	...	...	...	...	...	
...	66	7	7	14(*b*)	117	124	...	...	...	...	1	...	...	...	...	...	...	...	M
146	...	...	...	...	165	165	...	...	...	2	...	...	...	...	...	...	...	...	D
...	...	...	...	...	...	...	...	...	...	...	...	...	*4*	...	*40*	7 (*e*), (*k*)	*12*(*k*)	*44*(*k*)	
...	...	...	...	...	...	...	...	...	...	...	...	...	*2*(*f*)	...	*8*(*h*)	...	...	...	

(*f*) Pending issue of these vehicles forage carts will be utilised.
(*g*) Each wagon carries 8 miles of cable ; 2 additional miles are carried in each of the light spring wagons.
(*h*) 4 air-line wagons have 6 horses each, and 4 have 4 horses each. Each air-line wagon carries 5 miles of air-line material.
(*i*) Provides for 2 stations.
(*k*) Provides for 4 detachments.

Field

Units.		Lieutenant-Colonel.	Major.	Captains.	Lieutenants and 2nd Lieutenants.	Quarter-Master.	Total Officers.	Quarter-Master Serjeant.	Company Serjeant-Majors.	Company Quarter-Master-Serjeant.	Orderly-Room Serjeant.	Acting Armourer-Serjeant.	Serjeant Bugler.	Serjeants.*	Trumpeters and Buglers.	Corporals.	2nd Corporals.	Shoeing and Carriage-smith.
Balloon Company	M	...	...	1	2	...	3	...	...	...	...	...	...	1	...	1	...	1
	D	...	...	...	...	...	...	...	1	...	...	...	...	1	1	3	3	...
Horses allowed for annual training		...	...	*1*	2	...	...	...	...	...	...	...	...	*1*	...	*1*	...	...
Vehicles ,, ,, ...		...	...	...	...	...	...	...	...	...	...	...	...	...	...	...	...	...
Railway Battalion		1	1	6	9	1	18	1	6	...	1	1	1	25	12	24	24	...
Horses allowed for annual training		*1*	*1*	...	...	...	...	...	...	...	...	...	...	...	...	...	...	...
Vehicles ,, ,, ...		...	...	...	...	...	...	...	...	...	...	...	...	...	...	...	...	...

(*a*) Fully armed and trained soldiers, and available for duty in the ranks.
(*b*) One 4-horse for balloon, and one 2-horse for equipment, &c.
(*c*) Does not include the horse for the Adjutant.
* Includes 1 serjeant cook.

Units, R.E.—*continued.*

	Drivers.							Permanent Staff.			Attached.			Vehicles. Wagons.		Total Horses, including P.S. and Attached.			
Sappers.	For Vehicles.	For Spare Draught Horses.	For Pack Animals.	Spare.	Batmen.	Total Other Ranks.	Total All Ranks.	Adjutant.	Acting Serjeant Major.	Serjeant Instructors.	Medical Officer.	R.A.M.C. for Water Duties.	A.S.C. Drivers.	G.S. for Equipment, Balloons, &c.	Gas Reservoir.	Officers.	Riding.	Draught.	
...	20	2	...	2	6 (*a*)	33	36	...	...	1	...	...	1	...	...	...	...	...	M
22	...	...	...	...	...	31	31	...	...	1	...	2	...	...	...	...	...	...	D
...	...	...	*1*	...	...	...	...	...	...	*1*	...	...	...	*6*	*12*	*3*	*4*	*18*	...
...	...	...	...	...	...	...	...	...	...	...	...	...	...	*2*(*b*)	*3*	...	...	...	...
419	...	...	...	...	...	514	532 (*d*)	1	1	2 (*e*)	1	...	...	...	...	...	...	...	...
...	...	...	...	...	...	...	...	...	...	...	...	...	...	*4*	...	*2* (*c*)	...	*4*	...
...	...	...	...	...	...	...	...	...	...	...	...	...	...	*2*	...	...	...	...	...

(*d*) 60 per cent. of these numbers will be Special Reservists.

(*e*) If the total numbers of the Railway Battalion including Special Reservists, exceeds 600 an additional Instructor will be allowed.

ROYAL ENGINEERS

Unit.	Defended Port.	No. of Cos. Works.	No. of Cos. Electric Lights.	Majors.	Captains.	Lieutenants and 2nd Lieutenants.
City of Aberdeen (Fortress) Royal Engineers ...	Aberdeen ...	1(*a*)	...	...	1	2
City of Dundee (Fortress) Royal Engineers ...	Tay	1(*b*)	...	...	1	2
City of Edinburgh (Fortress) Royal Engineers ...	Forth	1 ...	... 1	1	1 1	2 2
Lanarkshire (Fortress) Royal Engineers ... ... Renfrewshire (Fortress) Royal Engineers ...	Clyde...	1 ...	... 1	1	1 1	2 2
Lancashire (Fortress) Royal Engineers	Mersey and Barrow	1 ...	... 3(*d*)	1	1 3	2 7
Glamorganshire (Fortress) Royal Engineers ...	Milford Haven Cardiff and Barry	1 ... 1(*c*)	... 1 ...	1	1 1 1	2 3 2
Northumberland (Fortress) Royal Engineers ...	Tyne ...	3 ...	... 1	1	3 1	6 2
North Riding (Fortress) Royal Engineers ...	Tees	...	1	...	1	1
East Riding (Fortress) Royal Engineers	Humber	1 ...	... 1	1	1 1	2 1
Hampshire (Fortress) Royal Engineers	Portsmouth	3 ...	... 4	*1	6	6 8
Wiltshire (Fortress) Royal Engineers ... ... Dorsetshire (Fortress) Royal Engineers	Portland	1 ...	... 1	1	1 1	2 3
Devonshire (Fortress) Royal Engineers	Plymouth	3 ...	... 2	1	3 2†	6 4
Cornwall (Fortress) Royal Engineers	Falmouth	2 ...	... 1	1	2 1	4 1
Essex (Fortress) Royal Engineers	Harwich ...	...	1	...	1	2
Kent (Fortress) Royal Engineers	Thames and Medway	3 ...	... 2	1	3 2	6 4
Sussex (Fortress) Royal Engineers... ... ... Kent (Fortress) Royal Engineers	Dover...	1 ...	... 1	1	1 1	2 2

* There is in addition 1 Lieut.-Colonel.
† Three Reserve officers will be added on mobilization.
‡ The Coast Battalion officer will carry out the duties of Adjutant.
(*a*) Includes 9 N.C.Os. and men for Telephones.
(*b*) Includes 15 N.C.Os. and men for Telephones.
(*c*) Includes 21 N.C.Os. and men for Telephones.

FOR DEFENDED PORTS.

Quarter-Masters.	Total Officers.	Quarter-Master-Serjeants.	Company-Serjeant-Majors.	Serjeants.	Corporals.	2nd Corporals.	Buglers.	Sappers.	Total, Other Ranks.	Total, All Ranks.	Permanent Staff. Adjutants.	Permanent Staff. Acting-Serjeant-Majors.	Permanent Staff. Other Serjeant-Instructors.	Medical Personnel attached (e).
...	3	...	1	4	6	6	2	87	106	109	...	...	1	
...	3	...	1	5	6	6	2	92	112	115	...	...	1	
...	7	...	1	4	5	5	2	80	97	204	‡...	...	1	
...		...	1	5	7	7	2	78	100				1	
...	7	...	1	4	5	5	2	80	97	204	‡...	...	1	
...		...	1	5	7	7	2	78	100				1	
...	14	...	1	4	5	5	2	80	97	444	‡...	...	1	
...		1	3	15	25	25	6	258	333				1	
...	11	...	1	4	5	5	2	80	97	348	‡...	...	1	
...		...	1	6	9	9	2	95	122				1	
...		...	1	5	7	7	2	96	118		...	...	1	
1	14	1	3	12	15	15	6	239	291	393	‡...	...	2	
...		...	1	4	6	6	2	69	88				1	
...	2	...	1	2	4	4	2	40	53	55	‡...	...	...	
...	6	...	1	4	5	5	2	80	97	156	‡...	...	1	
...		...	1	2	4	4	2	40	53				1	
1	24	1	3	12	15	15	6	239	291	705	1	1	3	
1		1	4	17	30	30	8	300	390					
...	8	...	1	4	5	5	2	80	97	237	‡...	...	1	
...		...	1	6	10	10	2	103	132				1	
1	17	1	3	12	15	15	6	239	291	521	1	...	2	
...		...	2	10	16	16	4	165	213				1	
...	9	...	2	8	10	10	4	160	194	267	‡...	...	1	
...		...	1	3	5	5	2	48	64				...	
...	3	...	1	4	6	6	2	60	79	82	...	...	1	
1	17	1	3	12	15	15	6	239	291	539	1	...	2	
...		...	2	11	17	17	4	180	231				1	
...	7	...	1	4	5	5	2	80	97	215	...	...	1	
...		...	1	5		8	2	87	111				1	

(*d*) The establishment for Electric Lights at the Mersey includes the following :—

	Officers.		Other ranks.
For Liverpool (1 Company) ...	3	...	90
For Cork (1 Company) ...	3	...	108
For Berehaven (1 Company) ...	3	...	85
For Lough Swilly (Detach.) ...	1	...	50 (To form part of Berehaven Company
Total	10		333

(*e*) An exact scale cannot be fixed. Approximate numbers have been shown for each District. Arrangements will be made according to local requirements.

ESTABLISHMENTS OF ELECTRICAL ENGINEERS TO BE

	No. of Cos.									
	Works.	Electric Lights.	Majors.	Captains.	Lieutenants and 2nd Lieutenants.	Quarter-Masters.	Total Officers.	Quarter-Master-Serjeants.	Company-Serjeant-Majors.	Serjeants.
Tyne Division for :—										
Humber	...	...	...	1	1	...	2	...	1	2
Portsmouth	...	...	1	4	10	...	15	...	4	15
Total	...	...	1	5	11	...	17	...	5	17
London Division for :—										
Portland	...	...	...	1	2	...	3	...	1	6
Plymouth	...	...	1	2	6	...	9	...	2	7
Falmouth	...	...	...	1	1	...	2	...	1	2
Harwich	...	...	...	1	1	...	2	...	1	2
Thames and Medway ...	...	...	1	2	2	...	5	...	2	8
Dover	...	...	...	1	2	...	3	...	1	5
Total	...	...	2	8	14	...	24	...	8	30

RETAINED PENDING THE RAISING OF LOCAL UNITS.

Corporals.	2nd Corporals.	Buglers.	Sappers.	Total, Other Ranks.	Total, All Ranks.	Permanent Staff. Adjutants.	Permanent Staff. Acting-Serjeant-Majors.	Permanent Staff. Other Serjeant-Instructors.	Medical Personnel attached. (a).	
2	*2*	*1*	*27*	*35*	*37*	...	...	...	...	
15	*15*	*8*	*207*	*264*	*279*	...	...	...	...	
17	*17*	*9*	*234*	*299*	*316*	...	...	...	...	*Also 1 Lieut.-Colonel and 1 Quartermaster-Serjeant.*
8	*8*	*2*	*74*	*99*	*102*	...	...	...	...	
8	*8*	*3*	*80*	*108*	*117*	...	...	...	...	
3	*3*	*2*	*29*	*40*	*42*	...	...	...	...	
3	*3*	*2*	*29*	*40*	*42*	...	...	...	...	
10	*10*	*4*	*95*	*129*	*134*	...	...	...	...	
6	*6*	*2*	*52*	*72*	*75*	...	...	...	...	
38	*38*	*15*	*359*	*488*	*512*	*1*	*1*	*4*	...	*Also 1 Lieut.-Colonel, 1 Quartermaster, 1 Acting Chaplain, 1 Quarter-master-Serjeant, 1 Acting Armourer Staff-Serjeant, and 1 Orderly-Room Serjeant.*

(*a*) An exact scale cannot be fixed. Approximate numbers have been shown for each District Arrangements will be made according to local requirements.

INFAN

—	Lieutenant-Colonel.	Majors.	Captains.	Lieutenants and 2nd Lieutenants.	Quarter-Master.	Total Officers.	Serjeant-Major.	Quarter-Master-Serjeant.	Serjeant-Drummers.	Cook-Serjeant.	Pioneer-Serjeant.	Shoemaker-Serjeant.	Armourer-Serjeant.	Colour-Serjeants.	Serjeants.	Orderly-Room Clerks.
Company	...	...	1	2	...	3	...	...	...	...	...	...	...	1	4	...
Machine-Gun Section... ...	...	...	...	(a)	...	(a)	...	...	...	...	...	...	...	...	1	...
Battalion	1	2	8	16(a)	1	29(b)	...(c)	1	1	1	1	1	1	8	35(d)	1(g)
Horses allowed for annual training...	*1*	2	...	...	...	...	...	...	...	...	...	...	...	...	*1*(e)	...
Guns and vehicles allowed for annual training	...	...	...	...	...	...	...	...	...	...	...	...	...	...	...	...

(*a*) 1 subaltern will act as machine-gun officer, 1 as signalling officer, and 1 as transport officer.

(*b*) The adjutant (shown under P.S.) forms part of the normal establishment of the unit, and is included in these totals.

(*c*) The acting serjeant-major of the P.S. will be left at the depôt on mobilization and replaced by the promotion of a colour-serjeant. An extra private is included in the establishment for this purpose.

(*d*) Includes 1 for machine-gun section, 1 for signalling, and 1 for transport.

(*e*) Includes 1 for machine-gun section, and 1 for signalling.

(*f*) Includes 31 signallers, 10 pioneers, 16 stretcher-bearers (bandsmen), 12 for machine-gun section.

(*g*) One a lance corporal. Trained to the duties and placed under the orders of the medical officer.

[INFAN]TRY.

Drummers and Buglers.	Corporals.	Privates.				Total other Ranks.	Total all Ranks.	Permanent Staff.		Attached.			Machine Gun.	2nd Line Regimental Transport Wagons.	Total Horses, including P.S. and attached.		
		Privates.	Drivers (1st Line Transport).	Orderlies for Medical Officer.	Batmen.			Adjutant.	Serjeant-Instructors.	Medical Officers.	R.A.M.C. for Water Duties.	Drivers A.S.C. 2nd Line Transport.			Officers.	Riding.	Draught.
2	5	100 (*p*)	2	...	3(*h*)	117	120	...	...	...	...	...	...	...	...	...	...
...	1	12	2	...	...	16	16	...	...	...	...	...	...	...	...	...	...
16	42(*e*)	812(*f*)	28	2(*g*)	30(*h*)	980(*i*)	1,009(*b*)	1	3(*k*)	2(*o*)	5(*l*)	6	...	...	...	...	...
...	...	...	...	...	...	...	...	...	...	1	...	...	2	4	4(*m*)	1(*n*)	6
...	...	...	...	...	...	...	...	...	...	...	...	...	1	2	...	...	...

(*h*) Fully armed and trained soldiers, and available for duty in the ranks.
(*i*) Battalions with pipes will have 1 serjeant-piper and 5 pipers in addition.
(*k*) Left at the depôt on mobilization.
(*l*) Includes a corporal.
(*m*) Does not include the adjutant.
(*n*) For transport serjeant.
(*o*) Two medical officers are included to ensure that there shall always be one present at training; only one will be trained with the unit in any year.
(*p*) Includes 1 pioneer, 4 signallers, and 2 stretcher-bearers. In two of the companies there are 2 pioneers; and in one company one of the signallers is a corporal.
(*q*) Serjeant or corporal, according to service. If a corporal, the total serjeants will be [re]duced and the corporals increased accordingly.

A CYCLIST

	Lieutenant-Colonel.	Major.	Captains.	Lieutenants and 2nd Lieutenants.	Quarter-Master.	Total Officers.	Acting-Serjeant-Major.	Quartermaster-Serjeant.	Serjeant-Bugler.	Cook-Serjeant.	Signalling Serjeant.
Company	...	...	1	1	...	2	...	...	...	...	...
Machine-Gun Section	...	...	...	1	...	1	...	...	...	...	...
Battalion :—											
Headquarters	1	1	...	...	1	4(c)	1	1	1	1	
8 Companies (including Machine-gun Section)...	...	...	8	9	...	17	...	...	...	...	...
Motor vehicles and bicycles allowed for annual training	...	...	...	...	...	...	...	...	...	...	...

(*a*) Includes 4 signallers.
(*b*) Fully armed and trained soldiers.
(*c*) The Adjutant (shown under P.S.) forms part of the normal establishment of the unit, and is included in these totals.
(*d*) May be serjeant or corporal.

BATTALION.

Transport Serjeant.	Colour-Serjeants.	Serjeants.	Orderly-Room Clerk.	Buglers.	Corporals.	Artificers.	Privates. Privates.	Privates. Drivers.	Privates. Orderlies for Medical Officer.	Privates. Batmen.	Total Other Ranks.	Total All Ranks.	Permanent Staff. Adjutant.	Permanent Staff. Serjeant-Instructors.	Attached. Medical Officers.	Attached. R.A.M.C. for Water Duties.	Motor Vehicles for Baggage, etc.	Bicycles.
...	1	3	...	1	4	...	45(a)	2(b)	...	2(f)	58	60	...	...	...	...	...	...
...	...	1	...	...	1	...	12	4(b)	...	1(f)	19	20	...	...	...	...	...	...
1	...	...	1(d)	...	...	3	...	2(b)	2(e)	5(f)	19	23(c)	1(c)	...	2(h)	4(g)	...	...
...	8	25	...	8	33	...	372	20	...	17	483	500	...	2	...	...	...	...
...	...	...	...	...	...	...	...	...	...	...	...	...	...	...	...	...	2	504

(*e*) Two men (one a lance-corporal) trained to the duties and placed under the orders of the medical officer.

(*f*) Fully armed and trained soldiers, and are available for duty in the ranks.

(*g*) Includes one corporal.

(*h*) Two medical officers are included to ensure that there shall always be one present at training; only one will be trained with the unit in any year.

OFFICERS TRAINING UNIT.

—	Commandant.	Captain.	Lieutenants.	Adjutant and Quartermaster.	Total Officers.	Company Serjeant-Majors.	Company Quartermaster-Serjeants.	Serjeants.	Drummers and Buglers.	Corporals.	Clerks.	Privates.	Total other ranks.	Total all ranks.
Headquarters	1*(b)	...	...	1(a)	2	...	...	...	...	...	2(e)	...	2	4
Company	...	1*(c)	4*(d)	...	5	1	1	4	2	6	...	86	100	105
Four companies	...	4	16	...	20	4	4	16	8	24	...	344	400	420
Total for unit	1	4	16	1	22	4	4	16	8	24	2	344	402	424

(a) Captain or Lieutenant; Regular or ex-regular.
(b) Lieutenant-Colonel or Major.
(c) Company Commander.
(d) Captains and Lieutenants.
(e) Regular or Territorial soldiers.
* The number of these to be found from ex-regular officers is under consideration.

Permanent Staff		2 Serjeant Instructors.
Horses for annual training...	4	1 for Commandant. 1 ,, Adjutant and Quartermaster. 2 ,, 1 G.S. wagon.
Vehicles...		1 G.S. wagon.

POST OFFICE STAFF CORPS.

	1 Major
	8 Captains
	14 Subalterns
Total	23

ARMY SER

Units.	Colonel or Lieutenant-Colonel.	Majors.	Captains.	Lieutenants and 2nd Lieutenants.	Total Officers.	Staff-Serjeant-Majors.	Company-Serjeant-Majors.	Staff-Quarter-Master-Serjeant.	Company-Quarter-Master-Serjeant.	Staff-Serjeants.	Serjeants.	Corporals.	2nd Corporals.	Wheelers. Staff-Serjeants.	Wheelers. Corporals.	Wheelers. Drivers.
DIVISIONAL TRANSPORT AND SUPPLY COLUMN—																
Headquarters—																
Transport	1(*a*)	...	...	...	2(*k*)	...	...	...	...	...	...	...	...	...	...	...
Supply	...	1(*b*)	...	...	1	...	...	...	...	...	...	...	...	...	...	...
No. 1 Company—																
Headquarters of Company ...	...	1	1	2	4	2*	1*	...	1*	...	4*	3	3	1	2	4
Personnel detached for 2nd Line Transport (*c*)	...	...	...	...	...	...	...	...	...	...	...	1	...	...	...	...
Supply details attached	...	...	1	...	1	1	...	1	...	1	1	2	3	...	...	...
No. 2, 3, 4 Companies—																
Headquarters of Company ...	...	...	1	2	3	2*	1*	...	1*	...	*	2	3	1	1	2
Personnel detached for 2nd Line Transport (*d*)	...	...	...	...	...	...	...	...	...	...	...	1	...	...	...	...
Supply details attached	...	...	1	...	1	...	...	1	...	1	2	2	1	...	...	...
Total—																
Transport	1	1	4	8	15(*k*)	8	4	...	4	...	7	13	12	4	5	10
Supply	...	1(*b*)	4	...	5	1	...	4	...	4	7	8	6	...	...	...
Horses allowed for annual training	...	...	...	...	...	...	...	...	...	...	...	...	...	...	...	...
Vehicles allowed for annual training	...	...	...	...	...	...	...	...	...	...	...	...	...	...	...	...
MOUNTED BRIGADE, TRANSPORT AND SUPPLY COLUMN—																
Headquarters of Company	...	...	1	2	3	2*	1*	...	1*	...	2*	3	3	1	1	2
Personnel detached from company for 2nd Line Transport (*n*)	...	...	...	...	...	...	...	...	...	...	...	...	...	...	...	...
Supply details attached	...	...	1	...	1	...	...	1	...	1	1	2	1	...	...	...
Horses allowed for annual training ...	...	...	...	...	...	...	...	...	...	...	...	...	...	...	...	...
Vehicles allowed for annual training ...	...	...	...	...	...	...	...	...	...	...	...	...	...	...	...	...

(*a*) C.O. of column and senior transport officer of the division.
(*b*) Senior supply officer of the division.
(*c*) Detailed as follows :—

Headquarters of division...	1 corporal, 3 drivers.
1 Yeomanry Regiment	7 drivers.
Headquarters of division of Artillery... ...	1 ,,
3 Field Artillery brigades	45 ,,
1 ,, (howitzer) brigade	11 ,,
1 Heavy Artillery battery and A.C.	4 ,,
Headquarters divisional Engineers	1 ,,
2 Field companies	2 ,,

(*d*) Detailed as follows :—

Headquarters of Infantry brigade	1 corporal, 2 drivers.
1 Field ambulance (A.S.C. drivers for wagons only—1 per section)	3 drivers.
4 Infantry battalions	24 ,,

(*g**) All officers and these ranks (except one of the farrier-corporals with No. 1 company) will be mounted.

VICE CORPS.

Saddlers.			Farriers.							Permanent Staff.		Attached.				Vehicles.			Horses including P.S. and attached.				
Staff-Serjeants.	Corporals.	Drivers.	Staff-Serjeants.	Corporals.	Shoeing and Carriage-Smiths.	Trumpeters.	Drivers and Privates.	Total other Ranks.	Total all Ranks.	Adjutant.	Serjeant-Instructors.	Medical Officer.	R.A.M.C. for Water Duties.	Veterinary Officer.	Ordnance Officer.	Cars and Wagons (one horse).	Water-carts.	Pair-horse Wagons or Vans.	For Officers.	For N.C.O.'s.	Draught.	Spare Draught.	Total.
...	...	...	...	...	...	...	...	...	2(k)	1	2(l)	2(q)	4(p)	1	1	...	...	...	...	...	...	...	...
...	...	...	...	...	...	...	...	...	1										...	...	...	...	...
1*	2	3	1*	2*	5	1*	72	108	112	...	...	...	...	...	...	...	...	...	...	...	...	...	...
...	...	...	...	...	...	...	74	75	75	...	...	...	...	...	...	...	...	...	...	...	...	...	...
...	...	...	...	...	...	...	9	18	19	...	...	...	...	...	...	...	...	...	...	...	...	...	...
1	1	...	1*	1*	1	1*	35	55	58	...	...	...	...	...	...	...	...	...	...	...	...	...	...
...	...	...	...	...	...	...	29	30	30	...	...	...	...	...	...	...	...	...	...	...	...	...	...
...	...	...	...	...	...	...	5	12	13	...	...	...	...	...	...	...	...	...	...	...	...	...	...
4	5	3	4	5	8	4	338	438	453(k)	1	2	2	4(p)	1	1	...	...	...	...	...	...	...	...
...	...	...	...	...	...	...	24	54	59										...	...	...	...	...
...	...	...	...	...	...	...	...	...	...	...	...	...	...	...	...	*4*	...	*68*	*42*		*72*	...	*114*
...	...	...	...	...	...	...	...	...	...	...	...	...	...	...	...	*4*	...	*34*	...	...	...	...	...
1	1	1	1*	1	1	1*	43	66	69	...	1(m)	...	2	1	...	...	...	...	...	...	...	...	...
...	...	...	...	...	...	...	31	31	31	...	...	...	...	...	...	...	...	...	...	...	...	...	...
...	...	...	...	...	...	...	9	15	16	...	...	...	...	...	...	...	...	...	...	...	...	...	...
...	...	...	...	...	...	...	...	...	...	...	...	...	...	...	...	*1*	*1*	*18*			*20*	...	*28*
...	...	...	...	...	...	...	...	...	...	...	...	...	...	...	...	*1*	*1*	*9*	...	...	...	...	...

(*k*) The adjutant (shown under P.S.) forms part of the normal establishment of the divisional transport and supply column headquarters, and is therefore included in these totals.

(*l*) 1 staff-serjeant rough rider mounted duties, and 1 staff-serjeant supply for dismounted duties, accounting, &c.

(*m*) A Regular Warrant Officer.

(*n*) Detailed as follows:—

Headquarters of brigade	1 driver.
3 Yeomanry regiments...	21 drivers.
1 Horse Artillery Battery and A.C....	7 ,,
1 Mounted Brigade Field ambulance	2 ,,

NOTE.—2 G.S. wagons, 2 sets of G.S. harness, and 2 sets of packsaddlery will be maintained all the year round by each company for instructional work; the wagons are included in these figures.

(*p*) Includes a corporal.

(*q*) 2 medical officers are included in the establishment to ensure that there shall always be one present at training, but only one will be trained with the unit in any year; on mobilization only one will be called up with the unit.

THE ESTABLISHMENT OF THE FOLLOWING COMPANIES WILL BE INCREASED OR REDUCED BY THE NUMBER OF DRIVERS SHOWN FOR THE REASONS STATED:—

District.	A.S.C. Company.	2nd Line Driver.		Cause of Variation.
		Increase.	Decrease.	
1	Highland Mounted Brigade Transport and Supply Column	7	...	For Yeomanry Regiment (Inverness-shire) allotted to West Riding Division.
	Highland Divisional Headquarters Company	5	...	6 additional for substitution of Field Artillery Brigade by Mountain Artillery Brigade and Small-arm Section Ammunition Column less 1 for Field Company located in No. 2 District
	Seaforth and Cameron Company	30	...	For 5 Infantry Battalions in Renfrewshire (2), Stirlingshire, Argyllshire, and Dumbartonshire.
2	Lowland Divisional Headquarters Company...	4	...	For 1 Air-Line, 1 Wireless, 1 Cable Telegraph Company, and 1 for Field Company allotted to Highland Division.
	Highland Light Infantry Brigade Company	30	...	For 5 Infantry Battalions in Ayrshire (2), Dumfriesshire, Roxburghshire, and Lanarkshire.
	Lothian Brigade Company	12	...	For 2 Infantry Battalions in Peeblesshire and Midlothian.
3	East Lancashire Divisional Headquarters Company	7	...	For Yeomanry Regiment Cumberland, allotted to Welsh Division.
	North Lancashire Brigade Company	15	...	For 2 Infantry Battalions in Cumberland, and 1 Air Line, 1 Cable, and 1 Wireless Telegraph Company.
4	Welsh Divisional Headquarters Company ...	...	7	Drivers for Yeomanry Regiment located in Cumberland provided by East Lancashire Divisional Headquarters Company.
	South Wales Brigade Company...	30	...	For 5 Infantry Battalions in Shropshire, Herefordshire, Carmarthenshire, Brecknockshire, and Monmouthshire.
5	Northumbrian Divisional Headquarters Company	3	...	For 1 Air-Line, 1 Cable, and 1 Wireless Telegraph Company.
	West Riding Divisional Headquarters Company	...	7	Drivers for Yeomanry Regiment located in Inverness-shire provided by Highland Mounted Brigade Transport and Supply Column.
6	North Midland Divisional Headquarters Company	...	7	Drivers for Yeomanry Regiment located in Northamptonshire provided by East Anglian Divisional Headquarters Company.

7	South Midland Divisional Headquarters Company	...	4	3 additional for 1 Air-Line, 1 Cable and 1 Wireless Telegraph Company, less 7 for Yeomanry Regiment located in Hertfordshire provided by East Anglian Divisional Headquarters Company.
8	Hampshire Brigade Company	6	...	For Infantry Battalion in Hampshire.
	Devon and Cornwall Brigade Company ...	6	...	For Infantry Battalion in Devonshire.
9	East Anglian Divisional Headquarters Company	14	...	For 2 Yeomanry Regiments allotted to South Midland Division and North Midland Division.
10	Kent Brigade Company	12	...	For 2 Infantry Battalions in Sussex.
	South Eastern Mounted Brigade Transport and Supply Column	...	7	Drivers for Horse Artillery Battery and Mounted Brigade Ammunition Column located in London District, provided by London Mounted Brigade Transport and Supply Column.
London District	1st London Divisional Headquarters Company	4	...	For 1 Balloon Company, 1 Air-Line, 1 Cable, and 1 Wireless Telegraph Company.
	London Mounted Brigade Transport and Supply Column	10	...	For Horse Artillery Battery and Mounted Brigade Ammunition Column allotted to South Eastern Mounted Brigade, and for ½ Infantry Battalion.

Note.—The units for which 2nd line drivers are provided above, with the exception of the Yeomanry Regiments, Horse Artillery Batteries and Mounted Brigade Ammunition Columns and Field Companies, are allotted to Army troops.

ROYAL ARMY

Units.	Colonel.	Lieutenant-Colonels.	Majors.	Captains.	Subalterns.	Quarter-Master.	Total Officers.	Serjeant-Major.	Serjeants.* For Nursing Duties.	Stewards.	Compounders.	Supernumerary.	Clerks.	Corporals. Cooks.	Packstore Keepers.	Cler .
Mounted Brigade Field Ambulance (2 sections) (a)—																
Personnel—																
(i) Bearer Division ...	...	...	...	2		...	2	...	...	...	...	...	...		4	
(ii) Tent Division (50 patients)	...	1	1	2		...	4	1	2	2	2	1	...	2	2	2
(iii) Transport, &c. ...	...	...	...	...	...	...	(d)	...			2			...	...	...
Horses allowed for annual training	...	*1*	*1*	*4*		...	...	*1*	...	...	*2*	...	...	...	...	...
Vehicles allowed for annual training	...	...	...	...	...	...	...	...	...	...	...	...	...	...	...	...
Field Ambulance (3 sections) (b)—																
Personnel—																
(i) Bearer Division ...	...	...	...			...	3	...							3	
(ii) Tent Division (150 patients)	...	1	2	3		1	7	1	2	2	3	...	3	3	3	...
(iii) Transport, &c. ...	...	...	...	...	...	...	(d)	...			3			...	...	...
Horses allowed for annual training	...	*1*	*2*	*6*		*1*	...	*1*	...	...	*3*	...	...	...	...	...
Vehicles allowed for annual training	...	...	...	...	...	...	...	...	...	...	...	...	...	...	...	...
General Hospital (k)	1	...	1	...	...	1	3	2			13				8	
Sanitary Company	...	...	1	2	2	...	5	...			4				5	
Schools of Instruction... ...	...	...	...	...	...	...	...	...			...				...	

* Includes for a Mounted Brigade Field Ambulance 1 Quartermaster-Serjeant, 1 Staff-Serjeant.
" " Field Ambulance 1 Quartermaster-Serjeant, 2 Staff-Serjeants.
" " General Hospital 2 Quartermaster-Serjeants, 3 Staff-Serjeants.

(a) Each section to consist of one-half of the Bearer Division and one-half of the Tent Division.

(b) Each section to consist of one-third of the Bearer Division and one-third of the Tent Division, approximately.

(c) 1 Permanent Staff Serjeant Instructor for technical medical transport duties;
2 Permanent Staff Serjeant Instructors for corps instructional purposes.

(d) The drivers for the forage carts will be furnished by the A.S.C.

MEDICAL CORPS.

Buglers.	Privates. For Nursing Duties.	Privates. Cooks.	Privates. Washermen.	Privates. Supernumeraries.	Privates. Clerks.	Drivers. For Vehicles.	Drivers. For Spare Draught Horses.	Drivers. Spare.	Bâtmen.	Total, other Ranks.	Total, all Ranks.	A.S.C. Drivers attached.	Permanent Staff. Adjutant.	Permanent Staff. Serjeant-Instructors. (c)	Vehicles. Ambulance Wagons (4-horse), Heavy, Mark V* or VI.	Vehicles. Ambulance Wagons (2-horse), Mark V* or VI.	Vehicles. Ambulance Wagons (2-horse), Mark I, Light.	Vehicles. G.S. Wagons, for Baggage.	Vehicles. Forage Carts.	Total Horses. Officers'.	Total Horses. Riding.	Total Horses. Draught.
2	34					...	...	...	...	40	42				...	...	...	...	...	...	...	...
...	10	2	2	2	...	...	...	...	...	30	34	2	...	1	...	...	...	...	...	...	...	...
...	...	...	...	...	...	20	2	3	6	33	33				...	...	...	...	...	...	...	...
...	...	...	...	...	...	...	...	...	...	...	...	...	...	...	16	...	8	4	2	6	3	30
...	...	...	...	...	...	...	...	...	...	...	...	...	...	...	4(g)	...	4	2	2(d)	...	...	...
3	117					...	...	...	...	126	129				...	...	...	...	...	...	...	...
...	21	3	3	9	3	...	...	...	...	56	63	3	...	1	...	...	...	...	...	...	...	...
...	...	...	...	...	...	19	3	3	10	38	3				...	...	...	...	...	...	...	...
...	...	...	...	...	...	...	...	...	...	...	...	...	...	...	...	12	...	12	3	10	4	27
...	...	...	...	...	...	...	...	...	...	...	...	...	...	...	...	6(h)	...	6(e)	3	...	...	...
2	18					...	...	...	...	43	46	...	...	...	...	...	...	...	...	...	...	...
...	86					...	...	...	5	100	105	...	...	...	...	...	...	...	...	1	...	...
...	...					...	...	...	...	...	...	...	1	3(l)	...	...	...	...	...	...	...	...

(e) The drivers for three of these wagons will be furnished by the A.S.C.
(g) Four horses each for training.
(h) Two horses each for training.
(i) One of the officers of the Bearer Division will perform the duties of transport officer.
(k) Only those numbers are included which refer to officers and other ranks of the Territorial Force who are paid and trained as such.
(l) One of these may be an acting serjeant-major.

APPENDIX 4.—EXAMINATION

SUB-AP

SYLLABUS OF THE EXAMINATION

	Yeomanry.	Artillery. Horse, Field, Heavy and Mountain.	Artillery. Garrison. Coast Defence Companies.	Artillery. Garrison. Coast Defence Heavy Batteries.	Engineers.
(a) 2nd Lieutenants. (Before promotion to rank of Lieutenant and within two years of his first appointment.)	Certificate A.*	Certificate A for Artillery.*	Certificate A for Garrison Artillery.*		Certificate A.*
(b) Lieutenants. (Before promotion to rank of Captain.)	Certificate B.†	Certificate B.†	Certificate B.†		Certificate B.†
(c) Captains. (Before promotion to rank of Major.)	1. Drill and manœuvre of a squadron acting independently or as part of a regiment. 2. Laying out a camp for a Yeomanry regiment. 3. Map reading. 4. General principles of the employment of Cavalry in the field; the duties of the Independent or Strategical Cavalry, the Protective Cavalry, and the Divisional Cavalry; dismounted action. A thorough knowledge of (a) the duties of Divisional Cavalry, and (b) dismounted action will be required. Cavalry in co-operation with the other arms on the battlefield. 5. Musketry.	1. Drill and manœuvre of a battery. 2. Application of fire; laying — direct and indirect; construction of cover for guns; passage of obstacles; marches. 3. Employment and conduct of artillery in the field. 4. Ammunition, stores and carriages. 5. Range-finding. 6. Map reading.	1. Practical examination in the duties of a Battery Commander in Coast Defence. 2. Riding.	1. Practical examination in the duties of a Battery Commander, and in taking up positions in the open and under cover. 2. Riding.	*For officers of all branches.* 1. The practical application in the field of the subject matter dealt with in the Manual of Military Engineering. 2. Company drill. 3. Riding (unless examined as a recruit officer). *In addition.* (*a*) Officers of Fortress Companies. "Military Engineering," Part II. Attack and Defence of Fortresses. Part IV, Mining and Demolitions. Good general knowledge of the arrangements of directing electric lights, and of the electrical communications of the fortress. The candidate to be capable of taking charge of a system of electric lights under ordinary conditions. (*b*) Officers of Railway Companies. "Military Engineering." Part VI. Railways. (*c*) Officers of Telegraph Companies. Army Manual of Telegraphy. (Field Telegraphs).

OF OFFICERS FOR PROMOTION, &c.

PENDIX I.

FOR PROMOTION OF OFFICERS.

Infantry.	Army Service Corps.	Royal Army Medical Corps.	Quartermasters of all Arms.
Certificate A.*	Certificate A.*	Officers are appointed to the Corps as Lieutenants.	Within 2 years of appointment a quartermaster, unless he has served as such in the Regular Forces, will be required to qualify in :— 1. Practical examination in packing and loading baggage, so as to facilitate its issue at the end of a march. Choosing the site of and laying out a camp.
Certificate B.†	Certificate B.†	Certificate B.†	2. Written examination in :— Army Forms to be used in peace and war. Making out returns and keeping necessary books for the receipt and issue of rations, forage, stores, equipment, etc.
1. The training of the company. 2. Battalion drill. 3. Infantry in attack and defence. 4. Riding. 5. Map reading. 6. Musketry.	1. Regimental duties, including company, foot, mounted and wagon drill; interior economy of a company on the line of march, and in the field; formation and defence of convoys. 2. Transport, general principles of construction, repair and care of vehicles, saddlery, pack-saddlery and harness required for military purposes, care and management of transport animals, various forms of transport, moving transport by rail and water, depôts and workshops, administration, organization, control, supervision and loading of transport in peace and war. 3. Supplies, judging quality of bread, meat, forage, groceries and other field supplies, scales of rations, formation and control of supply depôts, supply accounts and office work. 4. Mobilization of A.S.C. units.	Nil.	Quartermasters of Royal Army Medical Corps. 1. First aid as laid down for the recruit, if not a medical man. 2. Sanitation and other duties in camp, barracks, and on the line of march. 3. Army Forms, preparation of indents and vouchers for issue, receipt and repair of stores, etc. 4. Method of packing and loading field equipment and baggage. 5. Laying out camps. 6. Care of equipment, etc. N.B.—A quartermaster who has not served as such for one year in the Regular Forces, or has not passed the examination laid down for N.C.Os., R.A.M.C., before promotion to warrant rank in para. 285, Standing Orders, R.A.M.C., will be required to qualify in the above subjects within two years of his appointment.

* *See* Sub-Appendix II, page 176.

† *See* Sub-Appendix III, page 178.

Syllabus of the Examination for

	Yeomanry.	Artillery.			Engineers.
		Horse, Field, Heavy, and Mountain.	Garrison.		
			Coast Defence Companies.	Coast Defence Heavy Batteries.	
(d) **Majors.** (Before promotion to rank of Lieut.-Colonel or appointment to the command of a unit.)	An officer will be required :— To command a regiment when forming part of a larger force in a tactical exercise.	An officer will be required :— To command a brigade of field, or battery of heavy, artillery, as the case may be, in a tactical exercise with other troops.	An officer will be required :— To exercise a "Fire Command" in a coast defence action, and show a practical knowledge of the mobilization and fighting of a section of a fortress.	To command a battery of heavyartillery, in a tactical exercise with other troops.	An officer will be required :— To command a battalion acting alone in a tactical exercise, and to command a battalion in a tactical exercise when forming part of a larger force.

Promotion of Officers—*continued.*

Infantry.	Army Service Corps.	Royal Army Medical Corps.	Quartermasters of all Arms.
An officer will be required:— To command a battalion in a tactical exercise, when forming part of a larger force.	As for Captains before promotion to rank of Major, and, in addition:— 1. Organization for war of an army in the field. 2. Method of obtaining supplies and transport in war. 3. General duties of a staff officer administering transport and supply duties.	A written examination. 1. Army medical organization in peace and war. 2. Sanitation of towns, camps, transports, and all places likely to be occupied by troops in peace and war, epidemiology, and management of epidemics. 3. (*a*) The medical history of the more important campaigns and the lessons to be learnt therefrom. (*b*) A knowledge of the Army Medical Services of the more important powers. (*c*) The laws and customs of war so far as they relate to the sick and wounded.	

SUB-APPENDIX II.

SYLLABUS OF EXAMINATION FOR CERTIFICATE A.

I. Compulsory Subjects.

1. YEOMANRY.

Written Examination.

1st Paper.—200 marks—2 hours. Cavalry Training, 1907, Chapter VI and simple questions on Chapter VII.

2nd Paper.—200 marks.—2 hours. Combined Training, 1905; elementary questions on Chapters IV and VI.

Practical and Oral Examination.

(*a*) 100 marks.—Cavalry Training, 1907, Chapters III and IV, as modified by Appendix IV.
(*b*) 100 marks.—Tactical handling of a troop of at least 12 men.
(*c*) 100 marks.—Care of arms; mechanism of the rifle; elementary musketry practices. (Appendix to Training Manuals, 1905.)

2. ARTILLERY, HORSE, FIELD, MOUNTAIN AND HEAVY.

Written Examination.

1st Paper.—200 marks—2 hours. Field Artillery Training, 1906, Chapter III.—Gunnery.

2nd Paper.—200 marks—2 hours. Field Artillery Training, 1906, Chapter VIII.—Employment and conduct of artillery in the field. Combined Training, 1905, Chapter VI, Sections 103, 118, 119, 132, 136.

GARRISON ARTILLERY.

1st Paper.—200 marks—2 hours. Garrison Artillery Training, 1905, Volume I, Chapter I. Gunnery.

2nd Paper.—200 marks—2 hours. Garrison Artillery Training, 1905, Volume I, Chapter VII.—Attack and defence of a coast fortress. Chapter IX.—Manning and fighting medium and heavy guns.

Practical and Oral Examination.
(For Artillery only.)

(*a*) 100 marks—Squad drill (Infantry Training).
(*b*) 100 marks.—Standing gun drill of gun in use.
(*c*) 100 marks.—Explanation of the mechanism of gun and carriage fittings. Description of ammunition.

3. ALL ARMS (EXCEPT YEOMANRY AND ARTILLERY).

Written Examination.

1st Paper.—200 marks—2 hours. Infantry Training, 1905. Definitions. Sections—45–58, 76, 89, 89A, 126, 127, 128, 150, 169–171, 201–205.

2nd Paper.—200 marks—2 hours. Combined Training, 1905. Elementary questions on Chapters IV and VI.

In addition (for Engineers):—

FIELD AND FORTRESS COMPANIES—
3rd Paper.—200 marks—2 hours. Manual of Military Engineering, Part I, Chapters 1 to 10, 13.
(Field companies and land front fortress companies, good knowledge; for electric light fortress companies, fair knowledge.)

TELEGRAPH UNITS—
3rd Paper.—200 marks—2 hours. Army Manual of Telegraphy, 1897. Chapter V, pages 43–64, 79–94, 95–98.

Practical and Oral Examination.

ALL ARMS (EXCEPT YEOMANRY AND ARTILLERY).

(*a*) 100 marks.—Squad and Company drill (Infantry Training.)
(*b*) 100 marks.—Tactical handling of a section of at least 25 men.
(*c*) 100 marks.—Care of arms; Mechanism of the rifle; Elementary musketry exercises (Appendix to Training Manuals, 1905).

In addition (for Engineers):—

FIELD AND FORTRESS COMPANIES—
(*d*) 100 marks.—Manual of Military Engineering, Part I, Chapters 1 to 10, 13.
(Field companies and land front fortress companies, good knowledge; for electric light fortress companies, fair knowledge.)

ELECTRIC LIGHT FORTRESS COMPANIES—
(*d*) 100 marks.—Good knowledge of all details of electric light defence and electrical communications of the fortress.

Very good knowledge of one of the following:—
(1) Electrical work connected with electric lights.
(2) Engines and machinery connected with electric lights.
(3) Telephone system in use in fortress.

Candidates should be capable of taking charge of an electric light directing station.

LAND FRONT FORTRESS COMPANIES—
(*d*) 100 marks.—Elementary knowledge of the general arrangements and system of directing electric lights, and of the arrangement of the telephone system.

TELEGRAPH UNITS—
(*d*) 100 marks.—Army Manual of Telegraphy, 1897, Chapter VI, pages 106–135, and Appendices C and D. Chapter VII, pages 136–157.

BALLOON COMPANIES—
(*d*) 100 marks.—A fair knowledge of ballooning.

ROYAL ARMY MEDICAL CORPS—

Written Examination.

1st Paper.—200 marks.—2 hours.
Royal Army Medical Corps Training. Part I, Chapters II, III, VI; Part II, Chapter IX.

Practical and Oral Examination.

(*a*) 100 marks.
Squad and Company Drill (Infantry Training).
(*b*) 100 marks.
Royal Army Medical Corps Training. Part I, Chapters IV, V, VII, VIII; Part II, Chapter X.

II. Optional Subject.

3. ALL ARMS.

Semaphore Signalling (Training Manual—Signalling, 1907).
50 *marks.*

SUB-APPENDIX III.

SYLLABUS OF EXAMINATION FOR CERTIFICATE

I. Compulsory Subjects.

Written Examination.

1. ALL ARMS. (Alternative with No. 2 for candidates for Royal Army Medical Corps.)

(i.) 1st Paper. 200 marks—3 hours.

Field sketching, tactics and military engineering, map reading, scales, use of compass, attack and defence of a house, post or position. A simple problem of tactics, engineering and topography combined, entailing the employment of all arms.

(ii.) 2nd Paper. 100 marks—2 hours.

Military Law and King's Regulations. (Manual of Military Law and King's Regulations allowed for this examination.) Questions in subjects as for examination of lieutenants before promotion to captain, King's Regulations, Appendix XI (d) (ii).

HORSE, FIELD, MOUNTAIN AND HEAVY ARTILLERY :—

(iii.) 3rd Paper. 200 marks—2 hours.

Principles of employment of Artillery in the field (Field Artillery Training or Garrison Artillery Training, Vol. II); its technical management (Handbook of the Gun); horsemastership for Horse and Field Artillery (Animal Management.)

GARRISON ARTILLERY :—

(iv.) 3rd Paper. 200 marks—2 hours.

Garrison Artillery Training, 1905. Volume I.

FIELD AND FORTRESS COMPANIES :—

(v.) 3rd Paper. 200 marks—2 hours.

The Manual of Military Engineering, 1905. Military Engineering, Part II, Attack and Defence of Fortresses, Part IV, Mining and Demolitions.

ELECTRIC LIGHT FORTRESS COMPANIES :—

(vi.) 3rd Paper. 200 marks—2 hours.

Superior knowledge of all details of the electric light defence and electrical communications of the fortress.

Expert knowledge of one of the following :—

(1) Electrical work connected with electric lights.
(2) Engines and machinery connected with electric lights.
(3) Telephone system in use in the fortress.

LAND FRONT FORTRESS COMPANIES :—

(vii.) 3rd Paper. 200 marks—2 hours.

Fair knowledge of the general arrangements and system of directing electric lights and of the arrangements of the telephone system.

TELEGRAPH UNITS :—

(viii.) 3rd Paper. 200 marks—2 hours.

Army Manual of Telegraphy, 1897, Chapters III, IV, and V.

ARMY SERVICE CORPS :—

(ix.) 3rd Paper. 200 marks—2 hours.

Supply and Transport (Army Service Corps Training Manuals and Regulations for Supply, Transport and Barrack Services).

ROYAL ARMY MEDICAL CORPS :—

(x.) 3rd Paper. 200 marks—2 hours.

War Establishments.

Organization of Field Medical Units.

(xi.) 4th Paper (for candidates who have not obtained a "Medical" Certificate A).—200 marks—2 hours.

Royal Army Medical Corps Training, Part I, Chapters II, III, VI ; Part II, Chapter IX.

Practical and Oral Examination.

(*a*) 100 marks :—

The general system of organization of the army. The system of command, organization, discipline and administration of a squadron, battery or company in peace and in war.

(*b*) 100 marks.

Appendix XI (b), King's Regulations, Drill and Field Training.

(*c*) 100 marks.

Duties in the field, as applicable to each arm. Marches, outposts, map-reading, reconnaissances (including rough field sketches), attack and defence, including engineering details contained in Part I, Manual of Military Engineering, 1905, with the exception of Chapters XII, XIV and XVI ; and any duty or work which a captain may fairly be called upon to perform in the field.

In addition for Engineers :—

FIELD AND FORTRESS COMPANIES :—

(*d*) Practical and oral. 100 marks.

The subject matter under (v.).

A good knowledge.

ELECTRIC LIGHT FORTRESS COMPANIES :—

(*d*) Practical and oral. 100 marks.

The subject matter under (vi.).

A candidate should be capable of taking charge of a system of electric lights under any conditions.

A fair knowledge.

LAND FRONT FORTRESS COMPANIES :—

(*d*) Practical and oral. 100 marks.

The subject matter under (vii.).

A candidate should be capable of taking charge of an electric light directing station under ordinary conditions.

A good knowledge.

TELEGRAPH UNITS :—

(*d*) Practical and oral. 100 marks.

The subject matter contained in Army Manual of Telegraphy, 1897, Chapter VI, and Appendices C and D, and Chapter VII, pages 136–157.

BALLOONING COMPANIES :—

(*d*) Practical and oral. 100 marks.

A good knowledge of ballooning.

IN ADDITION FOR ROYAL ARMY MEDICAL CORPS :—

(*d*) (i) 100 marks :—Work of Medical Units in the field.

(ii) 100 marks :—Sanitation and other duties in barracks, camp, and on the line of march.

(iii) For candidates who have not obtained a "Medical" Certificate A (additional) :—

100 marks :—Royal Army Medical Corps Training, Part I, Chapters IV, V, VII, VIII ; Part II, Chapter X.

2. ROYAL ARMY MEDICAL CORPS. (Alternative to 1.)

Written Examination.

1st Paper. 200 marks—2 hours.

War establishments and organization of medical field units.

2nd Paper. 100 marks—2 hours.

Military Law and King's Regulations as laid down for lieutenants before promotion to captain in Appendix XI (d) (ii), King's Regulations.

Practical and Oral Examination.

(*a*) 100 marks.

Work of field medical units in the field, including corps drill.

(*b*) 100 marks.

Sanitation and other duties in barracks, camp, and on the line of march.

(*c*) 100 marks.

Map reading.

(*d*) 100 marks.

General system of organization of the army. The system of command, organization, discipline and administration of a company in peace time, and a field unit in war.

II. Optional Subjects.

All Arms.

Written Examination.

(i.) 300 marks—3 hours.

Military History and Strategy. (Prescribed period—Fortescue's "History of the British Army.")

APPENDIX 5.

STANDARDS FOR RECRUITS.

TABLE A.

Standards of Height.

The following are the standards of height—

Royal Horse and Royal Field Artillery—
Drivers, 5 ft. 3 in. to 5 ft. 6 in.
Gunners, 5 ft. 6 in. to 5 ft. 10 in.

Royal Artillery, Heavy—
Drivers, 5 ft. 4 in. and upwards.
Gunners, 5 ft. 6 in. „

Royal Artillery—
Mountain—Gunners, 5 ft. 7 in. and upwards.
„ „ as drivers, 5 ft. 4 in. and upwards.
Garrison, 5 ft. 6 in. and upwards.

Royal Engineers—
Drivers, 5 ft. 3 in. to 5 ft. 6 in.
Sappers, 5 ft. 4 in. and upwards.

Yeomanry—5 ft. 3 in. and upwards.
Infantry—5 ft. 2 in. „
Army Service Corps—5 ft. 3 in. to 5 ft. 6 in.
„ Drivers—5 ft. 2 in. to 5 ft. 4 in.
Royal Army Medical Corps—5 ft. 3 in. and upwards.
Army Ordnance Corps—5 ft. 3 in. and upwards.
Army Post Office Corps, 5 ft. 4 in. „

TEST A.

ALL UNITS EXCEPT CAVALRY AND INFANTRY.

Age.	Height.	Weight, *see* note (*b*).	Chest. Girth when fully expanded.	Chest. Range of expansion not less than
	inches.	lbs.	inches.	inches.
17	62 and under 65	110	32½	2
	65 „ 68	114	33	2
	68 „ 72	118	33½	2
	72 and upwards..	122	34½	2½
18	62 and under 65	112	33	2
	65 „ 68	115	33½	2
	68 „ 72	118	34	2
	72 and upwards..	122	34½	2½

TEST A—*continued.*

Age.	Height.	Weight, *see* note (*b*).	Chest. Girth when fully expanded.	Chest. Range of expansion not less than
	inches.	lbs.	inches.	inches.
19	62½ and under 65	114	33½	2
	65 „ 68	117	34	2
	68 „ 70	120	34½	2
	70 „ 72	124	35	2
	72 and upwards..	128	35½	2½
20	62½ and under 65	115	33½	2
	65 „ 68	120	34	2
	68 „ 70	123	34½	2
	70 „ 72	126	35	2½
	72 and upwards..	130	35½	2½
21	62½ and under 65	118	33½	2
	65 „ 68	121	34½	2
	68 „ 70	124	35	2
	70 „ 72	127	35½	2½
	72 and upwards..	132	36	2½
22 and over.	62½ and under 65	120	34	2
	65 „ 68	123	34½	2
	68 „ 70	126	35	2
	70 „ 72	130	35½	2½
	72 and upwards..	133	36	2½

TEST B.

CAVALRY AND ARTILLERY.

Age.	Height.	Weight *see* note (*b*).	Chest. Girth when fully expanded.	Chest. Range of expansion not less than
	inches.	lbs.	inches.	inches.
17	62 and under 65	110	32½	2
	65 „ 68	114	33	2
	68 „ 72	118	33½	2
	72 and upwards..	122	34½	2½
18	62 and under 65	115	34	2
	65 „ 68	115	34½	2
	68 „ 72	118	35	2
	72 and upwards..	122	35½	2½

TEST B—*continued.*

Age.	Height.	Weight, see note (*b*).	Chest. Girth when fully expanded.	Chest. Range of expansion not less than
	inches.	lbs.	inches.	inches.
19	62 and under 65	115	34½	2
	65 „ 68	117	34½	2
	68 „ 70	120	35	2
	70 „ 72	124	35½	2
	72 and upwards..	128	36	2½
20	62 and under 65	115	34½	2
	65 „ 68	120	34½	2
	68 „ 70	123	35	2
	70 „ 72	126	35½	2½
	72 and upwards..	130	36	2½
21	62 and under 65	118	34½	2
	65 „ 68	121	35	2
	68 „ 70	124	35½	2
	70 „ 72	127	36	2½
	72 and upwards..	132	36½	2½
22 and over.	62 and under 65	120	34½	2
	65 „ 68	123	35	2
	68 „ 70	126	35½	2
	70 „ 72	130	36	2½
	72 and upwards..	133	36½	2½

N.B.—The standard of height at which recruits may be taken is that given in Table A.

Notes on Standards and Tests.

No recruit will be enlisted who fails to fulfil the conditions of chest measurement, or chest expansion, laid down in the following tests :—

(*a*) The chest measurement of recruits will be taken by medical officers according to the directions given in the Medical Regulations ; but it is to be noted that the importance of accuracy is emphasized by the fact that a certain amount of expansion is required according to height and age ; the minimum chest being taken when the lungs are emptied of all air.

(*b*) There is no standard of weight, but the weights laid down in the various "tests" will be regarded as a guide, indicating the point at, and below which, a specially careful physical examination must be made ; and examining medical officers should pass as "fit" only such recruits whose failure to reach those weights is solely the result of insufficient nutriment, and not caused by constitutional taint.

APPENDIX 6.—TRAINING.

SUB-APPENDIX I.—TRAINING OF THE YEOMANRY.

Rank.	Training in first year of Service.	Subsequent.	
		Annual Training.	*Courses of Instruction.
Officers	(*a*) 40 drills, of which 20 must be performed before annual training in camp; † or, 14 days with a Regular unit before annual training in camp, and 20 drills. (*b*) The annual training in camp of his unit. (*c*) Recruits' course of musketry. (*d*) In addition to annual requirements he must obtain a certificate that he can ride sufficiently well to perform his duties.	(*a*) 10 drills to be performed before annual training in camp.† (Optional for field officers.) (*b*) Annual training in camp. (*c*) Annual course of musketry. (Optional for field officers.)	(*a*) Course at a school of musketry before promotion to the rank of Captain.‡ (*b*) 14 days' attachment to a Regular Cavalry regiment within 2 years before promotion to the rank of Major.§
N.C.Os. of rank of serjeant and above.	.. ..	As above.	
Other ranks ..	(*a*) 20 drills before the annual training in camp,† of which 3 days of at least 3 consecutive hours in field instruction must form part. (*b*) Recruits' course of musketry. (*c*) Annual training in camp.	As above.	

* In very special cases the O.C. Mounted Brigade may excuse an officer from attendance at these courses if circumstances justify it.

† No pay or allowances will be issued to officers or men who do not perform the necessary drills before annual training in camp.

‡ Until local schools of musketry have been established, officers may be allowed to pass an examination in musketry in lieu of attending a course.

§ In special cases where such attachment is impracticable, the O.C. Mounted Brigade may allow 20 drills with a Regular Cavalry regiment to be substituted.

Sub-Appendix II.—Training of the Artillery.

Rank.	Training in first year of Service.	Subsequent.	
		Annual Training.	*Course of Instruction.
Officers	(a) 45 drills, of which 30 must be performed before the annual training in camp.† (b) The annual training in camp of his unit, including gun practice. (c) In addition to annual requirements he must obtain a certificate that he can ride sufficiently well to perform his duties if he belongs to a mounted unit.	(a) 20 drills (of which 10 at least should be out-of-door drills) to be performed before the annual training in camp.† (Optional for field officers.) (b) Annual training in camp (including gun practice). (c) During the first 4 years of service, one period of 6 days' practice with a service brigade or at a coast defence work.	(a) 14 days' attachment to a training brigade or other Regular unit, before promotion to the rank of Captain. (b) A course of 14 days at a practice camp or coast defence work before promotion to the rank of Major.
Staff - serjeants and serjeants	.. ..	As above, except (c).	
Rank and file ..	As for recruit officers	As above, except (c).	(a) Before promotion to serjeant, 1 month or 30 drills with a training brigade (or Regular unit in the case of R.G.A.). (b) To obtain a certificate of ability to ride if he belongs to a mounted unit.

* In very special cases the G.O.C. Division, O.C. Mounted Brigade, or Coast Defence Commander may excuse an officer from attendance at these courses if circumstances justify it.

† No pay or allowances will be issued to officers or men who do not perform the necessary drills before annual training in camp.

SUB-APPENDIX III.—TRAINING OF ENGINEERS.

Rank.	Training in first year of Service.	Subsequent.	
		Annual Training.	Courses of Instruction.
Officers	(a) 45 drills, of which 20 must be performed before the annual training in camp,* or, electric light engineers, 18 drills, of which 12 are to be devoted to electric light and 6 to squad and company drill. (b) The annual training in camp of his unit. (c) Officers of field companies may, at the discretion of the G.O.C. Division, carry out a recruits' course of musketry (as for infantry). If this course is carried out 40 drills only will be necessary.† (d) In addition to annual requirements, a recruit officer of mounted units must obtain a certificate that he can ride sufficiently well to perform his duties.	(a) 15 drills to be performed before the officer attends the annual training in camp.* (Optional for field officers). Or, trained electric light engineers (as defined in para. 283), 6 squad and company drills, others, 18 drills, as for first year of service. (b) Officers of field companies may, at the discretion of the G.O.C. Division, carry out a course of musketry (as for infantry). When this is done, the number of annual drills may be reduced to 10. (c) Annual training in camp.	Before promotion to the rank of captain, 28 days' attachment to the School of Military Engineering or Electric Lighting or to a regular engineer unit. This course may be divided into two periods, each of 14 days. In the case of officers of electric light units who are members or associate members of the Institute of Electrical Engineers, this period may be reduced to 7 days, during which they must pass an examination to show that they are thoroughly qualified in the technical duties of their unit.
N.C.Os. of rank of serjeant and above	.. ..	As above.	
Rank and file ..	As for recruit officers	As above.	

* No pay or allowances will be issued to officers or men who do not perform the necessary drills before annual training in camp.

† Engineer units, other than field companies, will not carry out musketry prior to mobilization.

NOTE.—The above scheme may require modification as regards telegraph units for the Territorial Force after further experience has been gained in the training of these units.

Sub-Appendix IV.—Training of the Infantry (Including Cyclists.)

Rank.	Training in first year of Service.	Subsequent.	
		Annual Training.	Courses of Instruction.
Officers	(*a*) 40 drills, of which 20 must be performed before the annual training in camp.† (*b*) The annual training in camp of his unit. (*c*) Recruits' course of musketry.	(*a*) 10 drills to be performed before the officer attends the annual training in camp.† (Optional for field officers.) (*b*) Annual training in camp. (*c*) Annual course of musketry. (Optional for field officers.)	*Course at a School of Musketry before promotion to the rank of Captain.
Serjeants.. ..	.. ..	As above.	
Rank and file ..	As for officers	As above.	

* In very special cases the G.O.C., Division, may excuse an officer from attendance at this course if circumstances justify it. Until local schools of musketry have been established, officers may be allowed to pass an examination in musketry in lieu of attending the course.

† No pay or allowances will be issued to officers or men who do not perform the necessary drills before annual training in camp.

Sub-Appendix V.—Training of the Army Service Corps.

Rank.	Training in first year of Service.	Subsequent.	
		Annual Training.	Courses of instruction.
Officers	(*a*) 8 drills mounted and 8 drills on foot, which must be performed before the annual training in camp.‡ (*b*) The annual training in camp of his unit.	(*a*) 15 drills (of which 8 at least should be out-of-door drills) to be performed before the annual training in camp.‡ (*b*) Annual training in camp.	*2 courses of instruction before promotion to the rank of Captain: (a.) Transport course at one of the Transport Depôt companies (15 days). (b.) Supply course at A.S.C. Training Establishment at Aldershot (15 days).
Staff - serjeants and serjeants (Transport)	.. .. ..	As above.	

* In very special cases the G.O.C. Division or O.C. Mounted Brigade may excuse an officer or N.C.O., &c., from attendance at these courses if circumstances justify it.

‡ No pay or allowances will be issued to officers or men who do not perform the necessary drills before annual training in camp.

Sub-Appendix V—*continued.*

Training of the Army Service Corps—*continued.*

Rank.	Training in first year of Service.	Subsequent.	
		Annual Training.	Course of Instruction.
Rank and file (Transport)	(*a*) 20 mounted drills (riding and driving) and 8 drills on foot, which must be performed before the annual training in camp.‡ (*b*) The annual training in camp of his unit.	As above	*Before promotion to serjeant should undergo a course of instruction in Transport duties of 15 days' duration with a Transport company of A.S.C.
Staff serjeants and serjeants (Supply)	.. ..	As above.	
Rank and file (Supply)	(*a*) 8 drills on foot. Clerks in addition 8 attendances at the nearest A.S.C. Supply office for instruction in Supply clerical work, issuing, &c.‡ (*b*) Annual training in camp of his unit.	As above	*Before promotion to serjeant should undergo a course of instruction in Supply duties of 15 days' duration at the A.S.C. Training Establishment at Aldershot, or at a Supply office at an A.S.C. headquarter station.

* In very special cases the G.O.C. Division or O.C. Mounted Brigade may excuse an officer or N.C.O., &c., from attendance at these courses if circumstances justify it.

‡ No pay or allowances will be issued to officers or men who do not perform the necessary drills before annual training in camp.

NOTE.—Men enlisted for Transport duties should be, as far as possible, carters, drivers, grooms, with a proportion of farriers, shoeing-smiths, saddlers and wheelers. Men enlisted for Supply duties should be clerks, bakers, and butchers only.

SUB-APPENDIX VI.—TRAINING OF THE ROYAL ARMY MEDICAL CORPS.

Rank.	Training in first year of Service.	Subsequent.	
		Annual Training.	Courses of Instruction.
Officers of units, including quartermasters.	(*a*) A minimum of 30 drills, of which half must be performed before the annual training in camp.† (*b*) The annual training in camp of his unit, or attend an appropriate course of instruction in a Territorial Force Medical School or selected military institution. (Not to exceed 8 days in each case.) (*c*) An officer appointed to a field unit must obtain a certificate that he can ride sufficiently well to perform his duties.	(*a*) 15 drills to be performed before the annual training in camp.† (Optional for field officers.) (*b*) Officers of field units must do at least one annual training in camp in three. The Officer Commanding, Registrar, and Quarter-Master of General Hospitals train in Military Hospitals or Territorial Force Medical Schools (8 days).	When officers do not train in camp they must go through the course laid down for hospitals or at the Territorial Force Medical Schools (8 days).
		Sanitarians and other specialists, such as those holding a recognised hospital appointment, and who are not attached to combatant or belong to medical units may (not compelled to) come up every third year for either the annual training in camp or for a school course (8 days in each case).	

† No pay or allowances will be issued to officers or men who do not perform the necessary attendances before annual training in camp.

SUB-APPENDIX VI—*continued.*

Training of the Royal Army Medical Corps—*continued.*

Rank.	Training in first year of Service.	Subsequent.	
		Annual Training.	Courses of Instruction.
Regimental officers	The annual training in camp, or attend an appropriate course of instruction in a Territorial Force Medical School or selected military institution (not to exceed 8 days in each case.)	Annual training in camp.	Before promotion to major a course with a Territorial Force Medical School or selected military institution (8 days).
Serjeants.. ..	.. ..	(*a*) 15 drills at Headquarters and annual training in camp, or (*b*) 10 drills at Headquarters and a course at a hospital, or other selected institution, or Territorial Force Medical School in lieu of camp, or (*c*) for selected soldiers, the course at a hospital, or other selected institution or Territorial Force Medical School and the annual training in camp and no drills at Headquarters.*	
Rank and file ..	42 attendances at drill and instructions, of which one-half must be performed before the annual training in camp, should the recruit attend camp†; or, should the recruit not attend camp, the whole 42 attendances should be completed before the hospital course (which can be taken instead of the annual training in camp) is commenced.	(*a*) 10 drills at Headquarters and annual training in camp, or (*b*) 10 attendances at Headquarters and a course at a hospital, or other selected institution, or Territorial Force Medical School, in lieu of camp, or (*c*) for selected soldiers the course at a hospital, or other selected institution, or Territorial Force Medical School, and the annual training in camp, and no drills at Headquarters.*	

* By the 8-day hospital course is meant a course of 8 days, not necessarily consecutive, or 24 attendances, of which not more than three in one day may count, and of not less than 1 hour's duration each, at a suitable military or civil hospital, Territorial Force School, or other approved institution.

† No pay or allowances will be issued to officers or men who do not perform the necessary attendances before annual training in camp.

Sub-Appendix VII.—Training of the Royal Army Medical Corps, Transport Section.

Rank.	Training in first year of Service.	Subsequent.	
		Annual Training.	Courses of Instruction.
Officers ..	(*a*) 8 drills mounted and 8 drills on foot, which must be performed before the annual training in camp.† (*b*) If not a medical man, he must be certified as being trained in first aid. (*c*) The annual training in camp of his unit.	(*a*) 15 drills (of which 8, at least, should be out-of door drills), to be performed before the annual training in camp†. (*b*) Annual training in camp.	*One course of instruction before promotion to the rank of Captain, and to obtain satisfactory certificate, viz.:—Transport course at one of the Transport Depôt companies (15 days).
Staff-serjeants and serjeants	.. ..	As above.	
Rank and file..	(*a*) 20 drills mounted (riding and driving) and 8 drills on foot, which must be performed before the annual training in camp†. (*b*) Recruits must also be certified as being trained in first aid. (*c*) The annual training in camp of his unit.	As above ..	*Before promotion to serjeant should undergo a course of instruction in transport duties of 15 days' duration with a Transport company of Army Service Corps, and obtain satisfactory certificate.

* In special cases the G.O.C. Division or O.C. Mounted Brigade may excuse an officer or N.C.O. from attending this course.

† No pay or allowances will be issued to officers or men who do not perform the necessary drills before annual training in camp.

SUB-APPENDIX VIII.—EXAMINATION OF SUBALTERN OFFICERS IN MUSKETRY.

1. In order to qualify for promotion to the rank of captain, subaltern officers of yeomanry and infantry will be required to qualify at the School of Musketry. In very special cases, and until local schools of musketry have been established, they will be allowed to pass an examination in musketry, which will be held under the direction of the divisional or mounted brigade commander.

2. Examinations will be conducted by a board consisting of two officers of the regular forces, of whom the senior should hold rank not lower than that of captain.

3. The examination will include an oral and a written test. The former will be confined to ascertaining the ability of candidates to instruct in the musketry exercises and the care of arms. The latter should consist of 10 questions on the subjects treated in—

"Infantry Training," 1905.—Sections 51, 53, 72, 126, 127, 128, 134, and 163.

"Musketry Regulations," 1905.—Chapters 3, 5, 6, and 10.

"Appendix to Training Manuals," 1905.—Chapter II, Sections 1 to 3, 12 to 44, 47 to 50.

A total of 100 marks will be given for these questions.

4. The record of the proceedings will be prepared on A.F. A 2, and the questions forming the oral tests, with the opinion of the board as to the ability shown by each officer, will be recorded therein.

5. The board, after scrutinising the written papers and assigning marks for the answers given, will forward them with the proceedings to the divisional or mounted brigade commander, who will recommend candidates for a record of qualification, which will be published in orders.

APPENDIX 7.

ENACTMENTS RELATING TO THE MILITIA AND VOLUNTEERS APPLIED BY ORDER IN COUNCIL OF 19th MARCH, 1908, TO THE TERRITORIAL FORCE.

Order in Council.

Whereas His Majesty was pleased, by His Commission dated the seventeenth day of March, one thousand nine hundred and eight, to nominate and appoint His Royal Highness the Prince of Wales, in His Majesty's Absence from His Realm in Foreign Parts, to hold on His Majesty's behalf, His Privy Council, and to signify thereat His approval of any matter or thing whereunto His Royal Highness should be so authorized by writing under His Majesty's Sign Manual, and to do further on His Majesty's behalf any matter or thing for the purposes of the said Commission whereunto His Royal Highness should be authorized in manner aforesaid :

And whereas in virtue of the powers conferred upon Him by Section 6 of the Territorial and Reserve Forces Act, 1907, His Majesty has decided to raise and maintain a force, to be called the "Territorial Force" :

And whereas it is provided by Section 28 of the said Act that His Majesty may, by Order in Council, apply, with the necessary adaptations, to the said Force, or to the officers or men belonging to that Force, any enactment relating to the Militia, Yeomanry, or Volunteers, or to officers or men of the Militia, Yeomanry, or Volunteers, other than enactments with respect to the raising, service, pay, discipline, or government of the Militia, Yeomanry, or Volunteers :

And whereas it is expedient that certain enactments relating to the Militia specified in the First Part of the Schedule appended hereto, and certain enactments relating to officers of the Volunteers specified in the Second Part of the said Schedule, should be made applicable to the said Force :

Now, therefore, His Royal Highness the Prince of Wales, being authorized thereto by writing under His Majesty's Sign Manual, by and with the advice of His Majesty's Privy Council, doth on behalf of His Majesty, order, as it is hereby ordered, as follows :—

The several enactments specified in the First and Second Parts of the Schedule appended hereto shall apply to the Territorial Force and to the officers and men thereof in like manner as they apply to the Militia and to the officers and men of the Militia, and to officers of the Volunteers, respectively.

THE FOLLOWING ARE THE ENACTMENTS REFERRED TO IN THE FIRST AND SECOND PARTS OF THE SCHEDULE TO THE ORDER IN COUNCIL :—

9 / Gen. No. / 30

The Railway Act, 1842 (5 & 6 Vict., c. 55).

Railway companies shall convey military and police forces at prices to be settled.

XX.—And be it enacted, That whenever it shall be necessary to move any of the officers or soldiers of Her Majesty's forces of the line, ordnance corps, marines, militia, or the police force, by any railway, the directors thereof shall and are hereby required to permit such forces respectively, with their baggage, stores, arms, ammunition, and other necessaries and things, to be conveyed at the usual hours of starting, at such prices or upon such conditions as may from time to time be contracted for between the Secretary at War and such railway companies for the conveyance of such forces, on the production of a route or order for their conveyance signed by the proper authorities.

The Railway Act, 1844 (7 & 8 Vict., c. 85).

Certain companies to convey military, marine, and police forces at certain charges.

XII.—And whereas by an Act passed in the Sixth year of the reign of Her Majesty, intituled "An Act for the better regulation of railways, and for the conveyance of troops," it was among other things enacted, that whenever it shall be necessary to move any of the officers or soldiers of Her Majesty's forces of the line, ordnance corps, marines, militia, or the police force, by any railway, the directors thereof shall and are hereby required to permit such forces respectively, with their baggage, stores, arms, ammunition, and other necessaries and things, to be conveyed at the usual hours of starting, at such prices or upon such conditions as may from time to time be contracted for between the Secretary at War and such railway companies for the conveyance of such forces, on the production of a route or order for their conveyance signed by the proper authorities: And whereas it is expedient to amend such provision in regard to the prices and conditions of conveyance by any new railway or any railway obtaining new powers from Parliament: Be it enacted, that all railway companies which have been or shall be incorporated by any Act of the present or any future session, or which by any Act of the present or any future session shall have obtained or shall obtain any extension or amendment of the powers conferred by their previous Acts or any of them, or have been or shall be authorised to do any Act unauthorised by the provisions of such previous Acts, shall be bound to provide such conveyance as aforesaid for the said military, marine, and police forces, at fares not exceeding two pence per mile for each commissioned officer proceeding on duty, such officer being entitled to conveyance in a first class carriage, and not exceeding one penny for each mile for each soldier, marine, or private of the militia or police force, and also for each wife, widow, or child above twelve years of age of a soldier entitled by Act of Parliament or by competent authority to be sent to their destination at the public expense, children under three years of age so entitled being taken free of charge, and children of three years of age or upwards, but under twelve years of age, so entitled, being taken at half the price of an adult; and such soldiers, marines, and privates of the militia or police force, and their wives, widows, and children, so entitled, being conveyed in carriages which shall be provided with seats, with sufficient space for the reasonable accommodation of the persons conveyed, and which shall be protected against the weather; provided that every officer conveyed shall be entitled to take with him one hundredweight of personal luggage without extra charge, and every soldier, marine, private, wife or widow shall be entitled to take with him or her half a hundredweight of personal luggage without extra charge, all excess of the above weights of personal luggage being paid for at the rate of not more than one halfpenny per pound, and all public baggage, stores, arms, ammunition, and other necessaries and things (except gunpowder and other combustible matters, which the company shall only be bound to convey at such prices and upon such conditions as may be from time to time contracted for between the Secretary at War and the company), shall be conveyed at charges not exceeding two pence per ton per mile, the assistance of the military or other forces being given for loading and unloading such goods.

The National Defence Act, 1888 (51 & 52 Vict., c. 31).

Power of Government on occasion of national danger, or great emergency, to have precedence in traffic of railway.

IV.—(1). Whenever an order for the embodiment of the militia is in force, it shall be lawful for Her Majesty the Queen, by order signified under the hand of a Secretary of State, to declare that it is expedient for the public service that traffic for naval and military purposes shall have on the railways in the United Kingdom, or such of them as are mentioned in the order, precedence over other traffic.

(2). When any such order is in force as respects a railway, an officer on any part of Her Majesty's naval or military forces acting under the authority of a Secretary of State or the Admiralty may, by warrant, under his hand, addressed to the railway company working that railway require that such traffic as may be specified in the warrant shall be received and forwarded on the railway in priority to any other traffic, and the company shall comply with such warrant, and shall, so far as may be necessary, suspend the receiving and forwarding of all other traffic on such railway.

(3). If a director of or person employed by a railway company refuses or fails to comply with the exigency of the warrant, or obstructs the carrying thereof into effect, he shall be liable on summary conviction to a fine not exceeding fifty pounds, and any such officer as aforesaid may take such means as seems to him necessary for carrying (and if need be, by force) the warrant into effect.

(4). A warrant issued in pursuance of this section shall not be in force for more than one month after the date thereof unless renewed.

(5). An order made by Her Majesty in pursuance of this section may be revoked by Her Majesty at any time, and upon the militia being ordered to be disembodied shall cease to operate.

(6). There shall be paid, out of moneys provided by Parliament, to a railway company required to receive and forward traffic in pursuance of this section, such reasonable remuneration as may be agreed upon, or in default of agreement may be determined by arbitration.

(7). If any person suffers any loss by reason of anything done under the authority of a Secretary of State or the Admiralty in pursuance of this section, he may petition the Secretary of State or the Admiralty for compensation, and the Secretary of State or Admiralty may pay out of moneys provided by Parliament such reasonable compensation as may seem just: but no such compensation shall be paid in respect of any loss arising under a contract which was made subsequently to the date of an order under this section, or which, though made before, might have been determined subsequently to that date.

(8) For the purposes of this section—

The expression "secretary of state" means one of Her Majesty's principal secretaries of state; and

The expression "Admiralty" means the commissioners for executing the office of lord high admiral; and

The expression "railway" includes any tramway, whether worked by animal or mechanical power, or partly in one way and partly in the other; and

The expression "person" includes any person or body of persons, corporate or unincorporate; and

The expression "railway company" means any person as above defined who as owner or lessee of a railway or otherwise is actually engaged in working a railway; and

The expression "traffic" includes persons, animals, goods, and things of every description which are ordinarily carried, or are required by virtue of this Act to be received and forwarded, on a railway.

The Local Government Act, 1888 (51 & 52 Vict., c. 41).

Supplemental provision as to alteration of area.

59—(1) A scheme or order under this Act may make such administrative and judicial arrangements incidental to or consequential on any alteration of boundaries, authorities, or other matters made by the scheme or order as may seem expedient.

(2) A place which is part of an administrative county for the purposes of this Act shall, subject as in this Act mentioned form part of that county for all purposes, whether sheriff, lieutenant.

custos rotulorum, justices, militia, coroner, or other; Provided that—

(*a*) Notwithstanding this enactment, each of the entire counties of York, Lincoln, Sussex, Suffolk, Northampton, and Cambridge shall continue to be one county for the said purposes so far as it is one county at the passing of this Act; and

(*b*) This enactment shall not affect the existing powers or privileges of any city or borough as respects the sheriff, lieutenant, militia, justices, or coroner; but, if any county borough is, at the passing of this Act, a part of any county for any of the above purposes, nothing in this Act shall prevent the same from continuing to be part of that county for that purpose; and

(*c*) This enactment shall not affect parliamentary elections nor the right to vote at the election of a member to serve in Parliament, nor land tax, tithes, or tithe rent charge, nor the area within which any bishop, parson, or other ecclesiastical person has any cure of souls or jurisdiction.

(3) For the purposes of parliamentary elections, and of the registration of voters for such elections, the sheriff, clerk of the peace, and council of the county in which any place is comprised at the passing of this Act for the purpose of parliamentary elections shall, save as otherwise provided by the scheme or order, or by the County Electors Act, 1888, or this Act, continue to have the same powers, duties, and liabilities as they would have had if no alteration of boundary had taken place.

(4) Any scheme or order made in pursuance of this Act may, so far as may seem necessary or proper for the purposes of the scheme or order, provide for all or any of the following matters, that is to say—

(*a*) May provide for the abolition, restriction, or establishment, or extension of the jurisdiction of any local authority in or over any part of the area affected by the scheme or order, and for the adjustment or alteration of the boundaries of such area, and for the constitution of the local authorities therein, and may deal with the powers and duties of any council, local authorities, quarter sessions, justices of the peace, coroners, sheriff, lieutenant, custos rotulorum, clerk of the peace, and other officer therein, and with the costs of any such authorities, sessions, persons, or officers as aforesaid, and may determine the status of any such area as a component part of any larger area, and provide for the election of representatives in such area, and may extend to any altered area the provisions of any local Act which were previously in force in a portion of the area; and

(*b*) May make temporary provision for meeting the debts and liabilities of the various authorities affected by the scheme or order, for the management of their property, and for regulating the duties, position, and remuneration of officers affected by the scheme or order, and applying to them the provisions of this Act as to existing officers; and (*c*) May provide for the transfer of any writs, process, records, and documents relating to or to be executed in any part of the area affected by the scheme or order, and for determining questions arising from such transfer ; and

(*d*) May provide for all matters which appear necessary or proper for bringing into operation and giving full effect to the scheme or order ; and

(*e*) May adjust any property, debts, and liabilities affected by the scheme or order.

(5) Where an alteration of boundaries of a county is made by this Act an order for any of the above-mentioned matters may, if it appears to the Local Government Board desirable, be made by that Board, but such order, if petitioned against by any Council, sessions, or local authority affected thereby, within three months after notice of such order is given in accordance with this Act, shall be provisional only, unless the petition is withdrawn or the order is confirmed by Parliament.

(6) A scheme or order may be made for amending any scheme or order previously made in pursuance of this Act, and may be made by the same authority and after the same procedure as the original scheme or order. Where a provision of this Act respecing a scheme or order requires the scheme or order to be laid before Parliament, or to be confirmed by Parliament, either in every case or if it is petitioned against, such scheme or order may amend any local and personal Act.

The Friendly Societies Act, 1896 (59 & 60 Vict., c. 25).

Militiamen and volunteers.

43—(1). A person shall not, by reason of his enrolment or service in the militia, or as a naval coast volunteer, Royal Naval volunteer, naval artillery volunteer, or in any corps of yeomanry or volunteers whatsoever, lose or forfeit any interest in a friendly society or branch whether registered or unregistered which he possesses at the time of his being so enrolled or serving, or be fined for absence from or non-attendance at any meeting of the society or branch, if his absence or non-attendance is occasioned by the discharge of his military or naval duty as certified by his commanding officer, any rules of the society or branch to the contrary notwithstanding.

---

25 & 26 Vict., Cap. 4.

Officers' commissions in the army, &c., may be issued without Her Majesty's royal sign manual being affixed thereto.

I. It shall be lawful for Her Majesty, by Order in Council, from time to time, as occasion may require, to direct that all or any commissions for officers prepared or to be prepared under the authority of Her Majesty's Royal Sign Manual, may be afterwards issued without Her Royal Sign Manual, but having thereon, in the case of Her Majesty's land forces, except as hereinafter mentioned, the signatures of the commander-in-chief or the general commanding-in-chief, and of one of Her Majesty's Principal Secretaries of State, and, in the case of the royal marines, of the Admiralty, and in the case of military chaplains, commissariat and store officers, and of adjutants and quartermasters in the militia and volunteer forces, of one of Her Majesty's said Principal Secretaries; and every such commission issued and signed in pursuance of such Order in Council shall be conclusive evidence that the officer named in any such commission has been appointed or promoted by Her Majesty to the rank or office named therein.

Act not to affect Her Majesty's right to sign commission.

II. Nothing herein contained shall be construed to prevent Her Majesty from signing any commission, or to prevent any commission so signed from having the same validity and effect as if this Act had not passed.

The Regulation of the Forces Act, 1871.

Preparation, authentication and issue of commissions.

In section 6, the words "commissions shall be prepared, authenticated, and issued in the manner in which commissions of officers in Her Majesty's land forces are prepared, authenticated, and issued according to any law or custom for the time being in force."

APPENDIX 8.

CHAIN OF COMMAND.

DIAGRAM SHOWING CHAIN OF COMMAND.

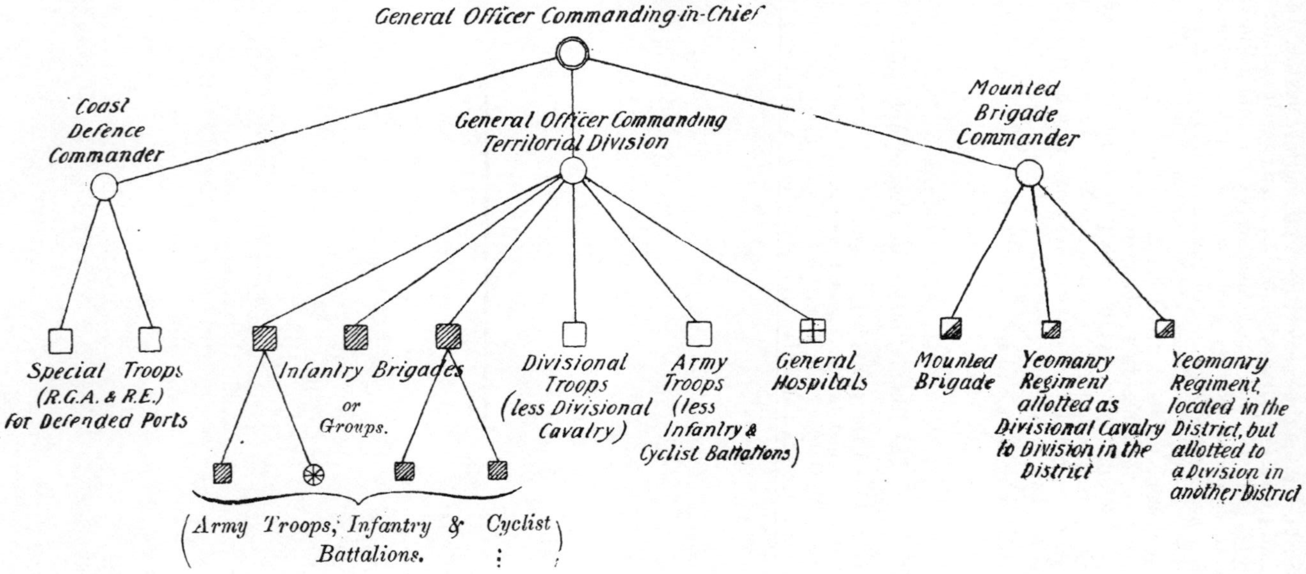

APPENDIX 9.—CHANNELS OF COMMUNICATION.

DIAGRAM SHOWING CHANNELS OF COMMUNICATION FOR TERRITORIAL FORCE AND COUNTY ASSOCIATIONS.

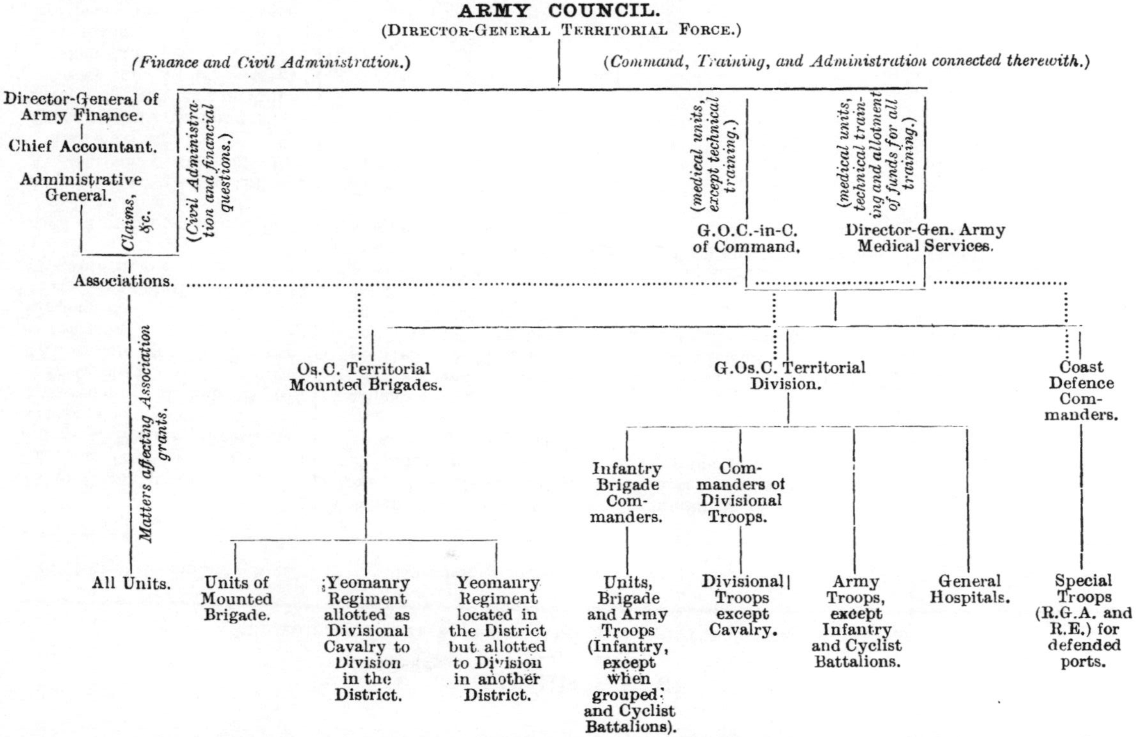

Note i.—The dotted line shows the channels through which Associations may communicate with officers of the Military Commands.

ii.—All letters for the War Office should be addressed, "The Secretary, War Office."

APPENDIX 10.

SUBJECTS OF CORRESPONDENCE AND AUTHORITY TO WHOM SUBMITTED.

Subject of Communication.	By whom sent.	Passed through.	To.
*War Organization .. *Annual Training .. *General Training Questions *Inspection .. .. *Attendance at Schools of Instruction *Allocation of Funds for Training *Discipline .. .. *Permanent Staff Discipline *Establishments ..	Yeomanry	Mounted Brigade Commander	G.O.C.-in-C.
	Units allotted to Infantry Brigades and Groups and Infantry and Cyclist Battalions of Army Troops attached	Infantry Brigade or Group Commander	G.O.C.-in-C.
	Units, except Yeomanry, allotted to Divisions	Divisional Troop Commander and Divisional General	G.O.C.-in-C.
	Army Troops attached, except Infantry and Cyclist Battalions	Divisional General	G.O.C.-in-C.
	General Hospitals	Divisional General	G.O.C.-in-C.
	Units allotted to Coast Defence	Coast Defence Commander ..	G.O.C.-in-C.
First Appointment of Officers in the lowest Rank	Presidents of Associations ..	—	G.O.C.-in-C.
Appointment of other Officers	Officer Commanding Unit ..	Association	G.O.C.-in-C.
Appointments, &c., of Permanent Staff	As above	—	O.C. Records.
Peace Organization of Units Administration and maintenance of Units, except when embodied .. Recruiting .. .. Provision and Maintenance of Ranges			

Provision and Maintenance of Buildings .. .. Facilitating Provision of Areas to be used for Manœuvres .. .. Facilitating the Attendance of Men at Annual Training .. .. Provision of Horses for Peace Requirements. . Provision of Equipment, Stores, Transport, &c., for Peace Requirements Provision of such equipment, Horses, &c., for Mobilization, as the Army Council may direct to be met locally .. .. Safe custody of Arms and such other Stores as are provided by the War Department .. .. Transport .. .. Conveyance of Men fully equipped to and from Annual Training ..	Yeomanry	Mounted Brigade Commander when necessary	†Association.
	Units allotted to Coast Defence.	Coast Defence Commander when necessary	†Association.
	All other Units	Divisional General when necessary	†Association.

* It must be left to the discretion of the Officers through whom this correspondence passed whether the particular case is one for decision by themselves or should be referred to higher authority. In certain cases the G.O.C.-in-C. will have to refer questions to the War Office.

† It will rest with the County Association to decide, in accordance with the Regulations on the subject, which cases must be referred to the Army Council, the Officers of the Military Command, or the Financial authorities, respectively.

APPENDIX 10—*continued.*

Subject of Communication.	By whom sent.	Passed through.	To.
Provision of Funds for the above Services .. Payment of Separation and other Allowances to Families of Men when embodied	All Units	—	Association.
Provision of Arms and such other Stores as remain War Department property	All Units	Chief Ordnance Officer ..	G.O.C.-in-C.

APPENDIX 11.

MEDICAL AND SURGICAL EQUIPMENT.

Medical Stores for Instructional Purposes.

At each headquarters of the R.A.M.C., where one or more Mounted Brigade Field Ambulances exist, the field medical equipment for a Mounted Brigade Field Ambulance (*see* appended table) will be stored.

At each headquarters of the R.A.M.C., where one or more Field Ambulances exist, the field medical equipment for a Field Ambulance (*see* appended table) will be stored.

This equipment will be demanded by A.M.Os. on A.F. I 1209, in duplicate, from the War Office, and will be available for instructional purposes.

It will be accounted for on A.F. I 1234, to be rendered in January of each year for the period ended 31st December.

Losses, damages and deficiencies of non-consumable articles, except such damages as are the result of fair wear and tear, will be dealt with on A.F. I 1230, in accordance with the King's Regulations, and the authority for writing any article off charge will be quoted in and will accompany the annual return A.F. I 1234.

Articles required to complete the equipment will be demanded on A.F. I 1209, in duplicate, to accompany A.F. I 1234, annually, or at such other time as may be found necessary.

Medical and Surgical Equipment for Camps.

Before the commencement of the training season the A.M.O. of the Territorial Force will make timely demands on the Regular A.M.O. of the Command, on A.F. I 1209, for medical and surgical equipment, in accordance with the following scale for the use of units and camps training within the area of his division.

He will only demand those articles which are absolutely necessary, and will arrange, as far as possible, for the transfer of the equipment from one unit to another.

For a Regimental Camp consisting of 500 or more men :—

Companion, medical, and water-bottle	No.	1
Haversack, surgical, and water-bottle	,,	2

For a Brigade Camp :—

Companion, medical, and water-bottle	,,	1
Haversack, surgical, and water-bottle	,,	4
Panniers, field, medical	pair	1
Box, field, fracture	No.	1
Pump, stomach	,,	1
Instruments, tooth	set	1

Losses, damages and deficiencies of non-consumable articles, except such damages as are the result of fair wear and tear, will be dealt with on A.F. I 1230, in accordance with the King's Regulations, and the authority for writing any article off charge will be quoted on the duplicate list of contents.

Medical officers in charge of regimental and brigade camps will see that the medical equipment is properly packed and returned to the District Loan Equipment store of the command at the termination of the training. Each article will be accompanied by an invoice or duplicate list of contents, in which losses, damages, deficiencies, and expenditure, will be carefully recorded. This document will be signed and dated by the medical officer in charge of the equipment and placed inside the article as a voucher.

Scale of Medical and Surgical Equipment for a Mounted Brigade ***Field*** *Ambulance and a Field Ambulance.*

Unit.	Medical Companion and Water-bottle.	Surgical Haversack and Water-bottle.	Field Medical Panniers (Pairs).	Reserve Field Medical Panniers (Pairs).	Field Surgical Panniers (Pairs).	Field Fracture Box.	Reserve Dressing Box.
Cavalry Field Ambulance	4	8	2	—	2	2	4
Field Ambulance	6	21	3	1	3	3	6

APPENDIX 12.

ROYAL ENGINEERS—TRADES, AND PROCEDURE IN REGARD TO THE RATING OF MEN FOR ENGINEER PAY.

1.—*Trades of Engineer Units.*

(i) The trades for Field Companies, Balloon Companies, and
9/Engineers/8 Telegraph Units should be as far as possible those laid down for regular Field, Balloon, and Telegraph Companies, respectively.

(ii) Electric Light Units should be formed of those having the same trades as for Works and Land Front Companies (*see* paragraph iii), preference being given to electricians, engine-drivers, smiths, and fitters.

(iii) Works and Land Front Companies should be formed of those who are connected with the engineering profession or employed as masons, joiners, quarrymen, skilled labourers or the like, and are of approved trades as shown below, viz. :-

Blacksmiths ; Boilermakers ; Bricklayers ; Cabinet-makers ; Carpenters ; Coppersmiths ; Coopers ; Engine-drivers ; Engine-erectors ; Fitters ; Gasfitters ; Instrument repairers ; Joiners ; Masons ; Metal-turners ; Moulders ; Painters ; Patternmakers ; Plasterers ; Plumbers ; Riveters ; Sawyers ; Slaters ; Tinsmiths ; White-smiths ; Wood-turners ; Electricians ; Telegraphists ; Telephonists ; Clerks, if suitable for training in electrical work.

(iv) Men who in civil life are employed in a specialized branch of any of the above trades, may be enlisted under the general trade term in the above list ; thus, men employed in a machine shop may be classed as either metal-turners or fitters ; men employed on electrical work as wiremen, jointers, &c., may be classed as electricians.

The nature of their special qualification should be recorded.

2.—*Procedure to be adopted in regard to the rating of men for Engineer Pay.*

The following procedure should be adopted in regard to the rating of men of Royal Engineer Units of the Territorial Force for Engineer Pay, viz. :—

(*a*) Provided no military workshop is available, a certificate of trade qualifications should be obtained from the man's employer, or other local source, in accordance with the certificate shown at the bottom of the front page of Army Form B 195.

(*b*) This certificate will be accepted on the recommendation of a Board of Officers consisting of the Regular Adjutant and one officer of the Territorial unit. A similar course will be followed in the case of subsequent increases of Engineer Pay, the entries being made on the back of the Form.

(*c*) The various rates of Engineer Pay will be as laid down for the Royal Engineers (Regulars) in the Pay Warrant (Article 874).

(*d*) The equivalent ratings for the qualifications specified in the footnote of Army Form B 195 are as follows :—

As in footnote to Army Form B 195.	Qualifications and Rating for Engineer Pay.	Article of Pay Warrant.
Very good	Superior (3rd rate)	876
Good	Skilled (4th rate)	876
Fair	Fair (5th rate)	876
Indifferent	Indifferent (6th rate)	—
Bad	Bad (7th rate)	—

Men who are "Very Superior" at their trades may be granted the 2nd rate of Engineer Pay.

The 1st rate of Engineer Pay will be granted only under very special and exceptional circumstances (Article 880, Pay Warrant).

(*e*) Mounted non-commissioned officers, drivers, trumpeters, and buglers will be rated in accordance with the provisions of Articles 875–879, Pay Warrant.

APPENDIX 13.

RATES AND CONDITIONS FOR TRAVELLING GRANTS.

Title of the grant.	Rate per mile on the distance from the head-quarters indicated to the place of training.	Arm of the Service.	Conditions of the grant.
Battalion parades	1*d*.... ...	Infantry units which have outlying companies with headquarters more than 5 miles from headquarters.	For each efficient member present on parade in a company which necessarily travels upwards of 5 miles to the place, within the unit's recruiting area, where battalion parade is held. The allowance will not be given for any company which is represented at the drill by less than 20 rank and file (exclusive of bandsmen). When more than one journey is undertaken by any individual member of a company, the travelling allowance may be drawn for each journey, provided the total amount claimed for the company does not exceed that payable in respect of one journey for each efficient.
Battery or company training.	1*d*.... ...	Artillery, Engineers (other than Electric Light Engineers), Infantry, Army Service Corps, Royal Army Medical Corps.	For each efficient member present at the training in a battery, company, or other unit which necessarily travels not less than 5 miles to carry out battery or company training. The allowance will only be granted on the certificate of the Brigadier or corresponding officer that the distance claimed for does not exceed that from the head-quarters of the battery, company, or other unit to the nearest suitable ground available for the purpose of battery or company training. In the case of Royal Garrison Artillery units this training may be done at works of defence. It is admissible in respect of each journey undertaken by any member of a battery, company, or other unit, provided the total amount so claimed does not exceed that payable for the battery or company in respect of six journeys for each efficient.

RATES AND CONDITIONS FOR TRAVELLING GRANTS—*continued.*

Title of the grant.	Rate per mile on the distance from the headquarters indicated to the place of training.	Arm of the Service.	Conditions of the grant.
Company training for unqualified men.	1*d*.... ...	Electric Light Engineers.	For each efficient who as an unqualified member necessarily travels not less than 5 miles from the headquarters of his company to perform the technical drills required for efficiency, and for each member of the necessary instructional staff. The allowance will be granted for each journey up to a limit of three journeys per man.
Musketry practice. (1903 course.)	*6*d*. for completing the course without reference to the number of journeys actually made but not to exceed a total of 9*s*. per man in any case.	Cavalry, Engineers (Field companies only), Infantry.	For each efficient member who passes out of the 3rd class, provided that the headquarters of his company, or the approved drill station of his recognised section, is more than 2 miles from its authorised range, or, if this range is unsuitable for the whole of the individual course or for collective practice, from the nearest suitable range. The same rates may be drawn for each efficient officer, staff serjeant, serjeant-instructor, and bugler who attends at the range when the practice is carried out, and for each efficient bandsman who attends the range on duty strictly connected with the musketry practice.

* In cases where the 1901 musketry course is adopted by a corps for the whole of its members, the rate will be 4*d*. per mile only, up to a maximum of 6*s*. per man.

When the 1901 course is fired and the individual practice can be performed at the ordinary range, but attendance at another range is necessary for the collective firing—

3*d*. per mile for individual practice ... }
1*d*. per mile for collective practice ... } Not to exceed 6*s*. per man in any case.

Where the 1903 course is completed at two or more ranges the rate will be divided in the proportion that the number of rounds fired at the various ranges bears to the total number of rounds required.

No travelling allowance will be issuable in respect of any practice dispensed with.

APPENDIX 14.

RULES AS TO LOANS, PURCHASE OF LAND, ERECTION OF BUILDINGS, &c.

1. A County Association may, with the consent of the Army Council, and subject to such conditions, if any, as the Army Council may think fit to impose—

(1) Purchase, take on lease, or exchange, or otherwise acquire land for the purposes of The Territorial and Reserve Forces Act, 1907;

(2) Sell, exchange, lease, or otherwise dispose of any land so acquired;

(3) Borrow such money as may be required for the purchase by the Association of land for the purposes of the Act of 1907, or for the purchase, erection, construction, alteration, or enlargement of any building or permanent work used or intended to be used for those purposes, or for the repayment of a loan raised for any such purpose;

(4) Secure the repayment of any monies so borrowed, with interest thereon at such rate as may be agreed, by mortgage of any land purchased or otherwise acquired by the Association, and, with the consent of the Army Council of any other property or revenues of the Association.

2. The council of a county or borough may, at the request of a County Association, purchase and hold or hire land on behalf of the Association, in the same manner as such council is by the Military Lands Acts, 1892 to 1903, authorised to purchase and hold or hire land on behalf of a Volunteer corps, and to lease the land so purchased or hired to the Volunteer corps.

3. As respects the matters dealt with in the foregoing regulations, the provisions of the Military Lands Acts, 1892 to 1903, set forth in the schedule* hereto, subject to the adaptations and modifications therein contained, shall apply so far as they relate to such matters.

4. When it is desired to acquire property for military purposes, the application should specify—

The exact situation and area of the property which it is proposed to acquire. (The situation should also be marked on a small map of the district.)

The purpose for which the property is required.

The price which it is proposed to pay.

The manner in which it is proposed to raise the purchase money, including the proportion which is to be raised from private funds.

---

* *See* Appendix 15, page 218.

Whether any, and if so what, liability will remain on the property after the purchase is affected.

Whether the property is subject to any charges such as land tax, tithe, &c., and, if so, the amount thereof.

Whether there are any restrictions as to the use of the land in the title. If mines or minerals are excluded from the proposed purchase, whether the mineral owner or lessee is bound to make good surface damage.

Whether there are any restrictions in the conditions of sale or the lease, as to the use of the property in the event of the disbandment of the unit.

If the property is already occupied by the County Association, the terms on which it is held.

If the property is not so occupied, but its acquisition will enable the Association to surrender other accommodation, the terms on which such other accommodation is held, and the amount of the saving to be effected by its surrender.

The application should be accompanied by a plan of the site and any existing buildings, and by the valuation of a local surveyor of standing, showing the sale value of the property, including that of any existing buildings, in the open market, and the period during which such buildings will probably last, ordinary care being assumed.

5. If it is desired to erect, construct, alter, or enlarge any building or permanent work, the application should specify, in addition to the particulars enumerated in paragraph 4, the terms in full detail on which the site is held, and should be accompanied by full particulars and plans of the proposed works, together with a report by a local surveyor of standing showing whether the estimate has been framed with due regard to economy, and whether the works can be carried out satisfactorily for the sum named.

6. When an Association wishes to employ the compulsory powers of the Military Lands Act, 1892, the procedure set forth in Section 2, Sub-sections 5 and 7 of that Act, will be observed, and the particulars specified in paragraph 4 supplied.

7. When an Association wishes to obtain a loan, whether from the Public Works Loan Commissioners or otherwise, the application will specify, in addition to the particulars mentioned in paragraphs 4 and 5—

The amount of the proposed loan.

The period, not to exceed 50 years, within which it is proposed that the loan shall be repaid.

If the loan is for the purpose of erecting, constructing, altering, or enlarging any building or permanent work, the surveyor's report will show, in addition to the particulars required under paragraph 5—

The sale value in the open market of the site.

The probable value in the open market of the land and works when completed, assuming that the works have been carried out in accordance with the plans and specification.

The period during which the buildings or works will probably last, ordinary care being assumed.

If the loan is for the purpose of the repayment of an existing loan which has been raised for any of the purposes mentioned in the Military Lands Acts, 1892 or 1897, the following further information must be furnished—

Full particulars of the loan which it is intended to repay.

The present sale value in the open market, duly certified by a local surveyor of standing, of the property forming the security for the loan. The surveyor's report will also state the period during which the buildings forming part of the property will probably last, ordinary care being assumed. Full particulars, plans of the property in question, and also a small map of the district, showing its exact position, should be furnished with this report.

Whether any, and if so what, liability will remain on the property after the existing loan has been paid off.

8. When it is proposed to obtain a loan, otherwise than from the Public Works Loan Commissioners, extending beyond the financial year, a statement will be forwarded to the War Office showing the arrangements proposed for paying it off, whether by annual repayments or otherwise.

9. When a Public Works Loan has been granted, no contract is to be entered into or building operations commenced until an intimation has been received from the Public Works Loan Commissioners that they are satisfied as to the title of the Association to the site.

10. When it is proposed to incur a loan for the purpose of carrying out building operations, tenders must be invited for the carrying out of the works, and a notification will be made accordingly when the application is sanctioned. If in exceptional circumstances other arrangements are considered preferable, the circumstances must be fully explained when applying for the loan to the Army Council.

11. When Public Works Loans have been approved for the purpose of erecting, constructing, altering or enlarging any buildings or permanent works, the money will be advanced by periodical instalments, upon the application of the Association, supported by a certificate of the engineer or architect in charge of the works, to the effect that work, in accordance with the plans and descriptions approved by the War Office, has been duly completed to the value of the sum applied for. Application for the final instalment should be made, when the work is completed, to the Army Council, and the work or building will be inspected on their behalf, and certified as in accordance with the approved plans, before issue is made by the Public Works Loan Commissioners. The applications for all other instalments should be made by the Association direct to the Public Works Loan Commissioners, Old Jewry, London, E.C.

12. In the case of special stores required for the work or buildings, but not included in the general contract for the construction, satisfactory evidence of the supply and cost of the articles should be furnished by the Association, together with the application for an instalment of the loan.

13. The rates of interest payable on loans granted after 9th September, 1907, by the Public Works Loan Commissioners, as laid down by the Treasury are—

When the period of repayment does not exceed—

30 years	... ...	$3\frac{1}{2}$ per cent.
50 „	... ...	$3\frac{3}{4}$ „

The capital will be repayable by equal annual instalments, the amount of interest on the outstanding portion diminishing with each instalment paid.

APPENDIX 15.

ACQUISITION OF LAND FOR MILITARY PURPOSES—MILITARY LANDS ACT, 1892.

Schedule.

PART I.

ACQUISITION OF LAND FOR MILITARY PURPOSES.

Power to purchase land.

1.—(1) * * * * *

(2) A *county association* may, with the consent of the *Army Council*, themselves purchase land under this Act for military purposes.

(3) The council of a county or borough may, at the request of *a county association*, purchase, under this Act, and hold land on behalf of the *county association* for military purposes.

(4) The *Army Council* shall, before giving their consent to the purchase of any land under this Act by *a county association*, send an inspector to the land for the purpose of ascertaining its capabilities of being used for military purposes with due regard to the safety and convenience of the public, and shall give or withhold their consent accordingly.

Machinery for purchase of land.

2. For the purpose of the purchase of land under this Act, the Lands Clauses Acts shall be incorporated with this Act, with the exceptions and additions and subject to the provisions following (that is to say):

(1) There shall not be incorporated with this Act, sections sixteen or seventeen of the Lands Clauses Consolidation Act, 1845, or the provisions of that Act with respect to affording access to the special Act:

(2) In the construction of this Act and the incorporated Acts, this Act shall be deemed to be the special Act, and the *county association* or council of a county or borough, as the case may be (in this section referred to as "the purchaser"), shall be deemed to be the promoters of the undertaking:

(3) * * * * *

(4) The provisions of the incorporated Acts with respect to the purchase of land compulsorily shall not be put in force until a Provisional Order has been made and the sanction of Parliament has been obtained in manner in this Act mentioned:

(5) One month at the least before the application for the Order, the purchaser shall serve, in manner provided by the Lands Clauses Acts, a notice on every owner or reputed owner, lessee or reputed lessee, and occupier of any land intended to be so purchased, describing the land intended to be taken, and in general terms the purposes to which it is to be applied, and stating the intention of the purchaser to obtain the sanction of Parliament to the purchase thereof, and inquiring whether the person so served assents or dissents to the taking of his land, and requesting him to forward to the purchaser any objections he may have to his land being taken.

(6) * * * * *

(7) Where the purchaser is *a county association* or the council of a county or borough—

(*a*) The *association* or council may, if they think fit, on compliance with the provisions of this section with respect to notices, present a petition to a Secretary of State. The petition shall state the land intended to be taken, and the purposes for which the land is required, and the names of the owners, lessees, and occupiers of land who have assented, dissented, or are neuter in respect of the taking the land, or who have returned no answer to the notice. The petition shall pray that the corps or council may, with reference to the land, be allowed to put in force the powers of the Lands Clauses Acts with respect to the purchase and taking of lands otherwise than by agreement, and the prayer shall be supported by such evidence as the Secretary of State requires:

(*b*) On receipt of the petition and on due proof of the proper notices having been served, the Secretary of State shall take the petition into consideration, and may either dismiss the same or direct a public local inquiry to be held by a competent officer as to the propriety of assenting to the prayer of the petition.

(8) Before a local inquiry is held in pursuance of this section the Secretary of State shall publish a notice of the intention to hold the inquiry—

(*a*) By affixing copies conspicuously on or in the immediate neighbourhood of the land proposed to be acquired; and

(*b*) By advertising the notice once at least in each of two successive weeks in some one and the same local newspaper circulating in the neighbourhood.

(9) If after the local inquiry has been held the Secretary of State is satisfied that the land ought to be taken, he may make a Provisional Order to that effect, authorising the taking of the land either by himself or by a *county association*, or

by a council of a county or borough, as the case may be, and may submit a Bill to Parliament for the confirmation of the Provisional Order, but the Provisional Order shall not be of any effect unless and until it is confirmed by Parliament.

(10) If, while the Bill confirming any such Order is pending in either House of Parliament, a petition is presented against anything comprised therein, the Bill, so far as relates to the Order may be referred to a select committee, and the petitioner shall be allowed to appear and oppose as in the case of private Bills.

Power to let lands.

3. Land acquired under this Act may be let by a *county association*, or if acquired by the council of a county or borough by that council, in any manner consistent with the use thereof for military purposes.

Payment of expenses.

4. Any expenses incurred by the council of a county or borough for the purposes of this Act shall be defrayed by the council of a county out of the county fund, and by the council of a borough out of the borough fund or borough rate.

Power of *county association* to borrow.

5.—(1) A *county association* may, with the consent of the *Army Council*, and subject to such conditions as *they* may impose, borrow such money as may be required for the purpose of the purchase by them of land under this Act.

(2) The money shall be borrowed on the security of the land acquired by the *county association*, and *with the consent of the Army Council, of any other property or revenues of the association.*

Powers of borough council to borrow, 38 & 39 Vict. c. 55.

6. The council of a borough may borrow for the purpose of acquiring land under this Act in like manner as they may borrow for the purposes of the Public Health Act, 1875, and the provisions of that Act shall apply accordingly, but the money shall be borrowed on the security of the borough fund or borough rate.

7. * * * * *

8. * * * * *

9. * * * * *

Provision as to land belonging to Crown, &c.

10.—(1) The Commissioners of Woods with the consent of the Treasury, as to land belonging to the Crown, the Chancellor and Council of the Duchy of Lancaster by deed under the hand and seal of the Chancellor, attested by the clerk of the council, as to land forming part of possessions of the Duchy of Lancaster, and the Duke of Cornwall or other the persons for the time being having power to dispose of land belonging to the Duchy of Cornwall, as to land forming part of possessions of that duchy, may lease land lor military purposes to a *county association* for a term not exceeding twenty-one years, but the lease shall cease to have effect if the land ceases to be used for military purposes.

(2) Where any land is vested in the Crown and is under the management of any commissioners or departments other than the Commissioners of Woods, and where land is held by any public department for the public service, the commissioners or department having the management of the lands may exercise, as regards

the land, any powers which under this Act may be exercised as respects land belonging to the Crown by the Commissioners of Woods.

(3) The Commissioners of Works may lease to a *county association* for military purposes any portion of such royal parks, gardens, and possessions as are under the management of those Commissioners for a term not exceeding twenty-one years, and subject to such conditions as the Commissioners think fit; but the lease shall be at all times revocable by His Majesty.

Power to lease land held for public purposes.

11.—(1) Any person, body of persons, or authority holding land for ecclesiastical or public purposes may lease any such land to a *county association* for military purposes for any term not exceeding twenty-one years, subject to the following provisions:—

(*a*) An ecclesiastical corporation sole below the dignity of a bishop shall not grant any such lease without the consent in writing of the bishop to whose jurisdiction he is subject, and of the patron of the preferment to which the land belongs, or the guardians or trustees of such patron:

(*b*) A lease of parochial property shall be granted under and in accordance with the provisions of section three of the Union and Parish Property Act, 1835, and the Acts amending the same:

(*c*) Where the land is vested in any trustees, commissioners, or other body of persons, a majority of a meeting of such trustees, commissioners, or other body of persons duly convened may grant a lease under this section and execute any instrument for that purpose:

(*d*) Where the land belongs to an administrative county, the county council may grant a lease under this section with the consent of the Local Government Board.

(2) A lease under this section shall cease to have effect if the land ceases to be used for military purposes.

Proof that land has ceased to be used for military purposes.

12. Any land leased under this Act shall be deemed to have ceased to be used for military purposes where there has not been such use for a period of one year, and a certificate of the fact of such non-user is given by *the Army Council*; and the certificate shall be conclusive evidence of the fact of such non-user.

Power to stop or divert footpaths.

13.—(1) Where a footpath crosses or runs inconveniently or dangerously near to any land leased under this Act, that footpath may with the consent of the vestry of the parish in which the same is situate, and on the certificate of two justices that the footpath to be substituted is convenient for the public, be stopped up or diverted.

(2) The provisions of the Highway Act, 1835, as to the obtaining of a certificate and the stopping up or diverting a highway where a person other than the inhabitants or vestry are desirous of stopping up, diverting, or turning a highway, shall apply so far as practicable to the obtaining of a certificate, and the stopping up or diverting a footpath under this section; with this exception that the certificate of the justices shall be conclusive in cases where it states the fact of their having viewed the footpath to be stopped up or diverted, and that the proposed new footpath is convenient for the public.

PART II.

BYELAWS AS TO LAND USED FOR MILITARY PURPOSES.

Power of Secretary of State to make byelaws as to use of land held for military purposes and securing safety of public.

14.—(1) Where any land belonging to a *county association* is for the time being appropriated by or with the consent of a Secretary of State for any military purpose, a Secretary of State may make byelaws for regulating the use of the land for the purposes to which it is appropriated, and for securing the public against danger arising from that use, with power to prohibit all intrusion on the land and all obstruction of the use thereof:

Provided that no byelaws promulgated under this section shall authorise the Secretary of State to take away or prejudicially affect any right of common.

(2) Where any such byelaws permit the public to use the land for any purpose when not used for the military purpose to which it is appropriated, those byelaws may also provide for the government of the land when so used by the public, and the preservation of order and good conduct thereon, and for the prevention of nuisances, obstructions, encampments, and encroachments thereon, and for the prevention of any injury to the same, or to anything growing or erected thereon, and for the prevention of anything interfering with the orderly use thereof by the public for the purpose permitted by the byelaws.

(3) "Land belonging to a *county association*" means any land vested in that *association* or in any person as trustee for that *association.*

Application of byelaws where right of firing acquired.

15 Where a *county association* has for the time being the right of using for any military purpose any land vested in another person this Part of this Act shall apply in like manner as if the land were vested in the *association,* and the same were appropriated for the said purpose, save that nothing therein or in any byelaws made thereunder shall injuriously affect the private rights of any person further or otherwise than is authorised by the grant of the right to use the land.

Byelaws as to highways.

16.—(1) A byelaw under this Act shall not interfere with any highway, unless made with the consent of the authority having control of the repair of the roads of the town, district, parish, or other area in which the highway is situate, but where it appears to the authority that any highway crosses or runs inconveniently or dangerously near to any land the use of which can be regulated by byelaws under this Act, the authority may consent to a byelaw providing to such extent as seems reasonable for the temporary diversion from time to time of the highway, or for the restriction from time to time of the use thereof.

(2) Any such highway, if a footpath, may (without prejudice to any other power of stopping up or diverting the same) be stopped up or diverted in the manner in which a footpath crossing or running

inconveniently or dangerously near to any land leased under Part One of this Act may be stopped up or diverted.

17.—(1) A Secretary of State, before making any byelaws under this Act, shall cause the proposed byelaws to be made known in the locality, and give an opportunity for objections being made to the same, and shall receive and consider all objections made; and when any such byelaws are made, shall cause the boundaries of the area to which the byelaws apply to be marked, and the byelaws to be published, in such manner as appears to him necessary to make them known to all persons in the locality, and shall provide for copies of the byelaws being sold at the price of one shilling for each copy to any person who desires to obtain the same. Notice and enforcement of byelaws.

(2) If any person commits an offence against any byelaw under this Act, he shall be liable, on conviction, before a court of summary jurisdiction, to a fine not exceeding five pounds, and may be removed by any constable or officer authorised in manner provided by the byelaw from the area, whether land or water, to which the byelaw applies, and taken into custody without warrant, and brought before a court of summary jurisdiction to be dealt with according to law, and any vehicle, animal, vessel, or thing found in the area in contravention of any byelaw, may be removed by any constable or such officer as aforesaid, and on due proof of such contravention, be declared by a court of summary jurisdiction to be forfeited to His Majesty.

(3) A byelaw under this Act shall be deemed to be a regulation within the meaning of the Documentary Evidence Act, 1868, and may be proved accordingly.

18.—(1) Where land has been leased under Part One of this Act, a byelaw made in respect of that land shall not be inconsistent with any condition contained in the instrument of lease. Byelaws in case of leased land.

(2) Where land has been leased under Part One of this Act subject to a condition that byelaws relating to the land shall be made with the consent of the lessor, or shall be made by the lessor subject to the approval of the Secretary of State, that condition shall be observed, and the lessor, acting with the approval of the Secretary of State shall have the same power of making byelaws in relation to the land as is conferred by this Act on the Secretary of State.

PART III.

SUPPLEMENTAL

19. * * * * *

20. Where any land is acquired under this Act or for military purposes under any Act with which the Lands Clauses Acts are incorporated, the person or authority acquiring the land may require that the compensation to be paid for the land be settled by arbitration and not by reference to a jury, and thereupon the provisions of the Lands Clauses Acts with reference to arbitration Power to have compensation settled by arbitration.

shall, if not already applicable, apply for the purpose of settling the compensation.

21. * * * * *

22. * * * * *

Interpretation. 23. In this Act the expression "military purposes" includes rifle or artillery practice, the building and enlarging of barracks and camps, the erection of butts, targets, batteries and other accommodation, the storing of arms, military drill and any other purpose connected with military matters approved by the *Army Council.*

In this Act and the enactments incorporated therewith the expression "land" includes any easement in or over lands, and for the purpose of Part One of this Act includes any right of firing over lands or other right of user.

Saving for New Forest. 24. Nothing in this Act shall authorise the taking of any land in the New Forest, or shall empower the Commissioners of Woods, to grant or lease, or give any licence over any land in the New Forest.

Application to Scotland. 25. In the application of this Act to Scotland, the following provisions shall have effect:—

(1) The expression "council of a county or borough" means the county council of a county or the town council of a burgh, as defined by the Local Government (Scotland) Act, 1889:

(2) The expressions "county fund" and "borough fund or borough rate," mean respectively the general purposes rate and the police rate:

(3) For the purpose of acquiring land under this Act a county council may borrow in like manner as they may borrow under section sixty-seven of the Local Government (Scotland) Act, 1889, and a town council in like manner as they may borrow under section fourteen of the Public Parks (Scotland) Act, 1878:

(4) The expression "Local Government Board" means Secretary for Scotland:

(5) A reference to any sections of the Lands Clauses Consolidation Act, 1845, shall be construed to mean a reference to the corresponding sections of the Lands Clauses Consolidation (Scotland) Act, 1845:

(6) Section eleven of this Act shall not apply to Scotland, and in lieu thereof the following provision shall have effect, namely,—

Any person, body of persons, or authority holding land for ecclesiastical or public purposes, may lease such land to a *county association* for military purposes for any term not exceeding twenty-one years, subject to the following provisions:—

(*a*) The minister of a parish who shall be in possession of a glebe shall be entitled to grant such lease as if the words "twenty-one years" had been substituted for the words "eleven years" in the third section of the Glebe Lands (Scotland) Act, 1866, provided that in all other respects the provisions of the said third section be observed;

(*b*) Where the land is vested in any trustees, commissioners, or other body of persons, a majority of a meeting of such trustees, commissioners, or other body of persons, duly convened, may grant a lease under this section, and execute any instrument for that purpose;

(*c*) Where the land belongs to a county council or a town council, that council may grant a lease under this section with the consent of the Secretary for Scotland;

(*d*) A lease under this section shall cease to have effect if the land ceases to be used for military purposes:

(7) The sheriff of the county shall give the consent and grant the certificate required under subsection one of section thirteen of this Act, and sections forty-two and forty-three of the Roads and Bridges (Scotland) Act, 1878, shall be substituted for subsection two of section thirteen of this Act:

(8) The expression "court of summary jurisdiction" means the sheriff or any two justices of the peace sitting in open court or any magistrate or magistrates within the meaning of the Summary Jurisdiction Acts:

(9) * * * * *

26. * * * * *

27. The powers given to the Commissioners of Woods by this Act shall extend to any allotment that may be made to and any land that may be purchased on behalf of Her Majesty, under the provisions of an Act of Tynwald, intituled the Isle of Man Disafforesting Act, 1860, but save as aforesaid, this Act shall not extend to the Isle of Man. **Limited application of Act to Isle of Man.**

28. * * * * *

29. This Act may be cited as the Military Lands Act, 1892. **Short title.**

THE MILITARY LANDS ACT, 1897.

1. The powers of a *county association* to borrow shall extend to the borrowing of such money as may be required for the purchase, erection, construction, alteration, or enlargement of any building or permanent work for the purposes of a *county association*, or for the repayment of a loan raised for any such purpose. **Amendment of law as to borrowing powers.**

2. This Act shall be construed as part of the Military Lands Act 1892, *as applied by these regulations*, and may be cited as the Military Lands Act, 1897. **Short title and construction.**

THE MILITARY LANDS ACT, 1900.

County or borough council may lease land and *county associations* may borrow on security of lease.

1.—(1) The council of a county or borough holding land on behalf of *a county association* under subsection three of section one of the Military Lands Act, 1892, *as applied by these regulations*, may lease the land or any part thereof to any such *association* for military purposes for a period not exceeding ninety-nine years.

(2) The powers of a *county association* to borrow under the Military Lands Acts, 1892 and 1897, shall extend to borrowing on the security of any such lease.

(3) If the land ceases to be used for military purposes, the lease shall vest in the *Army Council*, subject to repayment of any money borrowed on the security of the lease and not already repaid.

2.—(1) * * * * *

Provision as to byelaws.

(2) Where any land, the use of which can be regulated by byelaws under the Military Lands Act, 1892, *as applied by these regulations*, or this Act, abuts on any sea or tidal water, or where rifle or artillery practice is or can be carried on over any sea, tidal water, or shore, from any such land, byelaws may be made in relation to any such sea, tidal water, or shore, as if they were part of the land.

Provided that—

(*a*) If any such byelaw injuriously affects or obstructs the exercise, of any private right of any person in or over any such sea, tidal water, or shore, that person shall be entitled to compensation, and the compensation shall, in case of difference, be ascertained in manner provided by the Lands Clauses Acts with respect to the compensation for land taken other, wise than by agreement; and

(*b*) Any such byelaw shall not injuriously affect any public right within the meaning of this section unless made with the consent of the Board of Trade, but the Board of Trade, if satisfied after such inquiries and such notice and opportunity for objections as hereinafter mentioned, that a restriction of any public right is required for the safety of the public, or for the exigencies of the military purpose for which the area to which the byelaws apply is used, may consent to a byelaw restricting the public right to such extent as under all the circumstances of the case seems reasonable; and

(*c*) No such byelaw shall be made in relation to any sea, tidal water, or shore which may for the time being be vested in His Majesty, and under the management of the Commissioners of Woods, without the consent in writing of such Commissioners on behalf of His Majesty first had and obtained for that purpose, which consent such Commissioners are hereby authorised to give.

(3) The Board of Trade, before consenting to any byelaw under this section, shall cause notice of the byelaw to be given by advertisement or otherwise in the locality, in order that any such town,

harbour, and other local authorities and persons as are interested may have an opportunity for making objections to the byelaw, and shall consider any objections made and shall make such inquiries as appear to the Board necessary for the purpose of ascertaining that the byelaw will not unreasonably interfere with any public right.

(4) For the purposes of this section "public right" means any right of navigation, anchoring, grounding, fishing, bathing, walking, or recreation.

(5) Where an area to which byelaws under this section apply consists of any sea or tidal water, or the shore thereof, and the boundaries of the area cannot, in the opinion of the authority making the byelaws, be conveniently marked by permanent marks, those boundaries shall be described in the byelaws, and shall be deemed to be sufficiently marked within the meaning of section seventeen of the Military Lands Act, 1892, *as applied by these regulations*, if, while the area is in use for military purposes, sufficient means are taken to warn the public from entering the area.

(6) * * * * *

Extension of meaning of "land."

3. Section twenty-three of the Military Lands Act, 1892, *as applied by these regulations*, shall have effect as if the definition of "land" in that section included the bed of the sea or any tidal water, and also any right of interference with the free use of any land, and the Military Lands Act, 1892, *as so applied*, and as amended by this Act, shall be construed accordingly.

Amendment of 55 & 56 Vict. c. 43 s. 2, as to limit of time for compulsory purchase.

4. Notwithstanding anything in section two of the Military Lands Act, 1892, *as applied by these regulations*, the period of three years mentioned in section one hundred and twenty-three of the Lands Clauses Consolidation Act, 1845, shall be calculated from the passing of the Act confirming any Provisional Order under the Military Lands Act, 1892, and not from the passing of the Military Lands Act, 1892.

5. * * * * *

Short title and construction.

6. This Act shall be construed as part of the Military Lands Act, 1892, *as applied by these regulations*, and may be cited as the Military Lands Act, 1900.

THE MILITARY LANDS ACT, 1903.

Power of councils to hire land for military purposes.

1.—(1) The council of a county or borough may, at the request of *a county association* by agreement hire land on behalf of the *county association* for military purposes, for a period not less than twenty-one years, and may contribute towards the expenses incurred by another council in purchasing or hiring land for those purposes, and the expenses of so hiring or contributing may be defrayed in the same manner as expenses of purchasing, and the payment of those expenses, so far as they are in the nature of capital expenses, shall accordingly be a purpose for which the council may borrow.

(2) Land hired under this section on behalf of *a county association* may be leased to the *county association* in like manner as land held by the council of a county or borough under subsection three of section one of the Military Lands Act, 1892, and section one of the Military Lands Act, 1900, shall apply accordingly.

(3) Sections ten and eleven of the Military Lands Act, 1892, *as applied by these regulations*, shall apply to leases of land to councils hiring land under this section as they apply to leases of land to a *county association*.

Short title and construction.

2. This Act may be cited as the Military Lands Act, 1903, and shall be construed as one with Military Lands Acts, 1892 to 1900, *as applied by these regulations.*

APPENDIX 16.

DESIGNS FOR METAL TITLES TO BE WORN ON SHOULDER STRAPS.

Yeomanry.	Royal Horse Artillery.	Royal Field Artillery.
T Y SUSSEX	T R.H.A. CITY OF LONDON	T R.F.A. LANCASHIRE

Royal Garrison Artillery.	Royal Engineers.
T R.G.A. DEVONSHIRE	T R.E. HAMPSHIRE

INFANTRY.—Units bearing the same titles as regular regiments are to wear the same designation as is worn by the latter, with the addition of the letter "T" and the distinguishing battalion numeral :—

T 6 E. SURREY	T 4 SEAFORTH	T 6 S. R.

In other cases the design will be :—

T BRECKNOCK	T 2 MONMOUTH

The insertion of "shire" after the name of the county being left to the discretion of the County Association.

Light Infantry and Fusilier Regiments in addition to the territorial or other designation add the "Bugle" or the "Grenade" as the case may be :—

Army Service Corps.

T
A.S.C.
DEVON & CORNWALL

Royal Army Medical Corps.

T
R.A.M.C.
LONDON

INDEX.

[*References to Sections of T. and R. F. Act are printed in thick type.*]

A.

[References to Sections of T. and R. F. Act are printed in thick type.]

[*References to Sections of T. and R. F. Act are printed in thick type.*]

[References to Sections of T. and R. F. Act are printed in thick type.]

[*References to Sections of T. and R. F. Act are printed in thick type.*]

[*References to Sections of T. and R. F. Act are printed in thick type.*]

[*References to Sections of T. and R. F. Act are printed in thick type.*]

[*References to Sections of T. and R. F. Act are printed in thick type.*]

[*References to Sections of T. and R. F. Act are printed in thick type.*]

[*References to Sections of T. and R. F. Act are printed in thick type.*]

[*References to Sections of T. and R. F. Act are printed in thick type.*]

[References to Sections of T. and R. F. Act are printed in thick type.]

[*References to Sections of T. and R. F. Act are printed in thick type.*]

[*References to Sections of T. and R. F. Act are printed in thick type.*]

[*References to Sections of T. and R. F. Act are printed in thick type.*]

[*References to Sections of T. and R. F. Act are printed in thick type.*]

[*References to Sections of T. and R. F. Act are printed in thick type.*]

[*References to Sections of T. and R. F. Act are printed in thick type.*]

[References to Sections of T. and R. F. Act are printed in thick type.]

[*References to Sections of T. and R. F. Act are printed in thick type.*]

[*References to Sections of T. and R. F. Act are printed in thick type.*]

[*References to Sections of T. and R. F. Act are printed in thick type.*]

[*References to Sections of T. and R. F. Act are printed in thick type.*]

F.

[*References to Sections of T. and R. F. Act are printed in thick type.*]

[*References to Sections of T. and R. F. Act are printed in thick type.*]

G.

[*References to Sections of T. and R. F. Act are printed in thick type.*]

[*References to Sections of T. and R. F. Act are printed in thick type.*]

[*References to Sections of T. and R. F. Act are printed in thick type.*]

I.

[*References to Sections of T. and R. F. Act are printed in thick type.*]

[*References to Sections of T. and R. F. Act are printed in thick type.*]

[*References to Sections of T. and R. F. Act are printed in thick type.*]

[*References to Sections of T. and R. F. Act are printed in thick type.*]

[*References to Sections of T. and R. F. Act are printed in thick type.*]

[*References to Sections of T. and R. F. Act are printed in thick type.*]

[*References to Sections of T. and R. F. Act are printed in thick type.*]

[*References to Sections of T. and R. F. Act are printed in thick type.*]

N.

[*References to Sections of T. and R. F. Act are printed in thick type.*]

[*References to Sections of T. and R. F. Act are printed in thick type.*]

Para.

[*References to Sections of T. and R. F. Act are printed in thick type.*]

[*References to Sections of T. and R. F. Act are printed in thick type.*]

P.

[*References to Sections of T. and R.F. Act are printed in thick type.*]

[*References to Sections of T. and R. F. Act are printed in thick type.*]

[References to Sections of T. and R. F. Act are printed in thick type.]

[*References to Sections of T. and R. F. Act are printed in thick type.*]

[*References to Sections of T. and R. F. Act are printed in thick type.*]

[*References to Sections of T. and R. F. Act are printed in thick type.*]

[*References to Sections of T. and R. F. Act are printed in thick type.*]

[*References to Sections of T. and R. F. Act are printed in thick type.*]

S.

[*References to Sections of T. and R. F. Act are printed in thick type.*]

[References to Sections of T. and R. F. Act are printed in thick type.]

[*References to Sections of T. and R. F. Act are printed in thick type.*]

[References to Sections of T. and R. F. Act are printed in thick type.]

[*References to Sections of T. and R. F. Act are printed in thick type.*]

[*References to Sections of T. and R. F. Act are printed in thick type.*]

[*References to Sections of T. and R. F. Act are printed in thick type.*]

[*References to Sections of T. and R. F. Act are printed in thick type.*]

[*References to Sections of T. and R. F. Act are printed in thick type.*]

U.

[*References to Sections of T. and R. F. Act are printed in thick type.*]

[*References to Sections of T. and R. F. Act are printed in thick type.*]

V.

[*References to Sections of T. and R. F. Act are printed in thick type.*]

[*References to Sections of T. and R. F. Act are printed in thick type.*]

LONDON:
PRINTED FOR HIS MAJESTY'S STATIONERY OFFICE,
BY HARRISON AND SONS, ST. MARTIN'S LANE,
PRINTERS IN ORDINARY TO HIS MAJESTY.

3195472R00146

Printed in Great Britain
by Amazon.co.uk, Ltd.,
Marston Gate.